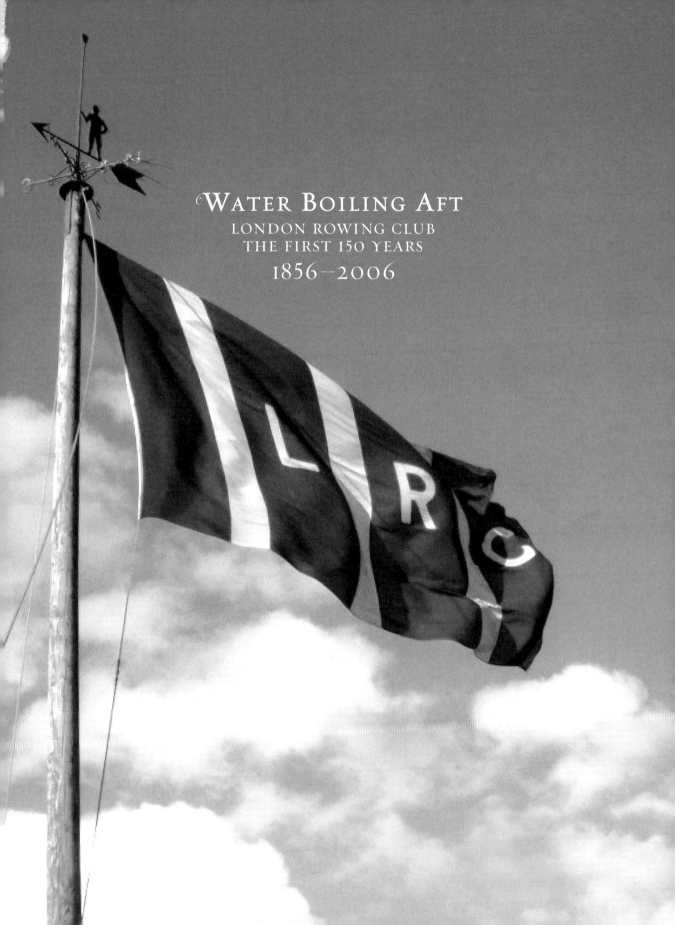

WATER BOILING AFT

LONDON ROWING CLUB
THE FIRST 150 YEARS

1856–2006

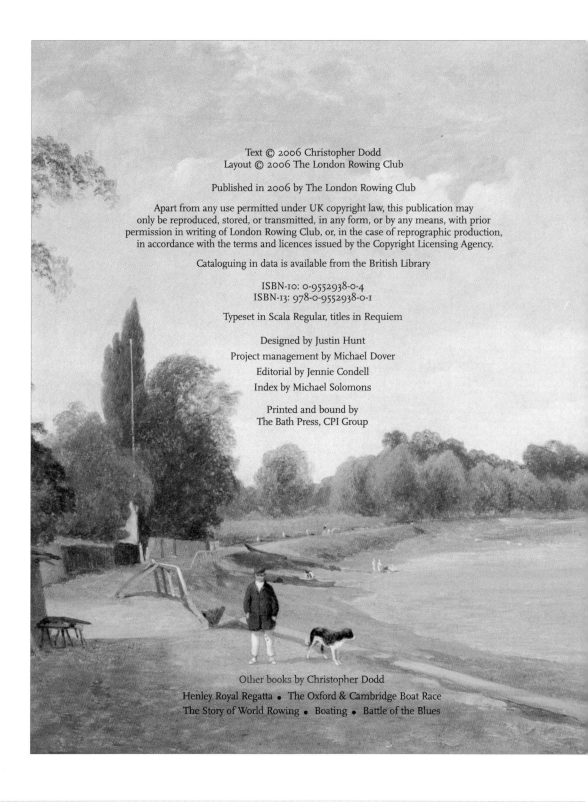

Text © 2006 Christopher Dodd
Layout © 2006 The London Rowing Club

Published in 2006 by The London Rowing Club

Cataloguing in data is available from the British Library

ISBN-10: 0-9552938-0-4
ISBN-13: 978-0-9552938-0-1

Typeset in Scala Regular, titles in Requiem

Designed by Justin Hunt
Project management by Michael Dover
Editorial by Jennie Condell
Index by Michael Solomons

Printed and bound by
The Bath Press, CPI Group

Other books by Christopher Dodd
Henley Royal Regatta • The Oxford & Cambridge Boat Race
The Story of World Rowing • Boating • Battle of the Blues

WATER BOILING AFT

LONDON ROWING CLUB
THE FIRST 150 YEARS
1856–2006

CHRISTOPHER DODD

Subscribers

Graham Anderson
Jonathan Andrew
Andrew Ardron
J.R.G. Auber
Mike Baldwin
Stephen Baldwin
P. M. Beard
R. P. M. Bell
Dr. Jurij Benn
Michael Billinghurst
Mark Blandford-Baker
John Brocklebank
James M. A. Brown
Hugh Burkitt
Ian E. Butler
R. Cameron Cooper
Prof. John P. Cann
Stephen J. Chilmaid
J. M. Clay
Richard Columbine
Nick Cooper
Timothy Cox
Simon Crosse
Mark De'ath
Michael Dover
Michael Delahooke
Bob Downie
Hugh Dulley
Christopher M. Drury
Henry W. Dunlop
Durham Amateur Rowing Club
Julian R. R. Ebsworth
Iain Edmondson
Steve Ellis
Miss J. T. Evans
Brian Fentiman
Martin B. Feuer
Paul A. H. Fitzwilliam
A. F. Foster
P. H. C. Fraser
Friends of Rowing History, USA
A. Gaylard
C J D George
Jayne Gorecki
Peter Halford
N. A. Hall
J. F. Hall-Craggs
George Hallowes
James Hamilton
Dave Hampton
E. S. Harborne
R. W. A. Hare
Guy Harris
Mark Harris
M. N. Haycock

M.B.D. Helm
A. W. Henderson
Henley Royal Regatta
Col. Michael Hickey
Keith R. Hicks
T. R. Holmes
J. M. Howard-Johnston
Jeremy Hudson
David & Judy Hunt
Justin Hunt
Dr. Simon Jefferies
C. A. L. Jones
Peter Jowitt
Ivor Kenny
Michael Kerrigan
Colin Kester
Dr. T. Killick
Christopher J. H. King
D. H. King
Dr. Tom King
Kings' Canterbury Boat Club
D. J. Kirmatzis
T. E. A. Lees
Bill Lewis
Daniel Lewis
Dennis Lightowler
J. W. Lindsay-Fynn
Ryan R. Lindstrom
Richard Linning
Anne and Paul Littleton
A. B. MacFarlane
R. G. V. Machin
Paul Mainds
Sam Mainds
Joan Matthewson
D. V. Melvin
J. N. Melvin
S. E. Melvin
Richard Metcalf
John Millbourn
Bill Miller
Miss C. A. Miller
Charles Moore
James Morrison
Ron Needs
Chas G. Newens
Steven O'Connor
John Ormiston
A. E. Owen
J. P. C. Palmer
Andrew N. Paterson
Ewan Pearson
John Pearson
Richard Philips
David Phipps

Martin Pinnell
Mrs Frances (M. H. N.) Plaisted
George Plumtree
Simon Porter
David A. H. Price
Robert Rakison
Nigel Read
Paul Reedy
Edward Lloyd Rees
Sacha Reeves
L. Reilly
John Rew
John A. Richards
Hugh Richardson
Simon Rippon
River & Rowing Museum
Clive Roberts
Juergen Saegebrecht
R. D. Scholle
Anna Scott
Alan Shrimpton
C. D. F. Smith
Nigel Smith
Christopher Sprague
Charles Stevens
Mark Stevens
Nick Strange
S. V. Suckling
David Tanner OBE
John A. Theophilus
F. L. Ter Voorde
Keith Ticehurst
Daniel Topolski
Dr. Robert Treharne Jones
Trinity Hall Boat Club
Andy Fiennes Trotman
David P. Trotter
Wim van der Zee
Roger Vincett
Christopher von Patzelt
J. D. Waite
N.I.C. Waters
Mark Watkin
A. S. Watson
Richard Way
Thomas E. Weil
Commander Anthony R. Wells, RN (Rtd)
Westminster School Boat Club
M. D. Williams
Paul Williams
A. Williamson
Brian Wilson
P. N. G. Wilson
Tim P. Wilson
Chris Woodall

Overleaf: *View of Putney reach with Beverley brook in foreground, c.1820. Oarsmen probably superimposed at a later date*

WATER BOILING AFT

I t was a great pleasure to be asked to write this account of London Rowing Club's first 150 years. Water Boiling Aft is a story of vision realised by engaging and dynamic people, many of whom appear in these pages. One hundred and fifty years means almost one hundred and fifty Henleys, several hundred crews, several thousand men manning boats, and a great ebb and flow of social events and other regattas which thread their way in and out of the tale. A thorough insight into one crew or one regatta would make a book in itself, so inadequacy and injustice are inevitably built into this text. Its form is partly dictated by the records and accounts of events available, and London is fortunate in having its annual reports intact for almost its first hundred years. It is also fortunate in having members with knowledge and enthusiasm, and more about those who have helped can be found in the acknowledgements.

Although the club is commonly referred to as LRC, its original and correct title is The London Rowing Club. The definite article has been dropped in the text for ease of reading, except where it is most relevant. Likewise, it should be taken as read that all office holders are honorary appointments except where indicated. The appendices include lists of all winning Henley crews and all who have represented London internationally. The glossary includes explanation of the tideway between Putney and Mortlake, the trophies and course landmarks at Henley, and information on other rowing bodies. Brief chapter-by-chapter footnotes are given at the end, and details of books referred to in footnotes are included in the bibliography.

It goes without saying that errors and omissions are the author's responsibility. Lastly, the novelist Paul Auster wrote that 'when a book floats out into the world, anything can happen.' This is true. This book is open, not closed. Many hands and lenses have contributed to it, and the lucky chap who writes the story of the next 150 years will have an easier time of it if members share their memories, diaries, photo albums, memorabilia, electronic images and accounts of their time at London with the club and/or the River & Rowing Museum. In a world where less is written down and where annual records are no more, nothing is irrelevant. When you are clearing out the attic, the garage or the hard drive, please remember that you make history too, and the secretary of The London Rowing Club and the rowing curator of the River & Rowing Museum would like to hear about it.

Christopher Dodd,
River & Rowing Museum, Henley-on-Thames, 2006.

CONTENTS

I

CALL TO ARMS 1856

CALL TO ARMS
1856

THE LONDON ROWING CLUB MADE ITS DEBUT on the bosom of old Father Thames on the evening of Thursday 22 May 1856. This bald, proud birth announcement followed a six week pregnancy after conception at a meeting at the Craven Hotel, Strand, where those summoned by a circular letter from Josias Nottidge resolved to 'form themselves into an association to be called the London Rowing Club, having for its object the encouragement of rowing on the River Thames, and the bringing together of gentlemen interested in that sport.'

This meeting took place on 9 April. The gentlemen present voted to spend a portion of the funds for the purchase or hire of boats, to hire rooms and to appoint a committee 'to deliberate upon the best means of forwarding the views of the meeting'. By the second meeting on 29 April, 106 men had declared their intention of joining. Elections for the committee took place on 8 May, Francis Playford becoming captain and his brother Herbert honorary secretary. A further meeting at the Star & Garter, Putney, on 15 May voted to obtain boats and hire premises, a move swiftly followed by the purchase of two outrigged eights, two outrigged fours, a gig and a randan, 'a three-man skiff rowed by a sculler and two oarsmen'. Rooms were engaged from Mr Heath of the Star & Garter and premises found nearby to house the boats. The London Rowing Club already comprised 140 members when it first went afloat on 22 May.

The speed of response to the call indicates a much longer gestation period than six weeks. The first clue to the founders' worries is given in the principles of the proposed club. The spectre facing amateur oarsmen on the tidal Thames was the decline and threatened extinction of older clubs. Their response was to gather 'a large number of members at a small annual subscription' instead of following the practice of attracting a few, who collectively faced an uncertain financial outlay. Members would enjoy 'a well assured immunity from any calls beyond their annual subscription' and 'perfect freedom from all fines' except those absolutely necessary for the protection of the property of the club. They would also enjoy a fleet of boats numerous enough to form racing crews without 'interfering with the usual pleasure-rowing of the rest of the members'.

Overleaf: London Rowing Club in 1859 with twelve-oar in background by Alfred de Prades, engraved by William Roffe. Eight (l to r): H H Weston, H H Playford, F Potter, J Paine, J Nottidge, G Schlotel, J Ireland, W Foster, G Dunnage. Skiff (l to r): F Layton, F Playford, J S Virtue, E Belfour. Sculler: A A Casamajor

Amateur rowing men, including Nottidge and his friends, were irritated by the dominance of Oxford and Cambridge and clubs closed to non-university men, such as those formed for graduates, or otherwise restricted, as in the case of Leander which was limited to 25 members. They were also faced with the changing nature of the river and were aware of environmental issues caused by traffic and pollution which discouraged amateur activity. In addition to the excitement and opportunities presented by the Industrial Revolution came its effect on the capital city and its river. The population of London grew from under two million people in the 1831 census to just under three million by 1856, a rapid and immense growth which increased the river traffic for people and goods, fuelled a huge railway expansion into the city's hinterland and caused a bridge building programme which, together with steam powered ships and underground trains, was to destroy the traditional watermen's way of life before the end of the century. It also brought pollution to a crisis point. The invention of the water closet in the mid-1840s ironically led to an increase in raw waste in the Thames before the accompanying modernised sewage system was complete. Matters came to a head in 1853 when the 'big stink' afflicted the noses of members of Parliament at the

The Houses of Parliament by William Lionel Wyllie RA. Although painted more than forty years after LRC was founded, this picture illustrates all the traffic problems of steam and sail which caused oarsmen to migrate to Putney

Final heat of the watermen's four-oar match for 100 sovereigns, won by Clasper's crew, 1848

Palace of Westminster. Stir in the fog turned into smog by belching factories, and it was no pleasure to go rowing there. The atmosphere is left for us today in the murky and moody images of Turner, Monet and Whistler. The light of their canvasses of Westminster, Chelsea and Battersea was not inspirational sunlight over London, but the grime of the metropolis.

The world in which the founders lived was one of expansion. Abroad, there was a nervous race to spread British influence wherever trade could be exploited and profit made; at home, burgeoning invention, industry and business, and crisis management of social change in a world which, on the 'Continent' as the Victorians viewed it, rumbled with revolt – much of it fanned by the London author Karl Marx's Communist Manifesto, published in 1848.

In March 1856 the Treaty of Paris concluded the Crimean war. Just beforehand, Palmerston's administration had replaced Lord Aberdeen's, and William Gladstone was chancellor. There was war with Persia and Britain interfered militarily in China. London had 33 per cent of the male workforce in Britain, including nine thousand civil servants and fifty-six thousand working in the professions. An explosion in news and titles took place after stamp duty on newspapers was abolished in 1855. Morse's electric telegraph dated from 1832, William Fox Talbot had taken his first recognisable photograph in 1835, and Reuter's news agency started in 1851. The bicycle had been around since 1839, the year of the first regatta at Henley. In 1840 the penny post started, and in 1843 the first public

telegraph line opened between Paddington and Slough. Isambard Kingdom Brunel's screw-propelled steamship, the SS *Great Britain*, was on the high seas. Tarmac was being laid on streets from 1845, and the Victoria & Albert Museum followed the Great Exhibition of 1851 as a permanent home for wonders of the world. The exhibition building in Hyde Park, the Crystal Palace, was rebuilt on Sydenham Hill in 1854. Tobacco in the form of cigarettes became available in that year. Alexander Parkes invented synthetic plastic, cellulose nitrate, in 1855, and in 1856 Bessemer's converter was to change the manufacture of iron and steel profoundly.

There was plenty to reflect on for the bankers and City men from whom the new rowing club drew most of its members as they took the train from the City or walked to and from Putney station of an evening, beneath the gaslights of the High Street. A new Limited Liabilities Act protected inventors from bankruptcy. Florence Nightingale's mission in the Crimea had opened eyes to health and sanitary issues, smoke abatement measures for the metropolitan area were taking effect, and Bazalgette's engineering works to tackle water and waste problems were under way. And there was a good read, Tom Brown's Schooldays, a newly available novel espousing the moral virtues of the English public school and its education, based on Rugby School, by Thomas Hughes, a journalist and oarsman.

'The flashing oars of a London eight seemed rapidly becoming a thing of the past', recorded Eugene Monteuuis, who compiled the reports of the London Rowing Club from 1856 to 1868. From the 1830s paddle steamers began to take possession of the river between Westminster and the village of Putney to the west. Increased turbulence and traffic was accompanied by a decline in the 'enlivenment and animation provided on those waters by the cutters of twenty different boating clubs', including 'the respective subscription rooms of Oxford and Cambridge, the invincible Leander, the St George's Club, the Thames and the Argonauts'. Some were extinct, and many shadows of their former selves.

14 July: Twelve members met and proceeded down to West India Docks where they dined as guests of the ship-owner Walter Bovill. The feed by Bovill on board the Sir Robert Sale at 6 o'clock was soup, fish, cold viands, cheese with a flood of claret and champagne; after that, songs, the party leaving by the 10.30 train, 28 present in all. The party went off very well, 'all more or less or rather more than less…'

At the meeting on 9 April 1856, Nottidge's intention was to form a subscription club whose members should meet periodically in town to discuss the interests of rowing and spend their surplus funds on promoting regattas. Two years beforehand, he had revived the old Royal Thames Regatta as the Thames National through his Thames Subscription Club, an advisory body 'to aid poor watermen and encourage and foster rowing generally',[1] but neither enterprise attracted much interest among amateurs.[2] Nottidge had looked at the Thames and mourned the decline into mere pleasure clubs, or worse, extinction, of the Waverley, the Thames, the Herne, the Argonaut, the Ilex, the St George's, the Wandle and the once great Leander. An eight from the tidal Thames had not been seen at Henley for years. Was rowing for amateurs and gentlemen dead, or could it be rekindled?[3] Most of those present at the inaugural meeting were active rowing men who were inclined to form a club which could put out crews worthy of contending against Oxford and Cambridge universities or other competent opponents. Herbert Playford caught the mood of the meeting when he asked: 'What's the use of a rowing club without boats? Let's have some boats as well as a club-room.'[4] Nottidge's cerebral approach was overtaken. The company gathered at the Craven Hotel set their sights on high level competitive rowing from the inception of The London Rowing Club. At the 1858 annual dinner, the idea of forming a club 'on a gigantic scale' was attributed to the 'mighty mind of

Josias Nottidge: convened the founders' meeting

a Playford'.[5] But Nottidge, himself an active competitor, became the first chairman and an enthusiastic and committed committee member. It is clear that his plans had been aired for some months, perhaps years, before the events of spring 1856, which may explain the alacrity with which the new club set up its base at Putney and put its first boats on the tideway. The new enterprise outstripped his subscription club in liveliness and influence, and the latter faded away in 1866.

The initial success of the club depended on a remarkable group prepared to turn enthusiasm to action. They included captain Francis 'Frank' Playford and secretary Herbert Playford, chairman Nottidge, joint treasurers James Virtue and John Ireland, and Alexander Alcee Casamajor, a tenacious oarsman and sculler who would become the secretary in 1858. The task they set themselves went beyond establishing the club itself; they led an assault on the pinnacle of amateur rowing, the Henley Royal Regatta, with spectacular and immediate success, even if the name of London failed to appear in the club's first year.

It is not recorded whether there was much debate about the location of the club. Again, the speed of setting it up suggests that Putney was in the minds of the founders from the beginning, even though the majority were London residents and almost all who owned up to a profession worked in the City. Putney, besides having associations with the republican Oliver Cromwell, the gloomy political philosopher Thomas Hobbes and the historian of the Roman empire, Edward Gibbon, had many great houses and country seats as well as more moderate, elegant villas with attractive grounds – country living in easy striking distance of London. But what made it possible as a rowing location was the arrival of the Richmond Railway Company's line in 1846, opening quick, easy and regular access to south London and beginning a house building boom to accommodate the professional classes who could afford the fares – an example being Hotham Villas, erected in the area then known as the Gardens, where Herbert Playford resided. The line linked Richmond to the London & South Western Railway's main line at Falcon Lane (Clapham Common). From 1848 the trains ran past the LSWR's terminus at Nine Elms to Waterloo.

By 1851 there was an hourly service which took twenty minutes, less than half the time taken by stagecoaches or the horse-drawn 'knifeboard' double decker

18 July: To Erith for excellent dinner at Crown, did not get back until 12.30 having been nearly run down off Greenwich by a steamer.

26 July: Rowed from Staines to Eton and then up to Surley to meet Westminster School; also had a 'slash' down with Eton in their outrigger.

— Leander Club's programme for July 1856

Frank Playford,
founding member,
secretary and captain

omnibuses that plied between Fulham High Street and Bank at ten-minute intervals. A few of these connected Roehampton, Wimbledon and Kingston via the old bridge at Putney. The first up train left Putney at 8.06, arriving at Waterloo at 8.30, and the railway catered primarily for Putney's numerous lawyers and bankers. Only four trains a day had third class accommodation, and fares – from nine pence single first class to five and a halfpenny third class – were too expensive for the working classes on a regular basis.

In 1856 the High Street was still among the best addresses, and from the railway station at the top end, the walk to the river passed several mansions set in grounds on both sides of the road, including Laurel House occupied by the singer Jenny Lind, known as the 'Swedish Nightingale'. The tower of St Mary's marked the approach to the river, and the southern end of the Chelsea Waterworks Company's new aqueduct was also visible from the High Street. The aqueduct took water pumped from Thames Ditton via a reservoir on Putney Common to the burgeoning districts of Chelsea and Westminster. You could not see the bridge until the very bottom of the street where it met the shore; here the carriageway curved to the right in front of the church before turning at the tollgate by the churchyard wall onto the wooden structure that crossed the Thames to Fulham.

This was the chief landmark and watermark of the members' new home. Old Putney bridge was known as Fulham bridge, and was the only crossing over the Thames between London bridge and Kingston when it opened in 1729. Before then, watermen provided the quickest way from Putney to Westminster and London, quicker than by the road on the south side to London bridge. The new bridge broke the power of the watermen and ferry interests who had long obstructed permanent crossings. The promoters spent £23,973 on the bridge and had to pay £8,387 9s 11d in compensation to ferry owners and pensions to impoverished watermen.

The bridge was a handsome wooden structure 768 feet long and 23 feet wide, including a four-foot footpath on the east side of the carriageway, designed by William Cheseldon, a surgeon at St Thomas's Hospital. It had pedestrian refuges above the piers on each side which were popular vantage and romantic assignation points. It was supported on twenty wooden piers with openings which varied from fourteen to thirty-two feet. Such gaps were a serious impediment to river traffic. In 1870 two openings were combined into one, and after damage caused by a barge in the following year, the centre opening was extended to seventy feet by replacing two wooden piers by cast-iron cylinders supporting an iron span.

The Fulham side's tollgate was a large one of stone astride the roadway. Most coach services terminated on the Fulham side because of the tolls, but even so, Putney was better connected to the city than anywhere on the south side of the river, even before the arrival of the railway.

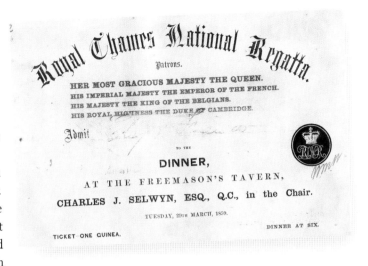

Ticket for dinner, Royal Thames National Regatta, 1856

There were fourteen pubs in Putney in 1856, and many of them jostled with shops at the bottom end of the High Street. The principal one was the Red Lion, an important meeting place and the home of the manor court. South of it was the White Lion[6] and the Bull. Nearby were the Falcon, the Queens Arms and the Lord of Exeter's Arms. Beside the gate to the church was the Rose & Crown, while close to the shore to the left was the Eight Bells, favourite haunt of watermen and rowing men. The walk to the club's rooms took members past the Eight Bells and the impressive Georgian terrace on the lower road to Richmond to the Star & Garter, situated between the road and the river. Further along was the Duke's Head with its meeting rooms and the handsome Winchester House standing next to it, while tucked up an alley off the south side of the road was the Bricklayers Arms. Further along came the Half Moon, a hostelry facing the Half Moon Field, which lay between the road and the riverbank. Behind the Half Moon was Biggs Row and several other small terraces dating from the eighteenth century, the centre of Putney's Irish community.

Most rowing took place upstream of the bridge and aqueduct, and the new members billeted at the Star and Garter would have found a lively stretch of water with a substantial, almost eighteen-foot rise and fall, and sometimes a strong stream countering an angry tide. They had the full gamut of rural quiet and wide open spaces, muddy beaches and dramatic changes of weather, and a strong ebb and flow often in conflict with the current pouring from the huge drain of the Thames Valley on its way to the estuary. Here was a place where a boat came alive, a place where, as it says on St Mary's sundial, 'time and tide wait for no man'.

On its westerly course upstream, the river passed between meadows and parkland on both banks, curving round a long Middlesex bend which was wooded as far as Craven Cottage, upstream of which was Lord Londonderry's The Old Crab-Tree Inn opposite Barn Elms on the Surrey bank. On the Middlesex side there was then a malt house and cottage and the site of demolished Brandenburgh House, where Queen Caroline had lived until her death in 1821. The sentinel at the end of the reach was a handsome chain bridge, the first such suspension bridge on the Thames, built in 1827 on the site of the present Hammersmith bridge. Its twenty-foot roadway was suspended sixteen feet above the waterway, and the span between the two Tuscan arched towers of the roadway was 688 feet. Octagonal tollgates guarded each end.

There was no building on the Surrey side save for a house or two and the beginnings of residential development near the bridge. On the Middlesex side was the waterfront of Hammersmith, a boatbuilder's yard and several handsome houses and eventually the famous Doves coffee house. The river turned sharply towards Surrey at the bridge and the long Surrey bend was built up on the Middlesex shore – West Middlesex water works, the church of St Nicholas, then Hammersmith Terrace, a malt house, a marine store, a printing office and the Red Lion leading to a ferry at the west end of Chiswick Eyot. Then came Parsonage House and Chiswick Church with Garrick's epitaph to Hogarth.

Gold Cup Regatta at Putney, 1856

Past a timber yard was the Duke of Devonshire's Chiswick House and its accompanying meadows, shaded by a fringe of trees along the river which by

CALL TO ARMS 1856   19

now was curving to the right again. On the Surrey side meadows were uninter-
rupted as far as the brewing village of Barnes whose riverfront, a jumble of
terraced dwellings, malt houses and the White Hart and Queen's Head, was
bisected by the LSWR's iron bridge carrying its rails to Richmond and
Hounslow. The manor house at Barnes had been occupied by Oliver Cromwell,
Edward Colston, the benefactor of Bristol, and several archbishops of
Canterbury. A long wall flanked the towpath here all the way round the bend to
the Ship, which marked the end of the 'championship course' used by the
university boat race and professional scullers for their matches, a distance of 4
miles 374 yards from the starting point in Putney. The boat race began in Henley
in 1829 and was raced from Westminster to Putney for the next five meetings, a
course on which the students suffered interference from sailing barges and
steamers. So in 1845 the seventh race between Oxford and Cambridge took place
from Putney to Mortlake Church. Coincidentally, the race became an annual
fixture in the same year as London was established in Putney.

   Thus far a complete S-bend has been described from Putney; the tideway
then turns left again past more of Chiswick on the Middlesex bank and Kew on
the Surrey shore, passing the Botanic Gardens, with the estate of Syon House on
the Middlesex bank after the Grand Union canal branches off at Brentford and
heads north to the Midlands. Isleworth nestles behind its eyot on the Middlesex
side, with its popular watering hole, the London Apprentice, and the Thames
turns south-east to Richmond with its half-lock and then south-west to Ham on
Surrey and Twickenham on Middlesex, the two linked by Hammerton's ferry.
Eel Pie Island hides Twickenham from the stream, and the tideway runs out
finally at Teddington lock. Although the Thames suited the rowing men better
upstream of Putney than on the turbulent London reaches in 1856, the river was
a busy highway for cargo between the port and the country. All the way up were
wharfs and barges transporting goods to and from the non-tidal upper reaches
of the Thames Valley, the Midlands via the Grand Union, and the west country
via the Kennet and Avon canal at Reading and other connections at Oxford.
There were many instances of interference from the sailing barges, strings of
lighters, and rampaging steamers, as accounts of boat races testify.

   When it came to competition, the new club was short of time. There were less
than three weeks between the first official outing on the ever-changing piece of
water that they made their home, and their prime target, Henley Regatta, which
took place on 9 and 10 June, and whose eligibility rules they fell foul of immediately. Henley required a year's existence as an entry qualification, which barred
London crews, but not its members. There were enough good oarsmen gathered
at Putney who were also full members of other clubs, and thus appeared a coxed
four made up of London men under the Argonaut flag which challenged for the

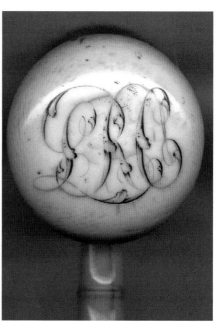

Right and below:
LRC gavel

Stewards' and the Wyfold cups. It comprised Nottidge at bow, Casamajor, Paine and Herbert Playford at stroke, with F Levien in the cox's seat. This crew was cemented by the discipline of sculling. James Paine had won the Wingfield Sculls – the amateur championship of England – in 1853, Herbert Playford in 1854 (following his brother Frank in 1849), and Casamajor in 1855. Nottidge, beaten by Paine for the Wingfields in 1853, won the Silver Goblets at Henley with Casamajor for the Wandle Club in 1855. In addition, Herbert Playford won the Diamond Sculls in 1854 and Casamajor the same in 1855. They were all, then, proven scullers and proven winners with great respect for one another. In 1856 these Argonauts won the Stewards' and the Wyfold. In addition Casamajor and Nottidge beat Playford and Paine for the Goblets, and Casamajor won his second Diamonds.

In the Stewards', the Argonauts beat Lady Margaret (St John's College, Cambridge) by two lengths in a heat. Lady Margaret were 'fairly in front' at Remenham where they put on a 'capital spurt', according to the reporter from *Bell's Life* in London. 'London, seeing this determination on the part of Cambridge, answered spurt with spurt, the Johnians got rather wild, and old Argo came in their clear length ahead.' When the holders, Royal Chester, withdrew from the final, the Argos rowed over to win goblets presented in lieu of gold medals. In the Wyfold, the Argos met the same Chester crew as had failed to defend the Stewards'. 'This was the most severe and beautiful race from the beginning to the end,'

Bell's reported. 'The Chester start was extraordinary; at the very first catch of the water their boat shot half its length ahead, and in twenty strokes the whole boat was nearly clear.' The Argos, on the Berks station, eventually clawed back the deficit inch by inch. Chester were not equal to the struggle: 'in a noble attempt to quicken to a spurt, their rowing was "thrown out". The brave Argonauts were now alongside. Mr Paine was rowing in the very best of his good form; Mr Casamajor was tearing away lion-like; Mr Playford rowing an admirable stroke, and Mr Nottidge was determination itself.' The steering of both ships was much to be commended, said Bell's. 'We did not observe in the course of the boats any waver of anxiety, or the slightest symptom of excitement.' Argonauts beat Chester by a length, but the reporter concluded that a turn of the wrist might have decided it. 'Mr Casamajor was much distressed at the finish, but he had rowed magnificently.' In the Goblets Casamajor and Nottidge, on the centre station, had a great tussle with Playford and Paine on Bucks before gaining the upper hand at Poplar Point, with Turner and Stocken of Exeter College trailing on Berks. Casamajor then defended the Diamonds 'as he liked' against J Stephens of Caversham, but not before Stephens held his Berks station as far as Remenham, keeping the holder out in the middle.

Messrs Nottidge, Casamajor, Paine and H Playford thus clocked up four Henley wins under a flag of convenience in 1856, and gave the London Rowing Club a magnificent start.

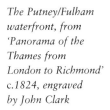

The Putney/Fulham waterfront, from 'Panorama of the Thames from London to Richmond' c.1824, engraved by John Clark

2 PLAYFORD, ARGONAUT WITH A BIG STICK

Herbert Harlee Playford, first honorary secretary of the London Rowing Club, lived ten minutes by foot from the River Thames at No 5 Hotham Villas, Putney, a new development just south of the lower road to Richmond. He was a ship broker, an activity booming at a time when a third of the world's merchant tonnage flew the British flag, and the Royal Navy's immense fleet was able to stamp out the shipment of slaves from Africa to the West Indies at the same time as enforcing free trade, including trade in narcotics, in China and the Far East. Honorary secretary Playford's correspondence book reveals an energetic campaigner, a dangler of carrots and wielder of a big stick, determined to set the club on a firm financial footing and equip it with premises and boats. His letters reflect the founders' robust agenda to set high standards by attracting members from elsewhere, by procuring the best available equipment, by providing good coaching, by initiating winter training, and by bonding through attractive social functions.

Herbert Harlee Playford, secretary extraordinaire

Playford, a former Diamonds and Wingfields winner, was at the height of his rowing powers as stroke of the 1856 Argonaut crew which was London's first adventure at Henley. He appears to have been as effective sitting at his davenport in Hotham Villas, pen in hand, as in a racing boat grasping an oar. 'Please see your friend Mr Green and get his subscription fee (two guineas) for London Rowing Club,' he wrote to Dr Easton on 1 December 1856. 'You proposed him and are liable. It is a great shame that gentlemen do not pay at once without giving me so much trouble in asking for it. Pray look to the matter soon as he will be in the black book next meeting.' Green sent a postal order and an acknowledgment was despatched on 5 December.

It was clearly the secretary's job to do the treasurers' bidding, and the flurry of correspondence emanating from Hotham Villas that month – preserved by Messrs Nissen and Parker's improved letter copying machine — is a reminder that 'pile them high and enrol them cheap' was the basis of the club's membership policy. In his clear hand and above his rippling signature, Playford's Parker (or at any rate, a steel nibbed pen probably made in Birmingham by Gillott or Mason, and flowing with the best ink of Mr Stephens) issued a string of invective into the penny post:

To A H Lucas: 'Unless I very soon get your two guineas I will county court you for the amount. I will no longer be treated in this un-gentlemanly way by any one.' To Frederick Catty: 'Your name standing so long in our black book looks very bad indeed, particularly as you are a member who has had so much rowing in the club as yourself, everyone knows you and likes you and it gives astonishment to hear your name mentioned as not having paid. Pray send me a Post Office order or cheque or if more convenient bring or send the money... Hoping you won't give me the trouble of writing again...' To Arthur Bird: '[the meeting decided that] unless you paid your sub fee that Mr Taylor would have to do so which he is quite ready to do according to the rules of the London Rowing Club, this seems to me to be very hard on him, it being two guineas out of his pocket from your negligence, *viz.* you are very wrong to say that you are not a member, you received from me a book of rules with notice of your election...'

Playford in full flow eschewed punctuation, so his fury has been edited in the following. First to John Podmore: 'For goodness sake to send me down your two guineas. It is very unfair to increase my troublesome post of secretary by causing me to write as frequently for your debt to the club. If you do not pay the money, I must.' But he concluded by hoping to see Podmore at the forthcoming dinner. And then this incandescent communication to J C Stahlschmidt: 'Thank you for your note. Your friend Mr Johnson is a very nice man — does he expect our hon. sec. to call for the debt of the club? He is the first man I ever heard think of such a thing. I have had trouble enough with the club without doing such jobs as that...' Henry J Johnson got it directly in the neck as well as his sponsor: 'Mr Stahlschmidt informs me that you require me to call for your two guineas, or send someone. Allow me to say that the usual manner for paying debts of honour is not by asking gentlemen to call for the money. I take upon myself the trouble of being the Hon. Sec. of London Rowing Club but never expected anyone to ask me to call for their sub fee - a Post Office man would cost you 3d, to send a man to call would cost the club 2s/6d. If you send me a cheque...' Johnson sent the money directly.

The first entry in the book is a letter to Messrs J Searle & Sons on the 9 May 1856 agreeing terms for the use of part of the boatbuilders' yard in Putney for £40 per year for 'two years certain' with an option for a further two years on the same terms. 'The club are bound not to build any boats on the premises, but of course should boats require new rowlocks or outriggers changed or any such trifles our own men would do like matters,' wrote Playford. He concluded that 'you will be expected to have the place cleared at once of all your boats which now stand there.' Presumably, then, London first launched from Searle's later that month.

A request to erect a building on the Half Moon playing field, which was upstream of the Searle's and lay between the river and the public house of the same name, was refused, despite Playford's barbed pitch in a letter to an associate of Mr Leader, the owner: 'The new club now numbers about 140 Gentlemen as members and will I doubt not soon double that number, as several Noblemen and Gentlemen are about to be connected with the club as patrons or members, and I feel that Mr Leader would obtain many tenants from among the members for the premises about to be erected in that locality.'

By November negotiations were advanced with Thomas Heath of the Star & Garter: 'I am ordered by the London Rowing Club to inform you that your proposal will be agreed to if you are inclined to accept £40 per year for the new rooms. Twenty of the members are willing to sign a document which shall guarantee this rent for six years. The rooms to be made ready for use on the first of March next.' The terms appear not to have been accepted by Heath, for on 1 December Playford wrote that in his opinion 'the trade you will get from the members and friends enables you to accept lower rent than you otherwise expect. I must beg you to favour me with an early reply, yes or no... I sincerely hope that you will consent to our terms as I am sure it is to your advantage to do so.' The wrangle continued into January when there is reference to £50 rent and an increase of £5 for the construction of a balcony. But the agreement was settled, and specially appointed rooms at the Star & Garter became the headquarters of the club until the 1870s.

Meanwhile, accounts were being paid to Searle and Heath and a cheque for £50 8s was paid to Messrs J & T Staples in Aldersgate Street for a silver claret jug and a short gilt vase. In February 1857 there appears a draft of a begging letter for contributions for a new four and eight for Henley. Playford set out the reasoning: 'I may be allowed to remark the universities are making great preparations for the coming regatta at Henley and evidently consider us formidable opponents. They have already ordered four new eights to be built. Chester too will also be there with the two-fold object of retaining the laurels won from the Oxford and Cambridge crews and regaining those acquired by the London crew.' He argues that people like himself can afford to contribute because they have had so much for their guinea. Meanwhile, there is a letter from R Jewett of Dunstan on the Tyne which says, 'Sir, I will build you an Eight and a Four oared cutter of cedar wood well finished and delivered to London for £65 cash'.

The significance of Chester is that in 1855 Royal Chester RC had won the Stewards' and Wyfold trophies – the first year of the latter – using a new design of four in which the keel was brought inboard, enabling the boat to have a smooth rounded hull. Harry Clasper tried this a few years earlier, but Chester's four was commissioned from another Tynesider, Matt Taylor, with spectacular success. Next year, when the London's 'Argonaut' crew won the Stewards' and Wyfold in a boat made by Jewett, Chester turned up in a Taylor keel-less eight and won the Grand and the Ladies' Plate. This feat resulted in Oxford ordering a boat for the 1857 Boat Race which they were to win by half a minute, having engaged the professional Taylor 'not to instruct us in the art of rowing, but to show us the proper way to send his boat along as quickly as possible'.

At this time when Tyne boatbuilders were leaders in design and innovation, it is not surprising that London turned to a maker far from home. Playford was circumspect as ever. He wrote to Jewett on 13 February that he should hear particulars regarding the boats in a few days. Then he switched tack. 'It is the general opinion here that the last few boats that you have built have not been well made, that the work has been done quickly but not with proper care and attention, that your only care seemed to be to get the boats finished quickly without giving yourself much trouble that the work was slurred over... that the boats consequently get twisted and out of shape before much work had been done in them.' He demands proper and neat work, strong and fast boats, well varnished – 'the boat you sent me was not half varnished' – stiff and strong. He concludes: 'Make these boats well and fast. We will put good men in them and they will win their races which will be a great advertisement for you and then we shall see who next year get the most orders to build boats for London, Oxford and Cambridge. Your reputation is at stake. Mind what you do.'

By May 1857 the club had turned its attention to boat housing again. Playford requested permission from Mr Wood to erect a shed, 70 by 39 feet, of wood and covered in felt, on Finches Field. 'It is only to be a sort of box placed on the ground, nothing whatever is to be driven into the earth, in fact it is to be a portable shed which can be taken in pieces and removed at any moment.' A postscript to his letter says: 'Don't you think I might have the honour of proposing you as a member of LRC?' On 5 June he wrote to Mr Salter: 'Dear Salter, you have got the job. We expect the boat house to be quite ready by this day in four weeks.' Instructions were given regarding a solid strong lock to the side door, bars on the windows at each end, and 'good strong fastening' inside the three other doors 'so that we shall be safe from robbers'. And then there was the roof: 'You must leave no cracks where birds can get in and drop their turds on our boats.' Salter apparently failed to comply in several respects. On 11 January next Playford wrote to him: 'There must have been something very wrong about your work in building our boathouse. The rain is now coming in

The Thames at Putney by moonlight, looking towards Fulham from the site of LRC, by F W Meyer (1869–1922)

and spoiling our new eight. This must be your fault and we beg that you will put it right at once (free of all charge).'

There were plenty of more mundane tasks to keep Playford striving at his pen in Hotham Villas of an evening. There are connections and arrangements to be made over a variety of matters. In June 1856 he requested the Oxford and Cambridge Subscription Club to assist London to act as umpires with their eight for the new club's scratch match. Westminster School was thanked for the use of boats. The arrangement whereby Argonauts were allowed to park their boats on Mr Cooper's lawn at Henley was nurtured for London.[1] Steamboats were hired for members and guests to follow club races, tideway events and the Boat Race, and tickets issued. Oxford and Cambridge were invited to make use of London's premises from 1857. Notices were issued to London's monthly meetings in the City, and to the annual dinner.

By 1858 the role was too much for Herbert. He retained his seat on the committee, while his brother Frank, who had been named joint secretary in 1857, took over as chief pen pusher, with Alcée Casamajor as understudy. Soon there was to be an assistant, paid, secretary to take care of much of the routine work, and in 1859 Frank succeeded James Paine as captain. The Playford brothers, together with Casamajor and Paine and others among the founding stalwarts, continued to bend to the mission of establishing the club as they did to their oars.

When his brother became captain, Herbert turned his attention to underpin the successes on the water during London's first two seasons by recruiting new blood and sustaining growth. The draft of his recruiting letter dated 12 October 1859 sets out his thinking about the place of London RC in the universe, and probably reflects the debate which started before Josiah Nottidge called his fateful meeting three years before. It advocates a kind of federal structure for London rowing. The club would be at the apex, running a winter training programme, constantly coaching and actively recruiting from other clubs. 'The club has now (in my view) taken up a position on the Thames with reference to other clubs in the neighbourhood similar to that of Oxford and Cambridge amongst their respective college clubs,' he wrote, citing Kingston, Richmond and Ilex as providing some of London's best oarsmen for both the Henley eight and private matches. 'We are very short of eleven and twelve stone men and such weights are absolutely necessary in the middle of a cutter.'

London crews are coxed by proper oarsmen, so instruction for young members 'or even boys' is good for getting some new young blood into the club. Men who already know the art are the most desirable additions, Herbert wrote, but 'any man who is willing to learn and has the necessary amount of strength, activity and youth will with due perseverance soon become an effective and skilful rower'. He proposes that the club shall go out every Saturday during the winter with either Mr Casamajor, Mr Ireland, his brother Frank or himself as coxswain 'to teach as well as we are able all those who are willing to profit by the opportunity.'

He also urges members to go out recruiting, without shame, among their rowing friends elsewhere. There should be 'no hesitation in asking a man to join London Rowing Club because he belongs to some other club [to] keep up the repute of the London river, which we shall do if assisted by other clubs on the Tideway throwing aside all petty jealousies and party feeling, uniting in the great cause of London against the world for amateur rowing.'

1 2 7 4 5 6 cox Stroke 3

THE DEFINITE ARTICLE 1856–1864

THE DEFINITE
ARTICLE 1856–1864

THE ARGONAUTS WHO WERE FOUNDING MEMBERS got London Rowing Club off to a rollicking start at Henley in 1856. This was the first regatta of the new club's season, and a punishing competitive programme was undertaken for the rest of the year. On 26 June the club staged a scratch competition for eights from Putney aqueduct to Hammersmith bridge, the prizes being silver oars and rudders. In a perfect Putney sunset, the occupants of a throng of boats on the river and ladies at the windows of the Star & Garter witnessed five eights, drawn by lot, battle it out. A dozen pairs trained for a week to take part in a pair-oared race from Putney to Hammersmith on 24 July. After three heats, Casamajor's boat fouled Dobree's during the final, and Pyle and Wray won the silver cups. On 9 August ten scullers, a club eight and two fours accompanied Casamajor sculling from Putney to Kew to retain the Wingfield Sculls – the amateur championship of England – there being no challenger.

Three London eights were entered for the Gold Challenge Cup at the Royal Thames National Regatta on 19 and 20 August. There was a fine start, report-ed *Bell's Life*, 'but before Mr F Playford (stroke of Yellow) had taken many pulls, he broke his oar, and tugged away at the water with the remaining part, until, his efforts useless, and thinking that [his] absence might do more good than his presence, he lightened the boat by leaping overboard near Hammersmith Bridge.' The Red crew won. London beat Albion in the four-oars, and beat

Overleaf: The Grand eight at Henley, 1858, with its caption (below). The crew named in the Henley regatta records is L Paine, Potter, Schlotel, Josias Nottidge, Farrar, J Paine, Casamajor, H Playford, cox Weston. Nottidge replaced Catty on the day when the latter was prevented from competing by his employer, the Bank of England

Margate 'as they liked' in the pair-oared gigs. The scullers' race was eventful. Cazaly (Albion) and Schlotel (London) fouled twice, while Gregory (Ilex) beat Thorn (London) over the line by a couple of lengths. Thorn won the junior sculls.

At Kingston-on-Thames Regatta composite crews appear when L F Chapman of the Triton Club and London's Nottidge beat Gregory of Ilex and Herbert Playford of London in the pairs. The London treasurer, John Ireland, won the junior sculls. London also won the outrigged gigs, and Casamajor and Nottidge, coxed by 'A Friend', beat H Playford and Pyle, with Dobree steering, in the non-outrigged pairs. London's *Nil Desperandum* beat Barnes and *Impromptu* in the junior fours.

The club wound up its first season with a four-oared race for goblets on 30 September. Five crews took part, and *Bell's Life* takes up a story which was to have familiar elements for generations to come: 'Considerable delay took place before a start could be effected, chiefly caused by the steerers of Yellow and Red having their crews in any place but the right one; after all, the start was a chance one, by some man on Hammersmith bridge giving the word "Off" before the right starter had them in proper order, but as they all went, sooner than cause further delay, the starter let them go.' Green, whose cox was named Drake, won by five lengths. There was much changing of position behind them. Red stopped off at the Star & Garter and White didn't go the distance. A good dinner at the Star & Garter followed.

*London beating
Oxford at Henley,
1857*

Bell's Life summarised London's first year in an article in December, which began by pointing out that the club's best oarsmen were long in the tooth. 'It remains to be seen whether its members will be able to surmount the difficulties now thrown in the way of London rowing – difficulties which have overthrown very mighty associations,' the paper said. The correspondent did not specify what these mighty associations might be, but he identified numbers as the key to future success: 'No number of the same men can long keep up rowing together at such a distance from town as Putney; but where the numbers are so great, the constant infusion of new and young blood may do much... The LRC... has necessarily assumed a high position... it will not do for them to play at boats, or they will be found unprepared when those ordeals are at hand which, triumphantly passed, alone can well secure their footing.'

Below:
*LRC silver
tankard won by
T N Talfourd,
July 1860*

The small band of competitors who had set a ripping pace on the
water also took measures to ensure that success was sustained. At the
club's first winter meeting on 13 November 1856 at Anderton's Hotel,
Fleet Street, it was reported that Mr Heath had offered to build new
rooms at the Star & Garter at an outlay of £300 if a guarantee of £50
per annum for six or seven years was ensured. Twenty members put
down the guarantee there and then. Then on 10 December forty-eight
sat at a table studded with trophies for the first dinner at the Albion
Hotel, Aldersgate Street, where they heard from their captain, Frank
Playford, that the club now had between 170 and 180 members, that it
possessed £100 worth of boats and had a further £100 in hand.
Playford singled out the Royal Thames Regatta as a beneficiary of a

1859.

LRC Grand eight at Henley, 1859

large number of entries – and fees of £100 – from the club. He also announced that the club might be considered as a great initiatory school for young men, and had given great impetus to rowing since its foundation. The evening contained abundant toasts and good glee from its notable singers, Messrs Cutler and Freeman.

In the mid-nineteenth century the regatta calendar began with Henley, which had established itself as the country's premier meeting in less than twenty years of existence. In 1857, the first year in which the Londoners could compete there under their own colours, they won the Grand and the Stewards'. The club followed this by collecting at least one of the regatta's glittering trophies each year until 1863. London members won the Diamond Sculls in all but one of those years – Casamajor in 1857, 1858 and 1861, Herbert Playford in 1860 and Edwin D Brickwood in 1862. The exception was 1859 when Brickwood won for the first time, but in the colours of Richmond.

Preparation for 1857 began in March when James Paine was elected captain and Frank Playford joined his brother Herbert as joint secretary. Races for club scullers took place in February and May. An eight for Henley was first got up in February, and on 27 May there was a race for six scratch eights from the Crab-Tree to Putney Pier. In the final, Red and Blue 'made a dead heat of it for the first place, with White close up to them, after a tremendous contest all the way down. As it was quite impossible to get the crews together again to row some other time, and being then quite dark, the plated tankards were, after some discussion and amidst laughter, tossed for between Red and Blue, when the former won.'

The club began a busy programme of closed and open fixtures, but Henley mattered to it most. The course that at this time ran from the eastern, Bucks, side of Temple Island to where the boat tents are today, and comprised three lanes, with a dog-leg turn upstream of the island and a bend on the Berkshire station shortly before the finish. The feats of the founding Londoners contributed to important changes at the regatta in 1857. New rules restricted the eight-oared Ladies' Plate to colleges of Oxford and Cambridge and the schools of Eton and Westminster as a consequence of Royal Chester's controversial win in 1856, and contestants for the four-oared Stewards' Challenge Cup were banned from the Wyfold because one Chester crew had taken both in 1855, and Argonauts had performed a similar feat in 1856.

London's Stewards' crew of 1857 was the same as the Argonauts crew of the year before, Casamajor and Nottidge having changed seats to put the former in the bow, with Paine at seat number 3 and Herbert Playford at stroke. H H Weston replaced Levien in the cox's seat. They set a record of 8 minutes 26 seconds in beating the Lady Margaret Boat Club. 'They were off like lightning,' reported the *Times*, 'and close together for three hundred yards, when the winners began to lead, and although the Cambridge men rowed at a clipping pace, they were unable to overhaul them.' The Stewards' and Wyfold fours combined for the Grand against an Oxford crew whose style was described as 'matchless'. An eyewitness account in London's report says that their early lead was clawed back by the Oxonians by the 'upper end of Remenham bay'. When London began to show again at the 'bush turn', both crews faltered suddenly, London when a man fell backwards in a faint and Oxford when

Such being the leading objects which the committee are earnestly resolved in carrying out, they cannot but indulge a well-grounded hope that this club will infer most invaluable benefits on the deserving watermen, as well as the gentleman amateur, and that from its establishment may hereafter be dated the revival of rowing on the Thames.
— *LRC report for 1856*

W H Wood's oar broke at the button. Herbert Playford said later that 'it is no joke to row for the Grand Challenge Cup against such a crew as that opposed to us… but we thought not so much of the honour which would accrue to ourselves; we knew we were winning a name to the club, and we thought to ourselves, if we win this race, the club will gain a name which would ever cling to it.' The verdict was a length and a quarter to London. Casamajor and Nottidge had a disaster in the Goblets when Nottidge's stretcher broke directly after the start and they had to abandon the race to two Oxford pairs, Messrs Warre and Lonsdale winning easily. This caused an upset beyond the unfortunate crew, for the London record states that 'a large sum of money exchanged hands on this event, the London visitors having booked the race as a dead certainty.'

The competitive season continued after Henley. Six coxed fours contested for tankards on 30 July, and as *Bell's Life* reported, 'the large gathering of well-known river faces strongly reminded us of old times, and afforded one of the best proofs how much The London Rowing Club has done to restore life and animation to the drooping prospects of the river.' There was an incident in the senior sculls at Isleworth Regatta when 'Schlotel soon got a clear length ahead; Driver, the Wandsworth waterman, rowing in front of him, as it was supposed, to direct his course which little bit of "coaching" nearly threw him out of the race, Driver fouling him off the Pavilion. Had Ireland, who was only a length astern at the moment, steered well, he would probably have won; but his defect in that respect enabled Schlotel to win by two lengths.' London's Walters and Ditton won the old-fashioned pair-oared gigs with cox Welsh. The reporter noted that 'If Mr Ditton's name be spelt backwards the reader will become enlightened,' signifying that the club's founder, Nottidge, was on the water. The club sent crews to Kingston, Barnes and the Royal Thames National Regattas, but did not confine itself to the Thames and tideway. A crew toured the north during August, winning a cup valued at £40 at Mersey Regatta on a course from Bromborough Pool to Rock Ferry slip, and winning the Ellesmere Cup for fours 'open to the world' and the Brackley Cup, described as a 'pair-oared race for four-oared gigs', at Manchester and Salford Regattas. At the grand annual dinner on 14 January 1858

Old Putney Bridge, aquatint, 1793

at the Freemasons' Tavern, Queen Street, Frank Playford reported that the membership now stood at 190 despite thirty members leaving during the year, and Josiah Nottidge said, 'When I advert to what Frank Playford has done, here I must say that the London Rowing Club without him would be like the play of Hamlet with the Danish prince omitted.'

Henley was a mixed bag for London in 1858. Playford and Casamajor won the Goblets and

THE CRAB-TREE INN, ON THE THAMES.—[SKETCHED BY OUR OWN ARTIST.]

The Crab-Tree Inn, 1869

Casamajor, 'the finest amateur waterman that ever got into a boat,' took the Diamonds. These two and the rest of their victorious 1857 Stewards' crew rowed over to retain that trophy, and then London lost the Grand to a good Cambridge crew, described as 'the music of many as of one'. London had to reshuffle on the morning of the race, because Frederick Catty, the number 3, did not show up. Nottidge was put in at four and Schlotel moved from four to three. London started askew on the 'Oxfordshire' station and were leading by three-quarters of a length after Remenham, increasing to a length. They then made two attempts to take Cambridge's water, but were forced to give way when Morland, the Cambridge cox, called for spurts. Weston, London's cox, was no match for Morland, who was immortalised by Sir George Trevelyan:

> *You may search the whole coast from Land's End to North Foreland,*
> *But where will you find such a steersman as Morland?*
> *Just look at him peering, as sharp as a rat,*
> *From under his rum little shaggy black hat.*[1]

Weston had to use his rudder hard to avoid catastrophe, and Cambridge reached the line with a half-length advantage. There was a fearful argument about Catty's absence, some accusing London of orchestrating a last-minute substitution of a better oarsman. Nottidge denied this by pointing out that he himself had been unwell on the morning of the race and had almost fainted in a Henley chemist's shop. The argument was fuzzy, and rumbled on despite Catty's explanation of his action. On 5 July he replied to a sharp note from Frank Playford and Casamajor, the joint secretaries: 'It is with much surprise and regret that I have read your note of the third instant. In reply I beg to mention that the captain and

Claret jug with engraved silver lid for Club Fours presented by the first president, James Layton, in 1861

crew are aware that I would not row at Henley Regatta because the governor of the Bank of England in which establishment I am a clerk, seeing by the newspapers that I was about to row, expressly forbade me from leaving the bank and if I had disobeyed this injunction I should have been dismissed from my appointment.

'With reference to a public or private explanation, it did not appear to me to be necessary as I sent a telegraphic message to Henley on the day of the race and my brother-in-law Mr Shearman who was at Henley the same day explained to the crew the reason of my absence; moreover last Thursday I saw the captain of the club and our Hon Sec Mr Casamajor and no mention was made as to the necessity of explaining a matter which was so well known to the crew and I believe to the club.

'The crew are aware how deeply I was mortified at not being able to row, indeed the mortification and anxiety with respect to my position in the bank made me so unwell that I was sent away on sick leave on the report of Mr Alfred Ince the surgeon to the bank and did not return for nearly a week... I have no desire to incur the censure of the club in addition to the mortification I have already suffered.'

Catty survived a motion of expulsion by thirty-one to ten, a narrow reprieve because the voting system used was one black ball in three to expel him. *Bell's Life* renewed hostilities on 6 January next year, causing London to take issue with the editor, Tom Egan, once a key figure in Cambridge University Boat Club as both cox and coach, who as a high priest of amateurism was the scourge of professionals' involvement in the university match. Under the *nom de plume* Pharos, *Bell's* wrote: 'As to the defaulter among the London crew and the consequent substitution of a better man so luckily at hand, the veil was so flimsy that to escape detection was next to impossible, and the motive so unworthy as to forbid investigation.' Long speeches at the annual dinner on 26 January 1859 had Nottidge defending his position, chairman Edmund Belfour declaring that 'Pharos' should be 'Un-Pharos', and Frank Playford castigating Pharos by quoting Egan's own report of the race and defending the measures taken. 'This Pharos says our conduct would not bear investigation,' he said. 'I will tell you whether it would or not. We took the greatest trouble to get Catty to Henley in time. We even had a man watching at the station until the last minute. Had Pharos used

H H Playford (bow) and A A Casamajor

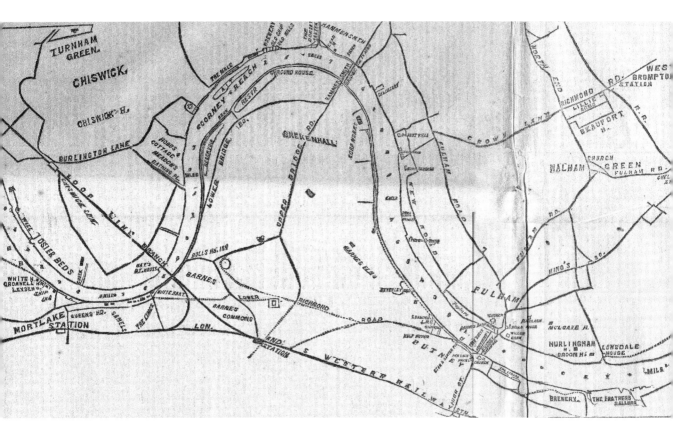

his eyes he would have found investigation was not shirked. I should very much have liked to have seen our captain [James Paine] face to face with the writer of that letter, and have heard Pharos make those assertions from his mouth which he has dared to write,' he said – as reported by *Bell's Life*, no less. 'I will suppose for an instant that they had met at the towing path in Putney, at high water; he would have had a swim, and a ducking too, and the latter he most certainly deserves. We have been treated, I consider, in a most low, blackguard manner; and told our conduct will not bear investigation. The editor, I think, was responsible for that letter, and had better have kept it out altogether than have allowed such insulting expressions to go in.' Captain Paine entered into the spirit of the thing. 'I think the author of that letter is an impostor and humbug,' he said, 'and as far as gentlemanly conduct goes, declare him to be a confounded sneak... I unhesitatingly say that it would afford me the greatest pleasure I ever experienced in my life to take him by the neck and heels, and throw him into that river, to which I think he is a complete disgrace.'

Catty's reputation was still under speculation more than one hundred and thirty years later: 'Catty, of course, had by then withdrawn from the scene with as much dignity as he could muster,' wrote Geoffrey Page in 1991. 'It is therefore interesting to speculate about his appearance in 1861 as the first captain of the

New York Times map of the Thames from Putney to Mortlake in 1869, on the occasion of the Oxford versus Harvard race. Harvard boated from LRC. This shows now-redundant landmarks such as Rose Cottage, the Dung Wharf and the Soap Works

A view of Putney, looking towards the old bridge from the Surrey bank

City of London RC. Whether it was out of pique because of his treatment by London, or from friendship with some of the other founders, or from a desire to form a new club with less competitive aims, it is now impossible to say.'[2]

London's records go some way to defusing such speculation, however. They show that Catty rowed in club races in twelve-oars, eights, fours and pairs, for the next five years. Moreover, during his tenure as captain of City of London RC he sat on the London committee, and took part in trial eights in 1862 and 1863. This was hardly a withdrawal from the London scene.

City of London was based at the Red Lion Hotel, Putney, where, incidentally, Leander had hired rooms in 1860, and it adopted the name 'Thames' in 1862 by kind permission of London's Frank Playford, who was the only traceable member of the old 1840s Thames Club. Catty resigned as captain in 1863 over disagreement with his committee's proposal for funding premises. His activities may be explained by the original objective of City of London, stated as 'organised pleasure or exercise rowing'. The first members were drawn largely from the drapery warehouses near St Paul's and were more concerned with wearing the designated white straw hat and ribbon than competition in boats. The club held a few races in 1863, but Thames's blooding in the open racing world came in 1865 when London initiated a race on the tideway for junior eights. London were triumphant, but Thames gained a taste for competition, and so a rivalry, which has lasted for a hundred and forty years, was born. In 1866 London and its neighbours started the Metropolitan Amateur Regatta, with London winning the senior eights event and Thames the junior eights event. Thames moved into a new boathouse at Putney erected by the Isleworth firm of Styles. Three years later, Catty's younger brother James, a London oarsman from 1862, was elected captain of Thames, and his reign coincided with the arrival there of 'Piggy' Eyre and George Vize who became hugely successful oarsman. The Wyfold four of 1870, containing Mickey Slater and A J Lowe recruited from West London Rowing Club, won the first Henley trophy for Thames, despite training from the Feathers at Wandsworth because of the club committee's disapproval of their activities. Eyre, Vize and Slater were in the winning Thames Cup crew two years later, Thames RC's first eight-oar trophy at Henley.[3] Years later, Eyre said that the younger Catty was 'best captain and coach I ever served under'. So far from disgraced, the name of Catty earned an honourable place in the development of the perpetual needle match between the two great Putney rivals.

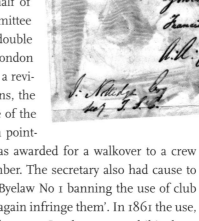

Presentation of report, 1858

Throughout these formative years, club officials were busy pushing their pens on behalf of members' welfare. Kingston Regatta committee were taken to task in 1858 for refusing the double sculls prize to Messrs Farrar and Schlotel. London demanded the prize or money returned and a revision of the rules to adopt 'Henley regulations, the result of many years' experience'. The cause of the trouble lay in scratching of entries, London pointing out that in the previous year a prize was awarded for a walkover to a crew which included a Kingston committee member. The secretary also had cause to write to a member to draw his attention to Byelaw No 1 banning the use of club boats on Sundays, and 'trusting you will not again infringe them'. In 1861 the use, wearing or display in any way of the club colours on Sundays was prohibited.

In December 1858 representations were made to Wandsworth Police Court over an unpleasant development at Barnes: 'With the view of assisting the proceedings of complaint under the Nuisance Act... we beg, as the representatives of a large number of gentlemen (viz. 250) to corroborate the evidence given on 27 October by the plaintiffs witnesses, as to the existence of a most disgusting and unhealthy effluvium, caused by the bone-boiling and soap works of Messrs Cowan at Barnes, which up to yesterday was not in the least abated. We have innumerable complaints on this subject, and are much astonished that so foul and obnoxious trade should ever have been permitted to be carried out in this hitherto salubrious neighbourhood. Hoping the proceedings will result in

Old Putney bridge,
1829

the annihilation of this terrible nuisance.' The soap works was to feature as a landmark on the course for many years to come.

There was an averted scandal in 1859 when Mr Tidbury received a letter which stated: 'The committee of the LRC being aware that it is the intention of certain members to propose the expulsion of Mr Tidbury from the club on account of his retaining certain monies of the Thames Regatta think it advisable to inform him of the fact that he may have the option of resigning previous to the motion being brought forward.'

London's second Grand win came in 1859. Founder members Herbert Playford in the stroke seat, Casamajor at number 7, James Paine at numbere 6 and Frank Potter at number 3, together with G and W Dunnage, W Foster and W Farrar, had the pleasure of beating Oxford in the heat and Cambridge in the final, a feat which fulfilled the club's chief aim in one event. Next year the Wyfold came London's way, plus the Silver Goblets in the hands of Casamajor and Woodbridge. In 1861 the eight and both fours failed and it was left to Casamajor to bring glory to London in the Diamonds, although the glory was there for simply turning up, because both his opponents were also members. He lost his early lead to Cox and then collided with him when he caught him beyond Remenham. The two of them got going again and Casamajor won, but if an appeal had been lodged, the regatta record says he would have been disqualified and the others made to row again. As it turned out, it was Alexander Alcée Casamajor's last race. He died suddenly from a 'breaking blood vessel' on the night of 7 August 1861.

The big boats returned to success in 1862. The Grand eight beat Trinity College, Oxford, by three lengths in the final, and four of the crew won the Wyfold easily. The next year was fallow on the honours board but noteworthy for the regatta's own report of the Wyfold: 'A protest was made by London Rowing Club, the holders, against the Kingston and Third Trinity crews, on the ground that a member of each crew had contended on a previous occasion for the Stewards' Cup. The objection was overruled by the Stewards, but on what principle it is difficult to imagine, as the qualification rule for the Wyfold expressly disqualified anyone who had contended, or was entered to contend, for the Stewards' Cup.' In 1864 London won the Stewards' itself, for the third time. Although Fenner and May won the Silver Goblets in 1865, larger boats did not succeed at Henley for another four years. The year 1864 marked the end of London's honeymoon at Henley.

LONDON ROWING CLUB,
Star and Garter Hotel, Putney.

On MONDAY EVENING, August 31, 1857,
An Amateur Performance

Will take place in the Rooms of the Club, commencing at a Quarter to Eight o'Clock precisely, with Mrs. C. Kemble's Petite Comedy, in One Act,

A WIFE'S FIRST LESSON.

Colonel Freelove	Mr. C. H. Wilkinson.
Lord Rivers	Mr. F. Tyars.
James	Mr. Fitzjames.
Lady Elizabeth Freelove	Miss Marie Wilton
Mrs. Davies	Miss Ida Wilton.

A SENTIMENTAL DITTY ...... by .... MR. QUINTIN TWISS.

After which, a Comic Drama, in One Act, by C. Dance, Esq.,

DELICATE GROUND.

Citizen Sangfroid	Mr. C. Wray
Alphonse	Mr. J. R. Sowray
Pauline	Miss Emily Sidney.

A Glee .... by .... The Messrs. Cutler.
A Cantata .... by .... Mr. Quintin Twiss.

To conclude with the Farce, in One Act, by J. M. Morton, Esq.,

A THUMPING LEGACY.

Fillippo Geronimo (Innkeeper)	Mr. R. Morrison.
Jerry Ominous (his Nephew)	Mr. C. Wray.
Bambogetti	Mr. C. H. Wilkinson.
Leoni	Mr. J. R. Sowray.
Brigadier	Mr. Charles Grace.
Rosetta	Miss Ida Wilton.

The Audience are requested as a favor to be in their Seats by the Commencement of the Performance.

Theatrical entertainment, 1857

Public relations, bonding and plenty of less grand activity on the water under-pinned these first years of prowess at Henley. Many of the members, including a considerable number of hardened 'ancient mariners', had been drawn to the London Rowing Club because rowing was its main aim. Edmund Belfour, in the chair at the 1858 annual dinner at the London Tavern, spoke of the foundation: 'It occurred to the mighty mind of a Playford to form a club on a gigantic scale, with the convenience of rooms and comforts such as no club had before possessed, and such as had never entered the minds of boating men... I found the Leanders liked gastronomony [sic] so much, and rowing so little, and I liked rowing so much, and gastronomony so little, that we parted company.'

In 1859 Frank Playford demonstrated his family characteristic of buttering up while exercising prudence when he sent an inkstand to Philip B Cooper Esq to thank him for allowing London to park their boats on his lawn at Henley. 'The committee were induced to select an article of such trifling value fearing that you might object to a memento more worthy of your acceptance,' the captain wrote to Cooper. Each year letters went to Oxford and Cambridge offering facilities, and both formed relationships with London. Oxford first used the boat shed in 1859, and Cambridge were offered the use of equipment and the services of the twelve-oar to pace them. The club chartered steamers to follow Oxford versus Cambridge and the Eton versus Westminster fixtures, a valuable source of income.

Attention continued to be paid to training and recruiting. Prizes for the club's junior scullers' race – junior in those days referred to status, not age – were donated by Charles Clifford, inventor of the 'plan for safely lowering ships' boats which bears his name', adding another event to the programme of open and closed fixtures. Delays in races on the tideway were lessened by the new practice of mooring stake boats at the starting place. By 1860 an annual supper was given to captains and engineers employed on the Iron and Citizen Steamboats companies for 'easing when the members are out rowing, and other little courtesies'. The prize for the first trial eights in 1862 was a hand-some epergne, or centre dish for the dining table, for each member, 'a great improvement on the old prize mug,' says the club record. In 1861, while fees were waived for the considerable number of members living abroad, entrance fees were also waived for candidates who had paid subs to other clubs for at least two years. In 1860 a regular gymnastic class was started under Professor Harrison of St James's Street, Haymarket. A meeting in February 1861 issued an ultimatum stating that 'members desirous of rowing in the club crews at the coming Henley Regatta are particularly recommended to practise at once.' Next year's annual meeting proposed more competition for young men in old-fash-

ioned boats, and there was a sculling race for coxes, London's Weston weighing
in at 5 stone 3 pounds and beating Kingston's Horn, two pounds heavier, by two
lengths from Craven point to Putney aqueduct. Among the comings and goings
at the club were the arrival of Charles Dickens Jr, son of the great novelist and
social commentator, and George A Henty, a future prolific journalist and children's writer. Many of their contemporaries would become much more famous
at the oar than the pen. Frank Playford was presented with a testimonial silver
tea and coffee service and a silver salver. Founder Josias Nottidge married
Amelia Helen Brice in 1860 at the British consulate and afterwards at Holy
Trinity, Geneva. Vice-president Edmund Belfour died in 1863, not, one hopes,
from a 'gastronomony' illness.

Charles E Innes was a member of a crew that rowed to Gravesend and back
in 1863 to honour the arrival of Alexandra, Princess of Denmark, who was to

marry the Prince of Wales. He wrote an account of it at the time of her jubilee,
fifty years later. 'The boat rowed in was what we used to know as the old
'Leviathan' a ten-oared ship's gig, a fine old roomy craft that we used for any
down river expeditions.' This was a boat from China which could be rigged
for ten or twelve, and Innes names thirteen men. The crew was Chas Boydell,
H N Custance, J Farley, F Fenner, C E Innes, J C F May, E C Morley, Jos Owen,
H H Playford, G Ryan, C Schlotel, E T 'Teddy' Weston, Richard Wright.

*Old Hammersmith
bridge, 1830*

With the tide at Chiswick

'We all wore dark blue thick jerseys, pea coats and LRC caps. We left the boat-house on the evening of 5 March and rowed to the Temple Pier where the boat was left for the night. On the next afternoon we started for Erith where we stopped for the night, distance about eighteen miles. Leaving Erith very early on the seventh we rowed down a couple of miles or so below Gravesend where we hung about, having a second breakfast in the boat, turned her head upriver, and waited till the princess's vessel and her consort steamed slowly up. The morning was fine and we tossed oars and cheered, then rowed nearer the leading ship easily keeping by her owing to her slow speed. Presently out came the princess on deck and most sweetly bowed to us, we at the time being the only boat near.

'We then rowed on up to Gravesend and got a good berth between pier and shore, not many yards below the gangway and had a full view of her landing.

We spent the rest of the day at Gravesend, seeing the decorations etc. We found that by many we were taken for a Danish crew of cadets and were fêted accordingly. Staying the night there at, I think, the Rosherville Pier Hotel, we rowed up next day to Putney, thirty-four miles, dining rather heavily at Greenwich on our way. I fancy that we began to meet the ebb somewhere about Westminster so it was a stiffish piece in.'

They carried all their luggage on board, too. One member of this crew, Ebenezer Morley, was involved in another adventure in May of that year. He and three other London members, the Rev R Wright, E Gollinge (trainer for the trip) and T Gregory (cook), rowed the boat in which they were in the habit of commuting between Barnes and Westminster to Hull. Their week took them across England on the Grand Junction, Grand Union, Old Union, Leicester Navigation and Erewash and Loughborough canals to the River Trent and eventually across the Ouse and Humber estuary and along the Yorkshire coast. They covered three hundred miles and negotiated 148 locks.[4]

4 CASAMAJOR, DEXTERITY AND DEVILMENT

Alexander Alcée Casamajor – A A to his friends – appeared on the London rowing scene apparently fully formed. He was an Argonaut before joining London at the outset in 1856, and was the greatest amateur oarsman of his time. He won his first public sculling match as a stripling at Barnes in 1852, and between then and his death from a breaking blood vessel in 1861, aged twenty-eight, he won the Diamonds five times and held the Wingfields – the amateur sculling championship of England – from 1855 when he dethroned Herbert Playford until he stepped down in 1860 after rowing over for five years. He won the pairs at Henley six times, the Stewards' five, the Grand four and the Wyfold once, a grand Henley total of twenty-one wins.

The *Field*, for which he was the aquatics editor from 1859 to 1861, noted that Casamajor's rowing career encompassed about sixty important races of which he won upwards of forty.[1] He was one of the small band of stalwarts who gave London its early successes on the Thames, the Irwell, the Mersey and the Lee in Cork.

Alexander Alcée Casamajor

At Henley-on-Thames, the *Field* enthused, 'not to know Mr Casamajor would be indeed voting oneself unknown'. Not only was he the best, monopolising all the great sculling races from 1854, said his obituary in *Bell's Life*, but 'his wonderful prowess as an oarsman and sculler, and unflinching pluck, at once directed attention to the boat in which he was pulling a match... It is entirely due to his forbearance in withdrawing or standing out that any gentlemen have appeared as winners from that time to present.'[2]

Assessments of Casamajor range from 'unassuming bearing, you wouldn't guess him to be such a determined opponent,' to his own quoted declaration that he always felt, while in conflict, his opponent to be his deadliest enemy, and that he was tearing his heart out.[3] Certainly some race reports indicate a demon on the water, not averse to washing down opponents when the opportunity arose. He was, apparently, never able to stand much training, and more often than not was violently sick after a race.[4] He had a very long back swing and clean blade-work, according to W B Woodgate. The report of his Diamonds final in 1857 says: 'Ere a dozen pulls had been taken Casamajor began to draw away, and then crossing over to his opponent's water took it, and whenever Paine went, so likewise did Casamajor, in and out, to the end of the race, which was won by four lengths.' The next year produced no challenger, and he rowed over.

In his last Diamonds in 1861, there was a sign of health problems when he suffered a severe attack of rheumatism before the regatta, but he was fit enough to triumph in an epic struggle against Brickwood and Cox, both club mates. Woodgate revealed Casamajor's motive for entering. Cox was a fast starter, used small blades and a rapid stroke and did not swing back further than for rowing. In a friendly spin against Casamajor and the professional Harry Kelley earlier in the year, he had led. 'It was said that it was to vindicate his reputation as being still the best sculler of the day that the old unbeaten amateur once more entered for the Diamonds, where he knew he would encounter Cox in earnest.'[5] He was by no means in good health.

Casamajor had the centre station, with Brickwood to his left on Bucks and Cox on Berks. He led off the start, but Cox darted away and had three lengths at Remenham. Casamajor quickened and quickened his stroke till his long swing back vanished, and his boat danced up and down, but he could not catch Cox. But after the Barrier, Casamajor suddenly changed his style, and went back to his old swing. From that instant, he held Cox, who may have been tiring, but both were still distancing themselves from Brickwood. Woodgate cites Casamajor's own report of his race in the *Field*, in which the aquatic editor said that he had thrown away his speed by bidding for the lead, and after changing at about the end of the first minute and a half, was 'now rowing longer and with all his power.' This was quite true, said Woodgate. Casamajor relapsed to his old style.

Cox crossed into Casamajor's water but was forced to move back onto the Berks station as the great man slowly caught up with him. Overlapping, the two collided and stopped. They restarted with Casamajor about a length down, but he quickly passed Cox, while Brickwood came up to challenge Cox for second place. Casamajor won by three lengths. No appeal was made, but the official regatta record says that had there been one, the verdict would have condemned Casamajor, and the others would have had to row again. It was the right result for Casamajor, but not the ideal way to terminate an outstanding career. He died on 7 August.

Casamajor's Wingfield Sculls brooch with six clasps, signifying his amateur championship of England from 1855 to 1860

Casamajor was a formidable oarsman as well as a sculler. He was a super-

THE BOAT USED BY
A.A. CASAMAJOR,
WINNER OF :—
WINGFIELD SCULLS 1855·6·7·8·9·60
DIAMOND " " 1855·6·7·8·61

*Casamajor's unique
V-section sculling
boat, maker
unknown. But did
he actually use it?*

human engine room occupant in fours or eights, led fainting from the London eight after beating Oxford University in the 1857 Grand, and 'again fearfully distressed' after beating Oxford in the trial heat for the same cup in 1859. Woodgate, a considerable sculler himself who rather begrudged Casamajor a shortage of tough opponents, analysed the master's stroke. 'In sculling with a very long swing back it is not a fault to commence the recovery of the body while the hands are still completing their journey home to the ribs. The body... should recover with open chest and well up, simply pulling itself up slightly, to start the back swing, by the handles of the sculls as they come home for the last three or four inches of the journey. Casamajor always recovered then, so did Hanlan [the professional who mastered the slide in the 1870s and the world in the 1880s]... the fact is, this very long swing back entails much recovery, and yet materially adds to pace.'[6]

Besides devilment on the water, Casamajor was also popular, pulling his

weight in the affairs of the club. On one of his row-overs to retain the amateur championship of the Thames he was accompanied from Putney to Kew by the London eight, a fleet of scullers and several other boats. He also spent three arduous years as secretary of the club, mentored by the Playford brothers into the efficient toughness expected of the official at the hub of the enterprise. He was also said to have devoted much time to yachting pursuits.

As with many of his contemporaries, Casamajor described himself as a gentleman. Casamajor is a Spanish name, and the family had many tentacles in Europe, including a Huguenot branch in Bristol who were prosperous ship owners and members of the exclusive Society of Merchant Venturers in the eighteenth century, with connections in Hertfordshire. The first clue to Alexander Alcée's place in Casamajordom is the census in 1851 which has him living with his mother in Noel Street, Islington. The 1861 census, in the year of his death, reveals that he was born as a British subject in Paris, and that he and his mother Emma, who was from Lyme Regis, lived at a lodging house in Clapham Road, Lambeth. The modern transcription of these censuses is confused by the name 'Alcée' and has Casamajor down as 'Alice', despite his description as 'son'. In the club annals his addresses are variously given as 14 Cornhill and 81 Gracechurch Street, and the *Field* employed him as a sub-editor before he became aquatics editor. None of this explains why he is interred in a pauper's grave in the Catholic division of Kensal Green cemetery. The twenty-six-year-old hero of the oar hardly died unnoticed: every flag on the river above Westminster was at half-mast on the evening of his death, and London's premises were 'entirely' closed on the day of funeral.

There is another mystery surrounding Casamajor, and that is his V-sectioned sculling boat which is still at his club. There it hangs in the long room, 29 feet 9$\frac{1}{2}$ inches long, twisted now but quite evil-looking, as if it would cut the water as a knife, and any opponents at the same time. Its label says: 'The boat used by A A Casamajor'. In his lifetime, boat building was a major industry, and a builder who made a boat used by a top-drawer club or star oarsman, let alone the greatest amateur sculler of the mid-nineteenth century, was on a hiding to prosperity.

Right and opposite:
*Details of
Casamajor's boat*

He would have marketed his product for all he was worth. In April 1860, *Bailey's* magazine reported that 'Harry Clasper, of Newcastle-upon-Tyne, has just finished a symmetrical outrigger of 32 feet long, and 12 inches wide, for Mr A A Casamajor, the courteous amateur champion of the Thames.' But this does not measure up to the surviving boat, and was made near the end of the champion's competitive life. Newspapers devoted considerable space to boat design and innovation, but nowhere in the reports of Casamajor's races is there any description of the V-section boat. The man himself was aware of design as well as technique in moving boats. He is quoted as saying that Matthew Taylor, builder of keel-less fours and eights in which Chester conquered Henley in 1855 and in which Oxford conquered Cambridge, has no equal 'at the job of combining the practical skill of the waterman with the mental intelligence of the amateur.' Physics tells us that the boat in question requires a tightrope walker to balance it, and the conclusion must be that the V-sectioned boat is an experiment that failed. If that were not so, correspondents would have been writing it up and scullers, professional as well as amateur, would have been queuing up to try it out.

VIRES ACQUIRIT EUNDO 1865–1878

VIRES ACQUIRIT EUNDO
1865–1878

EN YEARS INTO ITS EXISTENCE, The London Rowing Club entered a short but lean period on the major events results board. But it was not long before a 21-year-old oarsman called Gulston appeared, a tyro who was to occupy the stroke seat and the captaincy for a decade in which the club would dominate the major trophies as well as play a full part in the development of the sport. Before Gulston's spectacular debut as stroke of the Grand eight in 1868, there were several important changes to the way in which rowing at London and on the tideway was run. Herbert Playford began two years as captain in 1865, and his reign saw the introduction of the badge committee, a group of seasoned oarsmen whose job it was to recruit and train crews, with particular emphasis on forming the eight. The Layton Fours, a prize offered by the club's president, James Layton, was substituted by the Layton Pairs, presumably because the captain believed that rowing in pairs was the key to development. In February 1865 London's Charles Dickens Jr organised a meeting of clubs situated on the Thames from Teddington to Greenwich to try and agree on a common opening day. Dickens and Playford then initiated races for junior eights and pairs later in the year. London beat Thames in the final of the former, the first time that the two erstwhile rivals raced each other in eights.[1] This was the first stirring of the Metropolitan Regatta.[2]

In 1866 life memberships were created to boost income and pave the way for acquiring larger premises, and a new twelve-oar arrived, initiating an annual match between the two twelves. On 17 February London Rowing Club athletic sports were held at Lord Ranelagh's Beaufort House. The oval ground was about a third of a mile in circumference, with a stand 'dedicated to ladies' beside the winning post. The 2nd Middlesex Volunteer Band did its best to avert attention from threatening weather, and the *Sporting Life* estimated the crowd at over a thousand. The programme included races over 100 yards, 300 yards, 250-yard hurdles, an open mile and a two-mile race open only to London members. The officials included Dickens as secretary, Herbert Playford as judge, and

Overleaf: The LRC Four in Henley Reach by Alfred de Prades, 1880: S LeBlanc-Smith, A de Lande Long, F S Gulston and W Stout. The sculler is F L Playford and the mounted coach is F Fenner

LRC's Henley badge

committee member Ebenezer Cobb Morley as starter. *Sporting Life* gave a full account of the races and commented: 'Good order was maintained throughout, and only once did we hear the stewards' orders questioned, and that was by a parcel of blackguards who would talk above everybody else, and set authority at defiance in their eagerness to get their money on.' It went on to declare professional betting men as a menace to amateur athletic societies.

Despite its apparent success, this was the only time that London staged an athletics meeting, but it was not the only example of rowing men's broad interests or initiative in the sporting world. West London Rowing Club held a track and field meeting open to amateurs in 1863. In 1866 Walter Rye of the *Sporting Gazette* and Thames RC organised a steeplechase on Wimbledon Common, based on the Crick run at Rugby School depicted in Thomas Hughes's Tom Brown's Schooldays. This led to the establishment of Thames Hare and Hounds in 1867, the first cross-country club and a trail-blazer for the Amateur Athletics Association which was founded in 1880.[3] Equally significant were the activities of the London athletics meeting's starter, Morley, a Yorkshire-born solicitor who moved to 26 The Terrace, Barnes, in 1858. He joined the club's committee in 1860, rowed in the Grand eight of 1864 and served as the honorary solicitor for many years. But his greater claim to fame was as procreator of the Football Association in 1863, becoming the 'father' of the world's most popular game.

A natural organiser, Morley founded Barnes and Mortlake Regatta (which survived for eighteen years) and Barnes Football Club in 1862. His letter to *Bell's Life* suggesting set rules for football led to a meeting at the Freemasons' Tavern in Great Queen Street on 26 October 1863, where the FA was founded. Morley wrote the first draft of rules and became the first secretary, and he also fittingly scored the first goal in the first representative match, for London against Sheffield on 31 March 1866. Morley was also involved in organising athletics meetings on Boat Race day, and indulged in beagling and hunting with the Devon and Somerset staghounds and the Surrey foxhounds. He was a dispenser of free legal aid to the poor, a supporter of working men's clubs, a justice of the peace and he represented Barnes on Surrey County Council.[4]

Francis Stepney Gulston, captain 1869 to 1878, winner of twenty Henley medals

During Playford's two years as captain, Frampton May and Frederick Fenner won the Goblets in 1865, and there were successes, mostly by junior crews, at Barnes and Mortlake, Bedford and Kingston regattas. In 1866 W and A Shoolbred rowed over for the aptly named St Rollox's Cup at the Scottish National Regatta. Fenner became captain for 1867 and May for 1868, years in which London's arms were granted followed by the adoption of the motto 'Vires acquirit eundo' ('From Strength to Strength'). But the most important occurrence in Fenner's reign was the arrival of Francis Stepney Gulston, who distinguished himself in up-river regattas with the Oscillators Club, an outpost at Surbiton where boats were kept for London members who lived in that area. In his Oscillating days he rowed in a pair with the professional George Hammerton, a straight-backed and excellent stylist who taught Gulston to cultivate a long clean finish. He stepped into the stroke seat of London's 1868 eight and won the Grand, never taking the rating above 38 after the first minute. This was remarkable for fixed-seat rowing. Gulston was elected captain for the next season and began by winning the Oswald Plate at Durham against five others by one foot. He remained captain for eleven thrilling years, transferring his expertise, and that of his crews, from fixed to sliding seats.[5]

Gulston was 21 when he showed up at Putney from Magdalene College, Cambridge. He was reputed to enjoy an allowance of £300 a year from his mother on condition that he would not follow his inclination to enter the Navy.

He combined ability at the oar with great strength – in 1877 he launched an eight weighing 240 pounds broad-side from the raft at Henley, entirely unaided.[6] Between his first and last years as captain he led the club to four Grand victories, nine in the Stewards', three in the Thames, five in the Goblets and one in the Wyfold. Gulston himself won the Grand and the Goblets five times and made the Stewards' his own with ten wins from eleven starts – in 1872 the odds on London winning the latter were quoted as 'all Lombard Street to a China orange'. He was stroke of nine out of the eleven eights and five out of the eleven fours in which he rowed. Albert de Lande Long, who started out as the amateur champion of the River Orwell, stuck with him most of the way, rowing in all his winning Grand crews and eight of his Stewards' fours. Together they won three Henley events in 1872, and again in 1874. They were partners three times in winning the Goblets, and together in the London crew who won the presentation coxless fours in 1872.

Gulston in a sculling boat. He designed sculling blades and suggested broad blades to the world professional sculling champion, Ned Hanlan

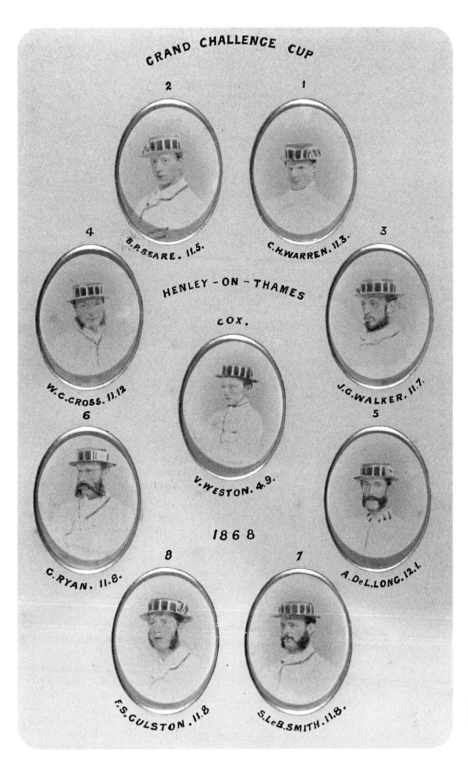

Portraits of London's Grand eight, 1869

*London's winning
Grand crew of 1874
and their reunion
picture in 1904*

Most of their victories were straightforward, but there were some incidents. In the Stewards' of 1868 University College, Oxford, successfully claimed a foul against the Oscillators Club. The umpire ordered the winners, London, to re-row against the college, but the latter conceded victory. Then in 1874, the Grand crew stormed through Eton, whose lead was two lengths at the White House, to win by two-thirds of a length in the last 150 yards. The Stewards' four had an inci-dent-packed final against Thames in 1876, a neck-and-neck race to the Barrier where oars touched and London got away as Thames eased. But Thames were half-a-length up at half-way and three-quar-ters of a length at the Point, where they came across towards London's Berks station. A foul occurred, and London got away first, and won by several lengths after their opponents, who included such legendaries as 'Piggy' Eyre and James Hastie, did not persevere. In 1878, Gulston's last outing in the Stewards', London beat the Shoe-wae-cae-mettes of Monroe, Michigan. The 'Shoes' started at a terrific rate. 'Their swivels rattled with a noise that might have been heard from one end of the course to the other; clouds of spray came from their oars; but their pace was undeniable.' But when London, 'admirably welded' and uniform in movement, drew level approaching the White House, the 'Shoes' increased their rate of striking from 45 to 48 before one collapsed and the rest stopped rowing.[7] The London record quoted an American as saying 'I guess we have been very sick all day' before pointing out that 'sick' in Yankee phraseology only means 'seedy'. The Monroe crew had made a great impression at Henley on this first occasion that American crews took part. But, unlike the students from Columbia College, New York, who were also on the card, the 'Shoes' were soon tainted with professionalism, and became the focus of new controversy in the amateur status question, of which we shall hear more later.

Gulston's time coincided with the most important development in rowing, before or since. Scullers in America were occasionally using seats that slid on rails, as were questing professionals on Tyneside. In 1870 the Yale six-oar used sliding seats in their race with Harvard. John Babcock patented them in America

There was a goodly company, especially of ladies, on the steamers and the Maria Wood, *where the band of the Royal Horse Artillery played some excellent music, varied by 'God Save the Queen' as the Prince and Princess of Wales passed over Putney Bridge on their way to the Hospital for Incurables.*

Report of the Metropolitan Regatta, 1879

On the water at Putney in 1872. From the bow: John B Close, F S Gulston, A de Lande Long, W Stout, and cox V Weston. Without Weston, this crew won the invitation event for coxless fours at Henley, and beat the Atalanta crew of New York on the Thames. With Weston coxing and S LeBlanc-Smith at bow, Close, Long and Gulston won the Stewards' at Henley in its last year as a coxed event. Gulston and Long also won the Goblets and the Grand in 1872

in 1871 and Harvard adopted them in 1872. But it was in England that the potential of the slide was first truly appreciated as the most important technical innovation since the introduction of the outrigger almost thirty years before.[8] While Gulston's badge committee was ratcheting up his men's fitness and commitment, he was looking out for any development which would keep London on top. He became a pioneer of the slide, introducing the seats for all London boats at Henley in 1872, a decision which stampeded other clubs into investing in wheels or rails. In 1873 Oxford and Cambridge used slides in the Boat Race, and in 1873 Robert J Cook and John Henry Walsh were among those who beat a path to London's new, handsome boathouse at Putney.

Bob Cook, an oarsman from Yale who later became an influential coach at his alma mater, was on a mission to learn English and Oxbridge ways. He was sent to Gulston by the former Yale oarsman George Smalley, the London correspondent of the *New York Tribune*. One day in February, reported Smalley, Cook experienced his first proper lesson in rowing from the finest teacher in England. In their first outing together in a tub pair, Cook exhausted himself trying to prevent being pulled round, while Gulston remained quite fresh. He learned 'to do as much work with half the fatigue'. And Cook was present when Walsh enlisted Gulston's help in a sliding seat experiment.

Walsh was a multi-talented editor of the *Field* who wrote under the pseudonym 'Stonehenge'. He was a fellow of the Royal College of Surgeons, a keeper of greyhounds, a broker of his own pointers and setters, a trainer of hawks, and

coach of a rowing club in Worcester where he applied his medical knowledge to train oarsmen without threatening their health. He was fascinated with mechanical things, his interest in gun safety leading to the design of the modern shotgun. Above all, he was passionate about sport. In 1856 his book British Rural Sports followed his treatise on greyhounds, and he began contributing to the *Field*, becoming editor during the next year.

It was no wonder, then, that Walsh instantly appreciated what the advent of the sliding seat meant to rowing. With Gulston's help, he arranged to test it mechanically. They selected a well-known amateur who had neither sculled in a wager boat for the past two years nor had ever used the slide. He was sent afloat in Mr Gulston's sculling boat to try the invention. The stretcher was too short for him, but after a few minutes, 'as soon as he had gained sufficient confidence to lay out, he began to slide, and was able to make a very fair exhibition,' said the *Field*.

Walsh observed that the very act of using the straps to bring up the body

Above *(left to right): Gulston, de Lande Long, Stout and Close*

draws the seat forward; and pressure of the feet on the stretcher drives the rower back to his former position. Using a diagram to illustrate the point, he shows that the apparent impossibility of getting the hands over the knees when the body is full forward is false because the straightened arms pass the knees before they start to rise when going forward, while the knees are lowered before the hands pass them when coming back.

The article goes on to consider comparative lengths of stroke. 'It has been practically found in rowing that a long, strong and comparatively slow stroke of 34 or 36 will win over a distance, although it will be beaten in a spurt by quick, sharp and comparatively weak stroke of 42 or 44 to the minute. Hence, length of stroke is to be desired – within certain limits, however, because it is clear that it cannot be advantageous to lengthen it so far fore and aft as merely to spread the water sideways without driving it back. The great reach forward and consequent swing has been overdone because excessive swing causes the modern boat to dip, and the power of the extensor muscles is applied disadvantageously.' The latter point, it says, can be demonstrated anatomically.

The second part of the experiment involved laying a tub four on trestles and supporting it on blocks. Gulston sat in the number 2 seat and rowed through the air instead of through water, while the beginning and finish of his strokes were marked by rods. On a fixed seat his blade moved 10 feet 4 inches, 6 feet 4 inches of it from beginning to 'centre'. On a slide of 9 inches in length, his blade moved 5 feet 2¹/₂ inches from 'centre' to finish and 11 feet 7 inches overall. By increasing both the pace of the stroke and the distance that the oar travels in the water by 18 inches on a 9-inch slide, the boat is moved further.

F L Playford, winner of the Wingfield Sculls, 1875

Gulston's demonstration and Walsh's analysis showed up the two advantages of slides. 'Gulston's stroke on the sliding seat is nearly 18 inches longer in the water,' said the *Field*, 'and even then is not nearly so long as he could make it if he were not prevented by his stopper and thowl. In other words, he can drop his oar into the water, and at once use his extensor muscles to advantage, and at the end of a sufficiently long stroke finish without dipping his boat, and without the loss of power which would of necessity have resulted in the same length of stroke on the old seat.'

Compared with a fixed seat, where the stroke is largely taken by the back and arms, the oarsman can bring the strong muscles of the thighs and legs into play.[10] The days of the short and stocky were now numbered, at least in top level rowing, while the era of the long-limbed was being advanced.

A second article in the *Field* is largely devoted to an argument with John Babcock who patented the slide in the United States.[11] Babcock wrote at length in the New York paper *Spirit of the Times* on the technicalities of the slide and the physiology of using it, usefully pointing out that his slide was only the beginning of what might be. The detail need not concern us here, save that the *Field* had to disabuse Babcock of his assumption that its articles had been written by Edwin Brickwood, the paper's aquatics correspondent, who used the pen name 'Argonaut'. The articles in question were unsigned, but there is little doubt that they emanated from the pen of Walsh, the editor. The anonymous *Field* writer is at pains to point out that he was once a colleague of 'England's most eminent surgeon', F C Skey CB, FRCS, at the anatomical school of St Bartholomew's Hospital, London. In 1869 the *Lancet* had published Skey's definitive piece on 'Muscular Action in Rowing'.[12]

By chance there is a letter headed 'Sliding seats' on the same page as the second *Field* piece 'in answer to an Oxford captain' which sets out the sequence of actions required to slide successfully, and concludes: 'To give an explanation of the stroke it has been necessary to analyse separately all the component parts; but in the execution all the various parts blend themselves into two motions, one backwards, the other forwards.' The letter is signed 'L.R.C.' – surely the hand of Gulston, by now the world's greatest expert at rowing air shots.

The conclusion to be drawn is that London, having stampeded slides into Henley, was once again a central player in a boat-moving experiment which further developed the science of rowing. This device was a long time in being accepted as the norm in competitive rowing for a number of reasons, one being that, broadly speaking, the manner of its use was divided between those who adapted the stroke to the slide, and those who attempted to adapt the slide to the stroke. The latter were more numerous on the east side of the Atlantic where the long season afforded plenty of time to attend to style and form. But as we can see, captain Gulston and doctor Walsh were inclined to the former approach.

Meanwhile, having witnessed the Boat Race and sat in a boat with Gulston, Bob Cook visited Oxford and Cambridge before returning home to introduce English selection methods, novice training and rowing style to Yale, the latter dubbed by the American newspapers the 'new English stroke'. Similar influences were at play simultaneously at Yale's rival, Harvard, where William Blaikie, captain in 1866 and effectively manager of the four who came to Putney to race Oxford in 1869, set out the ideas he learned in England in 'Ten years among the rowing men' in *Harper's Monthly*. He targeted objectionable primitive American training methods which, for example, discouraged eating vegetables or consuming liquid, thus causing boils and dehydration. His experiences of the 1869 encounter made physical fitness a lifetime concern for Blaikie. His book, How To Get Strong and Stay That Way, published in 1879, became a best seller.

The stroke that Cook brought back from England was described as follows:

Winners of the Grand, 1877.
Back row: Warren, Horton, Fenner
Middle row: Slade, LeBlanc-Smith, Gulston, de Lande Long, Trower
Front row: F L Playford and Dr Sheard (cox)

Winners of the Stewards, 1876. Standing: Fenner (coach), F L Playford. Seated: Warren, Gulston, LeBlanc-Smith

At the catch, light hands with blades buried to upper corner, shoulder drive beginning, no back wash, heads up, shoulders square, arms straight and knees natural.

Following the catch the power is quickly applied with shoulders and the slide is held still until the body swing is nearly complete.

Body swing follows the catch, legs about to go on. When the body swing is complete, the leg drive is complete, finishing with arms, continuing the application of power previously applied by body and legs.

The beginning of the feather is delayed until the lower corner of the blade is leaving the water. The wrists are then rolled down deliberately, without jar, the hands are very quickly shot away, knees down, elbows in, shoulder square, head up, away with the hand, shoulders with slide to follow.[13]

So Gulston's years at the oar were, as we have seen, action packed in more ways than one. When he hung it up in 1879, he might have done so in George Dunnage's superb building at Putney which opened in 1871, giving the burgeoning club a headquarters to outdo the 1867 edifice next door which had been erected by Leander to enable the exclusive socialites to leave Searle's yard at Stangate. For his last two years in the eight he had moved out of the stroke seat to make way for Frank L Playford, son of Francis, a rising star and a terrific sculler to boot, winner of the Diamonds in 1876 and the Wingfields five times from 1875–79. Gulston designed the sculling blades used by Playford, and he is also said to have been the first to suggest the use of broad blades to Ned Hanlan, the Canadian who combined mastery of the slide with showmanship to put himself on top of the professional sculling world.

Gulston probably witnessed the dead-heat in the club's twelve-oar race from the aqueduct to the top of Chiswick Eyot in 1876, when, after a half-hour rest and a toss for stations, Warren's crew beat Horton's by five feet on the return run from Hammersmith bridge to the Star & Garter. Gulston's period saw London take over the management of the Metropolitan Regatta and the introduction of the London RC Regatta which included events for watermen. Corporal Butt attended the club on Saturday evenings to give instruction in boxing, while gymnastic classes continued on two days a week during the winter for members and friends at Professor Harrison's, 8 St James Street, Haymarket (classes moved to Mr Castellotte's in Maiden Lane, Strand, in 1873). Winter Saturday rowing outings were co-ordinated with the times of trains from Waterloo.

The badge committee, born in 1865 to oversee coaching, training and preparation with an elected twelve-strong committee which then included Brickwood, Catty, Dickens, Fenner, May and Morley, clearly produced results. Its job was to examine candidates who wished to qualify for a proficiency badge, and its report of 1871 listed sixteen passes as well as noting that 'some members have come up for tuition who do not even know how to sit in a boat, much less how to handle an oar; and the member taking them out has found himself in great danger of a compulsory bath'. The committee set out what it was looking for: the examination of candidates for the title of 'oarsman' included their proficiency of position, swing, time and style. Although Monday attendance was regular, practice on other days should be better followed up. There was a need to stress continuance of practising after passing the exam, the report remarking that many miss this altogether, and reminding them that Mondays and Wednesdays are club nights.

Tuition was not confined to those who did not hold badges. Candidates were encouraged to ask friends to give preliminary lessons in a gig, and the young were exhorted to enter more races.

Ebenezer Cobb Morley, honorary solicitor 1862 to 1914 and founder of the Football Association

In a climate where rowing amongst amateurs was growing in popularity, a debate developed over amateur status. It was not a simple issue like how to use the sliding seat. Defining the amateur became a stew into which were stirred potions of class, habit, society and snobbery as well as notions of physical work, money prizes and love of sport for its own sake. London's luminaries played a big part in the debate. It was a crisis that crept up on a world where watermen

frequently took part in the same regattas, if not events, as amateurs. Some rowed for money, others for prizes. Josias Nottidge set up the Thames National Regatta for professionals and amateurs, Herbert Playford ran 'Sons of the Thames' regattas in old fashioned wherries to encourage young watermen scullers, and London itself instituted races for watermen's apprentices in 1859. In 1862 the *Rowing Almanack* – published by the *Field* whose aquatic editor was London's Brickwood – classified clubs under the headings 'gentlemen', 'tradesmen' and 'watermen'.

According to the historian Eric Halladay, the pioneers of London spearheaded a growth in amateur rowing among people who possessed a coherent philosophy that had its roots in the universities, with a set of values combining those of the enterprising middle class and the older rural gentry. It was an elusive, ill-defined 'gentlemanly' pattern of life unique to Britain.[14] This blend, confusing even for the people for whom it was the natural order, was way outside the comprehension of sportsmen across the English Channel or the Atlantic Ocean.[15] The need to come to terms with foreign crews eager to test themselves against the British was to have a decisive effect on the issue as it raged during

Frampton May, captain in 1868, and Fred Fenner, captain for 1867 – winners of the Goblets in 1865

Thames Cup winners on the water, at Henley, 1875

the last quarter of the nineteenth century, and the tensions amplified at the Paris International in 1867, the Philadelphia Centennial in 1876, and Henley in 1878. London members queried the status of the New Brunswickers who beat them in Paris, and questioned the status of the opponents who clashed with them in Philadelphia, while the stalwarts of Henley suspected the Shoe-wae-cae-mettes, London's opponents in the final of the 1878 Stewards', of not fitting their straitjacket. The 'Shoes' of Michigan could not have been the cause of the meeting initiated by London in April 1877, but they were victims of its outcome, having their entry for Henley refused in the following year.

The April meeting was also attended by Oxford, Cambridge, Thames and Kingston. There had been discussion about amateurs and definitions in the press and elsewhere since the 1830s, but the pressing element was now unquestionably foreigners – suspicion of the status of foreigners, the desire by some to meet and beat them and the desire by others to have no truck with them, cheats or not. The Putney definition that emerged took matters further than before, deciding that an amateur must be a civil or military officer – in 1877 three lieutenants, four captains and two lieutenant-colonels of the 1st Battalion Grenadier Guards were beaten by London in the first round of the Grand – a member of the liberal professions, the universities or public (i.e. private) schools, or a member of any rowing club which did not contain mechanics or professionals. It then excluded those connected with stakes or money prizes, those who had rowed with or against professionals for any prize, those who had 'taught, pursued or assisted in the pursuit of athletic exercises of any sort as a means of livelihood', those who have been 'employed in or about boats, or in manual labour', and anybody who worked as a 'mechanic, artisan or labourer'. The authors of the new rules destroyed what had been a largely unified world into pieces and spat it out, and set rowing on a pernicious course. A schism developed that took several generations to sort out.

LRC ran a Coat and Badge for watermen apprentices from 1875 to 1905. This badge was won by J Samson of Kew in 1887

Tankard for London Rowing Club Regatta eight-oared race, 1877

After the regatta in 1878 the Henley stewards, thus far relatively timid in this area, issued their own definition which followed the Putney one closely, adding require-ments for foreigners to be vouched for as amateurs by Henley's definition in their own countries. The pream-

HENLEY. 1874 & 1875.

F. L. Playford   F. S. Gulston   F. Fenner   A. de L. Long

S. Le B. Smith

Winners of the Stewards', 1875, with their coach, Fred Fenner

ble was concern over the status of the sculler G W Lee of Triton, New Jersey, as well as the 'Shoes' who were 'clearly not amateurs as the word was understood in England'. There was now no chance for the Michigan men to prove that they were gentlemen. A further Putney meeting in 1879 included representatives of Dublin University, and resulted in the founding of the Metropolitan Rowing Association, headquartered at London Rowing Club. It combined members of metropolitan clubs under one flag 'for the purpose of defeating the foreign or colonial invader'. In 1882 it changed its name to the Amateur Rowing Association (ARA), and a few years later when the amateur issue was still unresolved, it split into two, with the new National Amateur Rowing Association (NARA) allowing artisans to be amateurs. The ARA never actually formed a composite crew, and this avowed aim was expunged from its articles before the turn of the century.[16]

The amateur issue is well documented elsewhere,[17] but Richard Burnell points out in his history of Leander Club that much heartache over the definition of the amateur could have been avoided if the Henley and tideway hierarchy had recognised that the Paris International had provided a succinct answer in 1867. 'The races are open to amateurs only,' said the invitation. 'Are not considered

Winners of "Grand Challenge" — 1873 —

P. de. Barton. C.S. Routh John B. Close C.E. Routh. W. Pitchford
F.S. Gulston. A de C. Long
Highton. James B. Close.
(Swow.)

Winners of the Grand, 1873

amateurs: watermen, bargemen, long-shoremen, jacks-in-the-water, all men who belong to a boatbuilder's yard, and men who have been paid for rowing.' Leander, unsurprisingly, had turned down their invitation, Burnell says, because the captain 'no doubt mistrusted the intentions of the organisers, if for no other reason than because they were foreigners'.[18]

Frank Gulston won the Goblets for the last time with Labat in 1879 when Stuart LeBlanc-Smith, known as 'Sleb', followed him as captain. Gulston's twenty victories in Henley's top events for eights, fours and pairs added up to the most outstanding record in rowing to date – all the more remarkable if, as 'Guts' Woodgate once remarked, London ignored him when he first appeared. The club did not ignore him for long. He was outstanding on fixed seats and slides, renowned as captain and steersman. He was presented with a gold stop

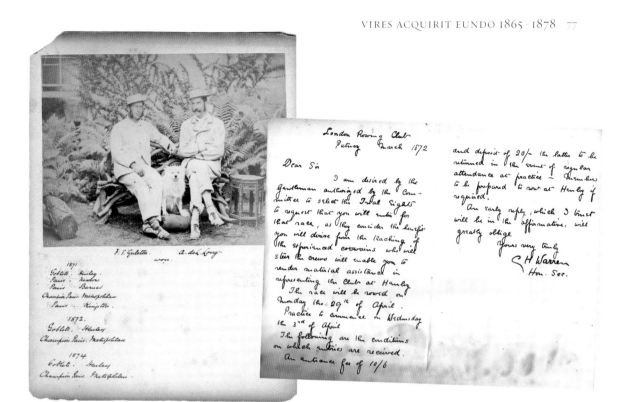

chronometer and chain to mark his decade as captain at a private dinner at the
Criterion. The most famous of his fours – LeBlanc-Smith, Gulston, de Lande Long
and Stout – is depicted in a painting by Alfred de Prades commissioned by
Long and presented in 1880. The crew is working on Henley reach, with Frank
L Playford taking avoiding action in his sculling boat, and coach Fred Fenner on
horseback on the towpath. Gulston lived to seventy-seven and died in Salcombe,
Devon. Lest London forget, the painting hangs in the members' room, and Rudie
Lehmann wrote a poem to remember Gulston by:

*Gulston with de
Lande Long*

*An invitation to cox,
1872*

> *They can't recall, but ah, I can,*   *With you to speed the hours along*
> *How hard and strong you looked, Sir,*   *No day was spent dully,*
> *Twelve stone and every inch a man,*   *Our stalwart, cheerful, matchless, strong,*
> *Unbeatable and uncooked, Sir.*   *Our undefeated Gully.*[19]

6 SHIPS OF THE LINE

London Rowing Club's avowed intent of building a large membership by attractively low subscriptions would have foundered if attention had not been paid to acquiring a fleet. Two outrigged fours and eights, a gig and a randan were purchased immediately – a randan being a kind of wherry, a speedy craft favoured by the river police and customs. It had three rowing positions, bow and stroke using oars and the man in the middle a pair of sculls.

Expenditure on boats and repairs is the largest item in early accounts after rent and rates for premises.[1] A draft letter appealing for funds for boats in addition to the annual subscription of one guinea appears in February 1857, and soon the secretary, Herbert Playford, is in detailed negotiations with Jewett of Dunstan for London's first tailor made boats, a sixty-foot eight and a four.[2] 'You say 16$^1/_2$ inches wide at front seat outside measure overall, this we fear will not be quite enough and leave it to your best judgment,' he wrote, citing a boat which the club has been using as 20 inches wide overall. 'You say 15 inches wide at the cox's seat. Are you sure this will do? I should think 18 inches would do better because our coxswains will most likely weigh ten stone – we always have men to steer, not boys as you do.'

Detail from LRC's boatbuilder's model, c.1880

There is evidence that London did use the Tyne practice of boys as coxswains early on, but clearly the supposition was that oarsmen would be coxing – particularly during the winter training when coaching was carried out from the cox's seat. 'You say 3 feet 3 inches between each seat – this we are sure will not do, we must have 4 feet, i.e. 8 or 9 inch seats and then 3 feet 3 inches or 4 inches as in enclosed diagram – it is all important our long legged men cannot reach out properly unless they have 4 feet altogether from the front edge of one seat to the front edge of the other.' Playford accepted Robert Jewett's other dimensions and then turned his attention to fittings and materials. 'The stretchers (foot boards) must not be quite so upright as you generally make them as London rowers always like them to slant a little as here and they must be made to move (shift to suit tall men and short men). Pray be sure that the inside keel (or back bone) is strong and firm, made of good wood. Mind you make the rudders neatly and well, and let the outriggers (irons) be strong and good, not short ones as we find when they are rather long that we get so much better leverage to work with which makes the boat go faster.' He gave scant attention to the four, however, bidding Jewett to 'make her as you please and according to your own fancy.' He instructed the builder to bring the boats himself and make adjustments free of charge – 'that is what all London boat builders do and it is certainly fair and just.'

There was a handicap race for scullers in 1864 that illustrates the variety of boats used by members, several of them probably privately owned. Thomson was in an old fashioned skiff, Paul an inrigged gig, Joyce an outrigged oak gig, Monteuuis and Gibbons in small blue tub boats, Lowe in the Devereux tub boat, Ryan in the boat in which the noted professional T Hoare rowed against Griggs, described as an old fashioned wager boat, and the remainder in outrigged sculling boats. The course was from the aqueduct against the ebb up the Surrey shore to a boat opposite the Crab-Tree, turning and finishing on the ebb at the steamboat pier. The starts given to the heavy boats were 'so ridiculously small that at Simmons's[3] they were all, or nearly all, fouling in a most agreeable way'. Men in sculling boats finished first and second, and a jolly good time was had by all.

Boats soon featured as prizes for London events. James Virtue and Herbert Playford first presented a sculling boat for the club junior scullers in 1858. In 1859 the prize boat was by the 'celebrated builder' Jewett, and two years later was a Harry Clasper. By 1858 there is a substantial list of larger boats. In October, twenty-one members rowed three outrigger eights which they had bought cheaply and presented to the club from Oxford to Putney in two days (with seven men aboard each). The inventory showed two further eight-oared cutters, three four-oared cutters, two randan skiffs and a randan gig, and the ten-oar Leviathan – 'all paid for'. The latter was built in China and 'purchased by us of a captain who brought her to England,' and used sometimes as a ten or a twelve. One of the four-oar gigs was that used by Belfour and Stratten and their friends for journeys through France, Holland and Belgium, and was presented to the club by them.

Herbert Playford's specification drawing for LRC's first purpose-built boat, sent to the Dunstan boatbuilder Jewett in 1857

Further evidence of London's attention to all aspects of rowing comes in February 1860 when a notice of a meeting remarks that 'the new twelve-oar which is now completed will probably have arrived by Saturday next.' This was the first twelve-oar, perhaps initiated by Herbert Playford who sent a proposal in 1859 for such a cutter by subscription, to cost £50 to £55 without oars. He argued that such a boat would be good for the standing of the club, for teaching young oarsmen and for umpire's crews, 'as she will be very fast'. Playford also had selection of the club eight on his mind, for a twelve-oar would be able to test speed against an eight and would allow a coach to view his entire squad of Henley contenders from the cox's seat. After its launch in 1860 a report says that the twelve leads an eight by about three lengths in two miles. 'With a scratch crew we started even with a Cambridge trained crew, out-started them, led for a mile, overlapped them at two miles, condition then told on us...'

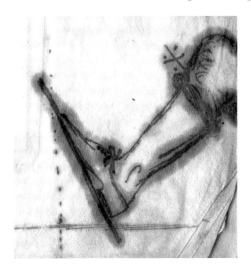

Herbert Playford's drawing of a foot-stretcher, 1857

A second twelve-oar appeared in 1866 and two replacements in 1875, made by Swaddle and Winship, another Tyneside boat-builder, for £110 each. They were 69 feet 8 inches long and 2 feet 3 inches amid-ships and had sliding seats. From 1866 there was a popular annual race between the twelves from the aqueduct at Putney to the top of Chiswick Eyot, the best recorded time being 12 minutes 48 seconds. The last race took place in December 1895 when both of the clapped-out survivors sank in rough conditions. Both boats shipped water from the start of the race, and the leading boat 'went down off Walden's, while their opponents only managed to get into the shore at the Crab-Tree before their boat sank also,' says the club record. Parts of the boats became furniture and can be seen in the clubhouse today. There was a revival in 1989, however, when a four-seat section was built by the club's boatman, Bill Colley, to bolt into the middle of a sectional eight. This sevent-six-foot monster was paraded during Henley Royal Regatta's 150th birthday celebrations, manned by a crew of veterans and, on one occasion, by twelve past captains of the club, and used for fund raising and promotional purposes.[4] The original 1860 twelve had a fitting memorial when it featured in the background of an oil painting of founder members by Alfred de Prades which was painted in the same year.

The relationship with Jewett continued for several years, with Playford keep-ing the boatbuilder on his toes, as this letter of February 1860 shows: 'I under-stand you are building a four-oar for Mr Woodbridge. Now if I give you the order for one it will be on condition that you do not give me the one you have begun for Mr Woodbridge and that you build her strictly as ordered for if she does not carry a crew of the weight she is intended for I will not have her at all – you know that several of the boats lately sent up have not carried the men they are for at all properly...'

Playford's reference in his original correspondence with Jewett to the 'inside keel' of the eight suggests that Jewett's boats were similar to those of another Tynesider, Matthew Taylor, whose revolutionary keel-less four was used by Royal Chester for their Henley victories in 1855 and whose keel-less eight was used by the same club to win the Grand and Ladies' Plate in 1856. Taylor's four was one of the earliest, if not the first, smooth-bottomed shells, the most important development in boat design since the outrigger, and arriving from the Tyne just as London Rowing Club came into existence. The next momentous advance was the introduction of the sliding seat, which became the design and rowing technique story of the 1870s. It coincided with the introduction of coxless fours, which began in 1867 when a crew from New Brunswick appeared with self-steering apparatus at the Paris Regatta, and these developments sent the racing boatbuilders back to their drawing boards.[5]

The notion of sliding had been around for some years. In 1870 a crew of professionals from Newcastle travelled to Canada and beat the New Brunswickers from St John at Lachine, using a technique of sliding on their fixed seats during spurts. In the same year the same technique was used by the Lancaster club John O'Gaunt, who lost the final of the Stewards' at Henley to the Oxford Etonian club and London RC. Also in the same year, an unknown sculler, R O Birch, used a sliding seat at King's Lynn Regatta, noted only by Edwin Brickwood, aquatic reporter and London member.

Next year, two Tyne crews visited America. James Renforth, world professional sculling champion in 1868 and the foremost professional oarsman of the day, died tragically during a race against the St John crew. Taylor's Tyne crew, meanwhile, used slides to beat an American crew which included the renowned Biglin brothers. The Geordies' victory was not spectacular. Later, however, they were decisive in a match on the Tyne against their rivals who were on fixed seats. The die was cast: in 1872 Frank Gulston's London crew used slides in their match on the Thames with Atalanta on 10 June, and there was an immediate run on the new contraption. All London's Henley crews were fitted with them, and others at Henley also adopted them, with Kingston and Pembroke College, Oxford, fitting them less than a week before the regatta. In two brushes against the fixed seated Lady Margaret, Pembroke improved their performance by fifteen seconds after changing to slides.

They could not wrestle the Ladies' Plate from the superb fixed seaters of Jesus College, Cambridge, but they won the Visitors' against the best Dublin four ever seen at Henley.[6] London, meanwhile, won the Grand, the Stewards', the prize for coxless fours (albeit by a row over) and the Goblets. This was the last time that a cox rode in the stern of boats in the Stewards'. They were made redundant in 1873, and in the Visitors' and Wyfold in 1874.

The Pembroke slides were on wheels, a mechanism that was soon afterwards discarded in favour of glass or steel grooved runners. Wheels returned in the 1880s.[7] The universities sat up and took notice of these developments, and in 1873 both eights in the Boat Race were on slides. In that year Brickwood and the captain of London, Gulston, conducted experiments with the *Field* newspaper which showed that a nine-inch slide added eighteen inches to the stroke, results confirmed by an Oxford experiment in 1873.[8] Meanwhile, Gulston's London crews were clearly mastering the slide, and they run the Grand for the next two years and the Stewards' for the next six. The 1873 Oxbridge presidents Rhodes and

LRC's launch Casamajor under construction at Tucker Brown and Co of Burnham-on-Crouch, 1952

Way and the former Cambridge giant Goldie, now stroking Leander, also did much to enhance sliding technique. So the 1870s brought much work to increase the length of the staterooms for the rowers while reducing the length of four-ones for the boatyards of the Tyne and the Thames, as well as in America where John Babcock had patented the slide in 1871. Waters, Balch and Co of Troy, New York, were fitting them to their fine sculling boats in moulded papier maché.

Launch Casamajor
on Llyn Padarn
during the Empire
games, 1958.
HRH Prince Philip,
patron of the club,
is on board

London Rowing Club stayed at the cutting edge of boat design. Frank L
Playford won the Wingfields in 1879 in a boat built expressly for him by Messrs
Phelps, Peters and Co of Putney. It was of Mexico cedar, with stern and rudder
in pine, with a 23-inch slide fitted with gunmetal swivel rowlocks patented by
Phelps and Co. The boat was 30 feet 6 inches long, $11^1/_2$ inches wide, $5^1/_2$ inches
deep at the well, $3^3/_8$ inches high at bow and $2^1/_2$ inches at the stern. Playford
used sculls from a design by Gulston 'who, by the bye, first put Hanlan up to the
idea of using broad-bladed ones,' says the club record. The Canadian Ned
Hanlan reigned as professional world sculling champion from 1880–84, and
was a master of the sliding seat.

In 1883 Frank Playford bought a six-oar inrigged skiff built by McAlister of
Dunbarton. It had fixed seats, was made of pine and cedar in two streaks, 'such
as is used for racing in Northern Ireland'. In 1885 Charlie Phelps converted an
old eight named *Bottlerack* for eight scullers. 'We believe this is the first eight-
sculler boat ever launched on the Thames,' says the club record. A race was
arranged between the club eight and eight professionals using the octuple.
The professionals won going upstream, and again going down after the crews
changed boats, despite the eight's rudder being faulty.

An exhibition at the Agricultural Hall, Islington, in 1884 serves to remind us
that boatbuilding was a huge, competitive industry, together with fittings and
rowing equipment. The late A A Casamajor's sculling boat was on show,
although the *Field*'s article does not go into sufficient detail to tell us if this was
the V-section boat which survives. The next entry is 'one of the earliest sculling
boats built by the late Harry Clasper, the inventor of the outrigger', but again, it

is unclear whether this refers to Casamajor's boat or another. Also exhibited was a racing four by Messrs Salter made in 1844; the paper boat built for the sculler Riley of Saratoga; and a tubular wager boat built in 1864 by Biffen for Richard Green, the professional Australian champion. This is almost certainly the *Cigar*, designed by George Green of North Shore, Sydney in 1863.[9] There were also maker's models from names such as Searle, Tagg, Messum, Burgoine and Turk. Amongst equipment exhibits are Champion and Co's home-trainer rowing machine consisting of a sliding seat, stretcher, outriggers, and sculls, 'all fitted and adjusted as in Hanlan's racing craft'; Messrs Spong and Co's new patent face-to-bow rowing appliance; and Mr F Woosnam of Southend's patent stowaway rowlock or crutch. Searle and Son of Stangate show a new rowlock or crutch, patented by Mr Renton, which can be affixed to an outrigger or to an ordinary boat. A few years later 'Guts' Woodgate, who introduced steering by moveable foot-stretcher to Britain after he saw the New Brunswickers perform in Paris in 1867, selects Mat Taylor, Sewell at Kings, Swaddle and Winship, and Jack Clasper, son of Harry, as the best boatbuilding practitioners.[10]

In 1884 also, the *Field* describes several inventions, among them a patent by Captain C W Morris for fixed oarlocks fitted to gunwhales which could be folded down when unshipped, the sole makers being W H Bailey's brass-founders of Albion Works, Salford; an improved rowlock by F D Grave of Boston, USA, 'the only fixed rowlock to have its oscillating movements made that, when the stroke is completed, it can be turned so as to feather the blade in the recovery of stroke'; and eight new models of bow-facing oars by William Lyman of Middlefield, Connecticut and F A Allen of Monmouth, Illinois, respectively. The newspaper judged both simpler than Spong's of Holborn. In 1886 a new patent rudder attachment (the 'X-L-All' by Hickman of Thames Ditton) was fitted to two London eights. It had a projecting bar on a long rod that was slid into the top of a groove so that it dropped to the bottom of its own accord, and 'can be shipped whether water is rough or smooth, without the least trouble'.

There were floods of patents for rowing machines and equipment in Europe, America and Australia over the late Victorian and Edwardian period. But in terms of boats, the major developments which shaped the racing shell were all in place by the 1900s – outriggers, smooth bottoms, sliding seats – and interest in detail both in the press and the London records declines. References to new club boats frequently omit the name of the builder, although the favoured firms are increasingly Thames-based, such as Sims or Phelps, and the most successful Tyne firm, Clasper, moved to Putney to where Westminster School now has its boathouse.

Coxless four which won the silver medal at the Olympic games, Berlin, 1936, suspended from the ceiling at the LRC clubhouse

*Trophy cabinets
made from pieces of
twelve-oar*

In 1893 Messrs Watts and Lowenadler presented the club with a new racing eight for Henley, and a single sculling boat for juniors. In 1897 controversial swivel oarlocks were fitted to all boats, but this did not last, because the 1927 record claims that swivels were introduced to eights for the first time. This was one of the changes made by the noted coach Steve Fairbairn when he arrived on

Case of models containing a single, pair, four, eight and twelve-oar, presented by G A Becker in 1880

the London scene. His first move was to lengthen slides to twenty-eight inches. A special meeting in 1926 voted for a levy of two pence per head per outing towards the boat fund.

The age of wood required a lot of maintenance to get the best out of the fleet, and in London's case a succession of Phelpses – Fred, Edwin, Jack and Tom – performed this task admirably, followed by Eddie Halpin, Frank Sims, and Bill Colley. Wooden boats and oars were subject to whippyness in wear and tear, and warping if they were abused or put on the rack incorrectly. Looked after properly, however, they serve generations of crews. The four built by Sims and Sons of Putney in 1936 for London's Olympic crew was designed with the minimum of ribs and cross braces and stayed in service until 1978, when it was sold to Bewl Bridge, a new club in Kent. They used it until 1987, when it was purchased back and restored by Colley, and now hangs in the long room.

In the 1960s the changing climate of international rowing brought new names in boatbuilding into the picture, and this is reflected in London's fleet both before and after the next big revolution, namely the arrival of plastics and fibres. With their precision of manufacture, their lightness, stiffness and indestructibility, composite materials soon spelt the decline of wood as the raw material of the boat and oar maker's art. In the 1960s the club acquired the H Leroy Whitney III, an eight by the American builder Pocock (founded by the sons of Aaron Pocock, an Eton boat builder), an eight by George Sims of Twickenham, and two sleek Italian Donoratico eights. By 1970 the captain was complaining that he only had seven eights, and a boat repair and renewal policy was put in place. Jeff Thorn of Sims at Putney built two new matched pairs, and two new coxed fours replaced two clapped-out coxless fours. In 1976 an eight by Karlisch of Germany joined the fleet, a marque from the top draw of

Casamajor's V-section sculling boat, c.1856, with a modern gull-wing single scull

cabinet making, and in the same year a new four was ordered from Putney's answer to Karlisch, Edwin Phelps. In 1977 two pairs and a four were purchased from Carbocraft, followed by coxed and coxless fours a year later. These were carbon fibre boats designed and made by John Vigurs, the international oarsman who rowed for London, Barn Cottage and Molesey during the 1960s. With the assistance of British Aerospace he made the *Carbon Tiger* for the British eight at the Montreal Olympics in 1976, and although this boat was not used in the Olympic regatta, its sister ship, the *Carbon Cub*, was sculled by the silver-winning double scullers Chris Baillieu and Mike Hart. Vigurs, together with his counterparts in East Germany, VEB, and West Germany,

*London's twelve-oar
at Henley, 1989*

Empacher, buried wood in boatbuilding, while Jerry Sutton of Laleham and Dick and Peter Dreissigacker of Vermont did the same for oars.[11] In 1979, £3,000 was raised by a sponsored row towards a boat for London's lightweight eight, a red Carbocraft, in which they won the world title. But the new materials were not quite the end of wood for London. A wooden Karlisch eight arrived in 1979, and two wooden fours by the same builder were purchased in 1984. However, a steady stream of plastic boats has joined the fleet ever since Carbocraft transformed into the Vespoli company in the USA and the Janousek Racing company in Britain. In 1981 forty-seven boats took part in the 125th anniversary row-past, and a year later London may have sent a boat to the Falklands war:

Backs of twelve-oar cabinets

'The *Gladstone Warwick* (500 pounds) was sold to the Royal Navy and steered away from the Embankment by the captain of HMS *Hermes* (23,000 tons) on Head of the River day. The Ministry of Defence has not said what part the eight played in the South Atlantic, but with Dave Hosking and many of the RN group boating from LRC in January deployed there, we can only guess at its tactical uses.'

In 1986 the captain of the club, Keith Mason, acknowledged the importance of equipment in his call to arms for the season – a typical season for a club with thriving groups of senior A, B and C oarsmen, plus novices, veterans and irregulars. His statement was a thinly disguised appeal to look after the boats as well as man them. 'Members join and row at London because of the attitude, atmosphere and traditions of the club, and not because it can offer newer boats than are available elsewhere... We must ensure that the equipment they use is as good as that of any crews they may meet.' And, he might have added, that it suits the level at which people row. Already by Mason's time, there were world-class heavy and lightweight crews who required the stiffest, lightest shells to suit their weight as well as veterans and beginners and intermediates who may prefer boats which are more forgiving and easier to balance. The addition of women to London's rowing programme further complicates the job of the boat manager, and the state-of-the-art in boat design is a moving standard. The boats used by the top crews in the Olympics of 2000 are different from those used in 1996, and the boats seen in 2004 are different again in detail from those of 2000. To take but two examples, aerodynamics has joined hydrodynamics in hull design, and material science has changed the profile and weight of outriggers. A fleet and its maintenance remain as important in 2006 as they did when the club was founded if a large number of people are to have the opportunity to enjoy rowing at a reasonable cost.

At the end of the period which this book covers, there were more than seventy rowing boats on London's books under three headings – racing, training and historic. The list includes fifteen eights, more than a dozen coxless fours and quads and twenty-five pairs from a range of builders that includes Karlisch, Carbocraft, Janousek Racing, Sims Racing, Eton Phoenix, Burgoshell, Stämpfli, Empacher, George Sims, Somerfield and Bill Colley, the last boatman to be employed by the club.[12] The biography of the boats illustrates the foibles of rowing on the tideway. A pair named *Edward Sturges* arrived in 2001 as a 'replacement for written off *Edward Sturges*'. Another nameless and written-off pair is described as 'bent round Hammersmith Bridge'. *Archie*, a Carbocraft pair is 'unloved, unused, damaged front canvas, new fin required, sold to Falcon RC'. The *Edgar Howitt* was 'split in two in traffic accident' and consequently had 'Too' tagged onto its name in the inventory. The list includes the *Gulston*, a Carbocraft eight with an extra four-seat section to expand it into a twelve. The name of Casamajor lives on also, in his case on the launch commissioned almost a hundred years after the club's foundation. The naval architect Alan Buchanan and his assistant Oliver Lee of Burnham-on-Crouch designed a thirty-two-foot boat with a beam of 5 feet 6 inches, capable of carrying half-a-dozen people at twenty miles per hour without creating a big wash. It has a hard chine hull in three-eighths-of-an-inch marine ply and was built by the Burnham firm, Tucker Brown and Co in 1952. *Casamajor* has been a familiar sight at tideway events ever since, having undergone at least two refits.

Boats come and go, but their names pay homage to the greats and the benefactors of the past. The *Lord Ampthill* and the *Jock Wise*, the *John Pinches* and the *Umbrage*, the *Peter Coni* and the *Ray Penney*, the *Farn* and the *Fothers* bear witness to a long and distinguished history of going rowing on the tideway and reaching out on the rowing waters of the world in competition and comradeship.

COMING OF AGE 1879–1914

COMING OF AGE
1879–1914

APPREHENSION WAS PROBABLY AN EMOTION felt by both Lord Londesborough when he became president of the London Rowing Club in 1879 and Ben and Horton when he became captain in May 1880, taking over from LeBlanc-Smith, whose reign was curtailed by illness. The great years of Gulston's crews, already immortalised in de Prades's grand painting presented by one of his comrades at the oar, Albert de Lande Long of Messrs Dorman, Long & Co, ironmasters of Middlesbrough, would be a difficult act to follow. Membership had reached 518, but the committee was worried about complacency. Nevertheless, London crews won the Thames Cup aginst Twickenham and the Wyfold against Third Trinity, Cambridge. Next year the Thames earned members' respect on Opening Day, when an easterly of gale force 'swept the river, transforming the water into a perfect sea' for the whole day. Two eights and several scullers ventured out, the eights reaching the White Hart at Barnes. The crews returned without accident, but sad news reached the boathouse that several people had lost their lives during the storm. The committee regretted that entries for club races were low, and the club's ball was also badly supported. Nevertheless, the Grand was secured – overcoming the 'terrible handicap of the Bucks station, right away round the fatal Poplar Point' – from Leander, who were a bare length behind, with Hertford College, Oxford, trailing in third.

The Grand crew of 1882 was substantially the same as the year before, but was out of form, and one man had to quit at Henley when he had a domestic crisis. Willoughby Grove kept London's end up in sculling when he won four championships during the season. A rugby match between London and Thames on the Half Moon ground, just behind the club, raised £11 15s for the widow and children of George Drewitt, a Putney waterman. In the same year Herbert Playford, the stalwart of stalwarts, a true London man before the club which he helped to create defined the concept, died.

When Horton resigned at the end of the 1885 season, his crews had landed both the Grand and the Thames twice more. There were changes at Henley in 1883 when it was deemed that if there were only two crews in a race, one would start on Bucks and the other on Berks, leaving the centre station fallow. London's Grand crew beat Jesus College, Cambridge, in a heat and Twickenham RC and Exeter College, Oxford, in the final. The Thames Cup crew was also victorious after H W Page was brought in at seat number 2 because W H Wells impaled his arm on an iron spike when the steps of the competitors' stand, 'put up in a ridiculously insecure manner', gave way. They beat West London in the final.

During this time a young sculler was making his mark. Jack Farrell won the Monteuuis prize boat in the club race for junior scullers, and the senior sculls at Barnes and Mortlake. In the Diamonds next year he 'fell over his sculls' at Phyllis Court. Farrell would later become a coach in Sweden, but his mention here serves to remind us that, while Henley crews took the limelight and continued to keep The London Rowing Club at the cutting edge of amateur rowing, the lower orders were performing up and down the river, well and often. The fears of the committee after Gulston's retirement were unfounded.

There was a notable death in 1883, that of the brilliant scholar and staunch athlete, Dr J H Moxon, who expired 'by a lamentable accident', the nature of which remains a secret. He was described as carrying off many prizes for First

Start of heat two of the Grand, 1886, with LRC nearest to camera on Berks station.

*F S Lowe, captain
1898 to 1904*

*LRC Regatta
programme, 1880*

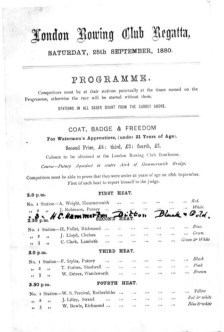

Trinity, Cambridge and London, 'one of the few who could mix with inferiors, as he did for some winters in managing the fen races of the Skating Association, identifying himself with them'.

In 1884 London won the Grand, beating Twickenham whose number 7 man passed out during the final. The Champion Cup at the Metropolitan Regatta was a dead heat between London and Thames on a course from Hammersmith bridge to the Star & Garter. There was another rugby match with Thames, this time for the benefit of 'Honest John' Phelps.

In the 1885 Thames Cup, London and Thames were level to the Point, when London drew away. In 1886 the junior crew won the trophy for the second year running, this time on Henley's new course which was buoyed on both sides and ran from just below the tail of the island to the Point, allowing two lanes only. The competition was extended to three days as a result, and the stewards' proposal to contain the number of races by limiting the regatta to 'first class crews' and dropping the Thames Cup was abandoned after fierce opposition from London, Thames, Twickenham and other clubs. London were continuously accident prone: the stroke seat in the Grand eight broke, the Wyfold four ran into a post, smashing number 3's rigger and putting him on his back, and the Stewards' four fouled Kingston and were disqualified. Accidents came thick and fast. The London report of the 1886 regatta at Moulsey [*sic*] says there were many fouls, and it was 'quite the exception for a race to be brought off without one'.

Next year, the rowlock of the stroke of the Thames Cup crew at Henley broke, and the Surrey crew in the twelve-oar race on the Tideway smashed its nose on a buoy at Rose Cottage and was beached by its crew before it sank. There are reports of a sculler having his cap blown into his slide, and of a sculler catching a crab that 'bore away the string of his rudder which so disconcerted him that he jumped overboard'. There was a terrible mishap for William Stout, the former star oarsman, when he lost his left foot in an accident at his nail and chain manufactory in Westgate Street, Gloucester. 'We understand that, although his foot is gone at the ankle, he will still be enabled, with the aid of a false one, to ride his tricycle, though he will not be able to play tennis,' reported the *Field*. But it was not all disaster. The ancient mariners manned the *Octopus*, rigged as an eight sculler, their combined ages amounting to 392 years; the average being forty-nine and their average weight thirteen stone.

In 1889 small calamities continued. The bow man in the Thames Cup crew, Charles Schlotel, hit a swan with his blade when leading the final, allowing Christ Church to get up by three or four lengths. The annual report said: 'For the mishap to the London second crew the [Thames] Conservancy can hardly be blamed, but the fact that this is the second occasion on which a swan has prevented a crew from winning rather seems to point to the necessity of removing the swans from the neighbourhood of the course during the races.' The report also complains that houseboats on the Berkshire shore obstructed vision. For the first time the club hired a barge from Oxford which was moored at Webb's yard – on the site of the present boathouses fronting the river along Wharf Lane – with provision for meals in a nearby boatbuilding shed. Members happily witnessed victory in the Wyfold. Back at Putney, the start of the Londesborough Fours was delayed by a string of barges progressing downstream and a torpedo boat coming up. The twelve-oar race was marked by fouls and a re-row on the following day. At the club scratch eights, 'there was nothing in it until P A N Thorn's boat struck a basket, which got fixed on the nose...'

In 1890 London won the Grand again after an interval of five years, an achievement attributed to three factors: firstly, 'a totally new style of rowing'; secondly, a very much improved build of boat, thirdly, the assistance of J F Stilwell, 'who inculcated the principles of the former and presided over the construction of the latter'. Unfortunately, details of the style and boats are not recorded. Stilwell cut his teeth at Henley with Ino Rowing Club in the Thames Cup in 1879 and subsequently made ten appearances in London crews. He won the Thames in 1880 and the Grand in 1884, and was beaten in the Grand in 1885 by a Jesus College, Cambridge, crew containing Steve Fairbairn and several who

Lord Ampthill, president of the London Rowing Club and ex-Governor of the Madras Presidency, visited Phelps's, the Putney boat-building premises, yesterday to view his new sculling boat, constructed to carry 17 stone, his lordship now scaling 16 stone 9 pounds, as against 12 stone 11 pounds, when of the 1889 Oxford crew.
— *Newspaper report, 24 March 1907*

*London beating
Leander in the final
of the Grand, and
crew portrait, 1881*

would later become disciples of his teaching of rowing, which would have a profound effect on London. The Jesus cox was Cecil Tyndale-Biscoe who was to use rowing for character-building at his school in Kashmir. Perhaps the London coaches could sense something about those Jesus men.

Unfortunately, the success of Stilwell's crew heralded bad times. Their neighbours Leander had made an appearance as winners in 1880, but until now had never been a serious power in metropolitan rowing compared with Thames and London, whose struggle for dominance at Henley was principally against talented Oxbridge colleges that came and went. In 1891, however, Leander won the Grand for the fourth time. While blues and college oarsmen were by no means unknown at London and Thames, Leander's 1893 offering of reduced subscriptions to the most successful oarsmen at the colleges of Oxford and Cambridge opened a conduit. Leander, with its boathouse in Putney, its newly accomplished oarsmen, its social attraction, became a popular place and a fearsome force. From a score of five Grand wins from 1839 to 1892, ten more were added in the next fifteen years.

Leander's rise was not the only factor at play at the turn of the century. London's example over forty years of producing crews to take on Oxbridge and providing good sport for working gentlemen clearly encouraged others: by the turn of the century amateur rowing was far stronger than in 1856. There were now many more clubs etching their names on the honours boards, including Vesta at Putney (1871), Kensington at Hammersmith (1873) and Auriol at Strand-on-the-Green (1873), not to mention the increasing foreign competition. Leander's ruse of recruiting blues was simple as well as being contrary to the *raison d'être* of clubs such as London, Thames, Molesey, Kingston and Twickenham on the Thames, plus burgeoning clubs in other parts of the country. Leander's accompanying masterstroke was to construct a Henley headquarters which opened in 1897, no doubt contributing to the membership total nudging 1,000. Meanwhile, London numbered more than 600 at this time and was growing, but the attraction of Leander at regatta time threatened to leach members away. The capital's club was suffering from another malaise, too, about which it could do nothing. An increasing proportion – between a quarter and a third – of its members was living abroad. This fostered links and spread the club's influence on several continents, but it did not help the captain to select his crews.

Even Leander was not strong enough to stop the Belgians from Ghent winning the Grand in 1906, 1907 and 1909. The Belgians were the early twentieth-century leaders of the foreign assault on Henley trophies. Sydney Rowing

Winners of the Thames Cup, 1880

Club followed by winning the Grand in 1912, and Harvard in 1914, prompting a 'death of English rowing' epitaph in the *Times*. But there is no doubt that it was principally Leander that was defending king and country against foreign assault at Henley and the Olympic games. The latter began in 1896 with rowing among the founding sports. Crews from Britain were in action in 1904 in Paris and 1908 at Henley, including London's first Olympic oarsman, J R K Fenning. The Amateur Rowing Association had formed in 1882 with fending off foreign crews as one of its aims, but it would be a long time before the governing body took such a task seriously. It was extremely wary of developments like the International Rowing Federation of 1892,[1] which began the European championships in the following year and wooed the ARA in vain. Two world wars would have to pass before the benefits of affiliating to the world body won the day. Meanwhile, Leander was the bastion in the young century, and Henley rules mattered much more than international standards.

In the decade during which Leander learned to strut their stuff, London suffered a litany of incident and accident. In 1892 'disasters, underserved and unexpected, followed thick on each other.' The captain was ill, the vice-captain was ill; two men were lost to the eight. 'The method of rowing was indifferent, a great want of life and finish being the chief characteristic.' And there was the largest deficit on record. Henley was worse than ever from every point of view. It was deluged on the first day, there were gales on the other days and the notorious 'bushes' wind off the Bucks bank made things worse. James and Farran were out of the Grand, Bradshaw and Baker were laid up during training, and stroke Vaux did not live up to his old form. They were, nevertheless, leading Thames by a canvas in the first heat when Bradshaw slipped his button and caught a crab. Jack Farrell was beaten by the Parisian sculler McHenry in the Diamonds, an event eventually won by Ooms of Neptunus, Amsterdam, the first foreigner to win the most prestigious sculling event in the world. The Stewards' four ran out of steam early in their race, the Thames Cup eight went down to Balliol, having 'no finish, and could not go a racing stroke'. The lively Wyfold four were doomed on the second stroke of their first race when steersman Thorn slipped his button and the boat was driven onto the island by the wind.

Winners of the Wyfold, 1875

Winners of the Grand, 1883

Matters did not improve as the season wore on. The club was empty handed at the Metropolitan Regatta, won only the Garrick pairs at Molesey, and at Reading an unruly horse ran away with all the boats and broke them up, only Thorn's sculling boat escaping damage. Thorn won the senior sculls when his opponent ran into a gig. Thorn won again at Kingston, and the season's first crew successes were the winning of the junior fours and eights. The club sent entries to Goring and Streatley Regatta for the first time, and F H Willis and F S Lowe won the challenge pairs. But there was disgruntlement in the single sculls. Thorn was winning easily when the ferry punt to the committee barge fouled him deliberately. His boat was smashed up, and his opponent Beddington, from Thames, was declared the winner by two feet. Beddington requested to row the race again, which the two did later between the bridges of Putney and Hammersmith. Beddington was the victor again, 'marred by the fact that Bubear, his trainer, sculled alongside and coached and steered him all the way.' As for Goring Regatta, 'This is the first occasion on which the club has sent crews... and unless the railway arrangements improve it will not be easily induced to send them such a distance again.'

The season rounded off in Paris in October with a saga of a waterlogged boat, collision, equipment failure and defeat.[2] The only good thing to say about 1892 was that, contrary to custom, no accident occurred during the twelve-oar race.

In 1893 the final of the Grand was lost to Leander. Lord Londesborough resigned the presidency and the young Lord Ampthill, Etonian and Oxford graduate who had been president of the Oxford Union and Oxford University Boat Club in the same year, succeeded, to preside over nearly forty years of indifferent results – indifferent, that is, as far as winning pots at Henley was concerned. In 1894, slackness of attendance made it difficult to get sixteen men to Henley, and the senior, second and junior eights failed to win any races at all. In many cases there was 'absolute ignorance of the use of the slide'. Clearly the badge committee was slipping. Several men would have done better with a 'prolonged course of instruction on fixed seats'. At Molesey 'the course was

Henley after a race, by Dickinson and Foster, 1894

disgracefully kept... the umpire's launch nearly ran into the London crew in the Thames Cup eights, and considerably retarded their pace by sucking them.'

There was falling income from bedroom rents, meals, sale of grandstand tickets on Boat Race day, and a disastrous rugby match against Thames at Richmond. But membership was rising, and if they wished, members could take part in a lively calendar of club events, there being fifteen such competitions from February to the following March, from scratch eights to handicap sculls. The twelve-oar race got up to its old tricks. The boats set off in bad light at Putney and were in pitch darkness at the Crab-Tree, after which a steamer ran into Charles Schlotel's oar and damaged it. Both crews stopped, 'but as the umpire could not be seen in the fog, went on, and Schlotel... won by a little more than a length, but was disqualified.' The umpire should have stopped the crews at the clash and disqualified Schlotel there and then, or ordered a re-row, snapped the annual report.

Then, in 1895, came a year with something to shout about. London won the Stewards' for the first time in seventeen years, and the Wyfold as well. The brothers Guy and Vivian Nickalls won the Goblets and the trophy that now accompanied it, the Nickalls Challenge Cup, presented to the regatta by their father Tom, a London founder member. 'Had the new boat in which they raced at Henley been better built their victories would have been easily secured,' said the captain's report, comparing their performances at the Royal Regatta and at the Metropolitan.

The Nickalls brothers were not pretty to look at, but they had undeniable pace, pace which they needed in particular in their heat against Crum and Pitman of New College when they lost three lengths by hitting the second post after the top of the island. They were a length up at Fawley and held off defeat by the same margin. In the final, Broughton and Muttlebury of Thames collided twice with skiffs on the course when trailing, and declined a proffered re-row because they judged the race lost before the incidents occurred.

The Nickalls brothers were in the stern of the Stewards' four who beat the Argonauts of Canada by two feet, having been behind at the grandstand when stroke and steersman Guy looked across. There was never more than half a length to either crew. The name Nickalls also featured in the Diamonds. The brothers were drawn against each other, and so Vivian withdrew. Guy lost to the Hon Rupert Guinness of Leander in the final.

Winners of the Wyfold, 1889 (top), and pictured at their reunion in 1919

Guinness went on to win at the Met, but lost the Wingfields to Vivian Nickalls.

Exceptional scullers were emerging at this time, and there was an epic race in the trial heat of the Wingfields between Guinness, Guy Nickalls and Vesta's Harry Blackstaffe. Blackstaffe led Nickalls from London's boathouse to beyond Craven

Steps, when Nickalls passed him at Walden's Wharf and had a length and three-quarters at Harrods. Guinness had not shown any threat, but had pulled up to a quarter of a length behind Blackstaffe, when, at the distillery, the latter stopped, completely rowed out. Nickalls had a length and a half over Guinness at the bridge and had to steer out to avoid a collision as Guinness spurted. Nickalls was caught at Chiswick Eyot, and Guinness led by two and a quarter lengths at the ferry, in

Jock Wise, winner of the Wingfield Sculls, 1913

rough water. The wind then drove him into the bank at the meadows, where he broke off a large piece of his left scull. Meanwhile, Nickalls had been struggling for some time because one of his gates had come open. He caught up a lot before Barnes bridge but trailed there by six lengths, helped by Guinness having to stop to pull up his shorts. Nickalls scrambled on to overlap Guinness when his scull sprang from its rowlock and he flipped out of his boat. In the final, Vivian Nickalls had a ding-dong race with Guinness to Hammersmith, where Nickalls passed under the bridge half a length in front. Guinness then experienced difficulty with his left scull, and Nickalls went right away. The Irish brewing heir was to reverse this result a year later.

Next year London won the Stewards' again, using swivel oarlocks that they found very advantageous. The Nickalls brothers won the Goblets for the third time together. The coaching committee was doing better than in the recent past, but it was noted that Thames 'were able to replace their vacancies with the brothers Guinness for the regattas after Henley, while London had to re-arrange their crews out of their existing material.' At Walton, for example, London were kept out at the post in the sun for more than half an hour while Thames were taking Guinness on board. The Grand eight suffered a recurrence of sickness and want of weight. The French club Encouragement, from the Marne in Paris, had astonishing pace. Rupert Guinness won the Diamonds again, in which Vivian Nickalls 'lacked life'.

The club's president, Lord Ampthill, finished second in the handicap sculls at the club regatta, having been given twenty-five seconds against H W Stout who was scratch. Seventeen entered, and Ampthill, sculling in a best boat, would

Hirsute LRC crews at Henley, 1886 – a good year for photographs, a bad year for trophies

have got there first if he'd not made an error in recognising the judge's boat.

Swivels were fitted to all London boats at all regattas in 1897 following the success in the Stewards' the year before, and a new club race for tub pairs was started to encourage tubbing among juniors. The Henley course was reduced to 110 feet wide and moved towards the Berkshire side to reduce the shelter of the woods on the Bucks side, and it moved thirty-five yards upstream to avoid a fallen tree at the start. There were extra starting punts from which a line was thrown to the bow men, thus keeping the boats still in a wind. Coincidentally with these changes, perhaps, there were records in the Stewards', Ladies' Plate and by the American sculler, Ten Eyck, in the Diamonds when he beat Blackstaffe.

In 1898 the London eight, coached by A G Aldous, won at Kingston, Staines, Moulsey [*sic*], Walton, the Metropolitan and Reading, but not at Henley. Other crews also had success, although there were accompanying mishaps, such as the London pairs race being swamped by a police launch. There were many new members. A change of rule in the Wingfield Sculls whereby professionals were no longer allowed to steer contestants from the bows of accompanying eights made London's F E Thorn the first amateur to do so. He guided his brother C H R Thorn. Ben Howell, an American at Trinity Hall, Cambridge, who had won the Diamonds in a record time of 8 minutes 29 seconds, later set a record for the Wingfields when he beat Harry Blackstaffe in the final in 22 minutes 56 seconds, beating Vivian Nickalls's 23 minutes 30 seconds set four years previously.

As far as the Henley honours board was concerned, this was a gloomy period

for London. Membership topped 600, a record, in 1899, and there was success in
fours at other regattas that year, but the only movement noticed by the club at the
Royal Regatta was the re-positioning of the course further towards the Berks station
to try and neutralise the shelter created by houseboats and trees on the Bucks side.
You can sense the frustration in the club reports at this time: in 1900 there was
another unsuccessful Henley, where the London crews 'lacked watermanship', but
were fairly successful overall, winning senior eights at five regattas and senior
fours at four. Goring and Streatley Regatta was still not finding favour at London.
'The attractions of the regatta are not great, the course is bad, the means of access
difficult. The committee... must either exclude entirely the skiff and dongola races
or put them at such periods as need not interfere with the orthodox part of the
regatta.' At Walton in 1901 the senior eight 'were not apparently prepared to
row a moderately fast stroke.' Rating 32, they were beaten by Kingston at 36.
But Holman Hunt, son of the pre-Raphaelite painter William Holman Hunt,
sculled well during that season, winning the junior-senior sculls at Marlow.

New members included Frederick J Furnivall, a maverick intellectual,
educator and oarsman who in 1896 founded the Hammersmith Sculling Club
for Girls (now the mixed club known as Furnivall Sculling Club). Furnivall's club
differed from such institutions as London in many respects, and represented a
world of rowing whose only overlap with the great racing clubs at the start of the
new century was shared water on the Tideway. Working girls were recruited
from among Furnivall's students and the waitresses at the ABC café that he
frequented. They were taught to row and introduced to river picnics, tea parties,
concerts, and winter classes in elocution and singing. The last were unpopular,
and stopped when Furnivall admitted that girls came to the club 'not to improve
their minds but to relax them'. The club organised outings for orphan children,
and teas for the elderly in the clubhouse. In 1900 members of Working Men's
College's music and dramatic society were invited on Boat Race day to 'see the
race, scull, dance and sing'.[3] Quite unlike the goings on at Henley remembered
by Sir Bertram Cubitt, KCB, when he reminisced about Henley in the 1880s and
1890s: 'London used to put up at the Red Lion, and training was severe.
The reaction on the last night was very great, and the police, though few, were
constantly in evidence – except in '86, when the LRC locked them up in their
own cells. The crew particularly disliked the peal of the church bells just over
them. One year, two of the second eight climbed to the belfry and tied up the
bells, which remained silent for the rest of that regatta.'[4]

The brilliant exception to the season of 1902 was a new sculler who earned a
mention in dispatches: 'As regards sculling, which with one brilliant exception

seems to be a decaying art in the club, the success of A Hamilton Cloutte, was most gratifying.' He put himself out of Henley's Diamonds by hitting a pile, but later won the Wingfields in a dramatic race. Cloutte lay second to Raymond Etherington-Smith of Leander for most of the way, and was seven to eight lengths down at Barnes bridge after he was involved in a collision with another boat. He then stormed after the Leander man, and they ran into each other. Etherington-Smith got away first but was caught by Cloutte on the line, and his half-hearted claim of the foul was dismissed by the umpire. The club had a good junior eight, lightweight at under eleven stone to a man. The senior eight tried a new design of swivel rowlocks at Walton. Next year was a bad one on all counts. There was a record membership of 776 but a lack of heavy men, lack of practice, lack of funds and so on. The club's favourite boat builder, George Sims, died. Cloutte lost the Wingfields to Frederick Septimus Kelly of Leander, and was beaten by the same for the second time in the Diamonds.

Cloutte bore the London colours for nine consecutive years in the Diamonds. In 1904 his first race was against Kingston's Douglas Stuart, who hit the booms. Next year it was Cloutte who hit the booms and lost to A A Stuart of London. In 1905 he lost the final to L F Scholes of Toronto. That was the nearest he came to winning, although he also reached the final of the Wyfold in 1904 when Birmingham RC were given the verdict after a messy race involving two fouls and locked oars. Henley success eventually came for Cloutte in 1911 when he appeared in Thames colours partnering his friend Julius Beresford. They won the Goblets, and he raced with Beresford twice more in that event.

London changed tactic by starting its juniors on fixed seats in 1904, and making them race on fixed seats as well. The racing record was disastrous. The Wyfold was lost to Birmingham RC as described above. At Kingston, the Coronation Cup crew for Thames Cup eights rowed and lost with seven men after the eighth didn't show up. The junior eight lost to Cooper's Hill, the boat club of the Royal Indian Engineering College, at Staines, and to Ibis at Molesey, both using fixed seats and, in their first race, a four lost to Royal Chester at Salford Regatta.

The chief concern of the committee in 1905 was lecturing the members on the financial straits confronting them. But the Wyfold four won, and elsewhere there was a smattering of good results, once more indicating that the seed-corn for the seekers of glory at the top regatta soldiered on. The magazine *Punch* was having fun as usual at Henley, suggesting that boating men fitted a mirror in front of them to 'look where you are going'. Hamilton Cloutte said he tried this and 'found

Webb's Wharf in Wharf Lane, Henley, where LRC's first houseboat rented for members during the regatta was moored in 1889. The watercolour, painted in the same year, is attributed to Janet Cooper

the bank more readily than ever'. A recruitment crisis followed next year, plus an outbreak of mumps in the club, and the bow man of the eight failed to show up at Marlow. But, again, the Wyfold was secured. This was the Henley when the Belgians won the Grand for the first time, and this was the first year that Henley occupied four days. The Royal was now the only regatta in Britain that had not moved to a weekend, but it held out only until 1911 when the finals were held on a Saturday. A unique fixture took place on the tideway when Harvard raced Cambridge from Putney to Mortlake in eights, the verdict going to Cambridge.

On Henley water, London's record continued to lack lustre. Nothing came the club's way until the Wyfold in 1914. In 1907 the club imposed a restriction on the number of regattas for which they would pay entrance fees and boat cartage. W E Green put down £500–£1,500 for prizes to revive the club fours event that was re-named the Green Fours, and £1,000 for general purposes. The Belgians won the Grand again. When the Olympic Regatta came to Henley in 1908, the Stewards refused entries from foreigners for their regatta, which preceded the games, 'in order to prevent any possible loss of entries for the Olympic regatta'. That season, London had a good second eight and two good fours, but no scullers. In 1909 the Belgians returned to win the Grand, having lost the Olympics to Leander's carefully prepared 'old men's crew', experienced toughies some of whom were hauled out of retirement, who had enjoyed weeks of training, unsullied by foreigners, on the Olympic course. London's only senior wins were the eights events at Staines and Molesey, although at Staines the most important event was wrecked by a launch. London's Club Eights was rowed on fixed seats, and there was a serious collision in the first Green Fours race. Next year saw the opening of a novelty indoor tank at London, and trial eights were revived after a lapse of a year. Stewart Bradshaw became the first London member to umpire at Henley.

Despite the new training facility, the captain's report for 1912 says that the Henley crews were not complete until they 'took up residence on the course'. London's four had success after Henley, partly attributed to Thames's winning Stewards' crew being away on Olympic duty in Stockholm. F S Watts presented the club with a new eight. In 1913 the Prince of Wales, a student at Magdalen College, Oxford, took tea at the clubhouse after following the Boat Race. There is a sad newspaper clipping reporting Cloutte's

Menu for annual dinner, 1906

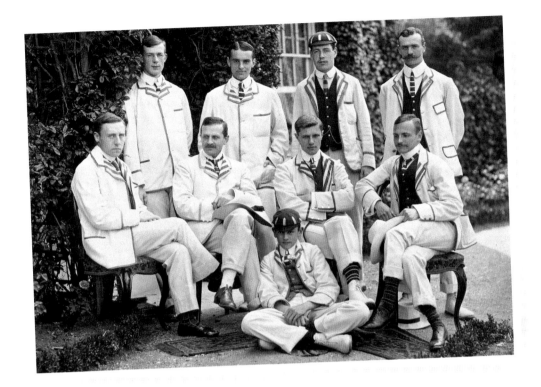

fall from grace, reporting that Arthur Hamilton Cloutte, aged forty-two, of Wimbledon Park was sentenced to six months hard labour for embezzling £200 from his employers, Baring Brothers. When arrested, Cloutte said: 'The game is up. There is no defence, and I make none.' He was described as a diligent worker for the bank for twenty years who had invested disastrously in mining, and the defalcations at the bank were thought to amount to more like £3,000. The bank did not sue for more because Cloutte was known to have a wife, five young children, a widowed mother and sisters to support. Also in 1913, the club purchased the freehold of its premises from Lord Westbury for £3,000. London's Claude 'Jock' Wise won the Wingfields, beating the 1912 Olympic champion Kinnear, and Charles Innes died. A former lightweight bow man and club secretary, he was an enthusiastic cyclist who, with Ebenezer Morley, pioneered bicycle touring abroad.

There is no question that in many senses the European world of the Victorian and Edwardian reigns was to end in 1914. But in daily life there were many developments during the period spanned by this chapter. In terms of industrial power, if steam was still king, changes were signalled by the arrival of the motor vehicle, the spread of electric light, the novelty of the telephone, and feat of the Frenchman Bleriot in flying across the Channel in 1909. Developments on the home stretch paralleled the expansion and imperial grandeur of London. Public transport became quicker and easier with the abolition of tolls on Hammersmith, Putney

One of four Grand eights stroked by G R Davis, seated, second from right, from 1902 to 1905

London Rowing Club tankards (left to right): *Junior trial eights, 1881; LRC Scratch eights, 1892; LRC Scratch eights 1895; twelve-oar race, 1876, won by E B Woodford*

and Battersea bridges in 1880. New landmarks included Putney's new bridge in 1884, and Hammersmith's new chain bridge, to a design by Bazalgette, which opened in 1887. Ten years later a new marker was built on the Surrey shore downstream of this bridge when the soap works and sugar refinery developed by Lewis Cowan was acquired by Harrods and replaced by a grand furniture depository. Designed by William George Hunt, it was constructed between 1896 and 1908. In 1888 there was a new embankment in Putney, and an additional bridge to carry the District Railway to Wimbledon opened in 1889. Those who ventured further downstream would have passed through a new Battersea bridge from 1890 and found the grandiose Tower bridge guarding the Pool of London from 1894.

At the club, extensions had added a sitting room and bedrooms, a washing room, committee room, and new entrance hall by 1893. Fulham Football Club moved to the Half Moon field for a season in 1895, but their fans were reluctant to make the journey across the river. Generally, there was huge boom in amateur rowing clubs in the forty years running up to 1914. Rowing institutions developed to support it. The great amateur debate rumbled into the new century when, eight years after the formation of the Amateur Rowing Association, a third of its members split to form the National ARA in 1890 to champion the cause of the artisan amateur. The secretary of the ARA, Rudie Lehmann, personally believed in reconciling factions, but his members were less so inclined. The argument was vitriolic at times. Such as a letter signed 'Corinthian' in the *Field* attacking the NARA as non-amateur and personally attacking its leading lights, the Rev Propert of Thames RC and Dr Furnivall. Propert replied: 'I cannot forget that I belong to a society – the Church – in which such invidious distinctions are unknown.' He condemned his stabber in the back as unworthy and ignoble, and Furnivall wrote to the paper that there is at least one Christian on the committee of Thames. In 1901 Lehmann signed an agreement with the International Rowing Federation, which was wooing the English associations, but the ARA stood aloof from trucking with foreigners, and from reconciliation with the NARA, until after

Above: *Grand Challenge Cup commemorative oar, 1890*

the Second World War. The Tradesmen's Rowing Clubs Association is in being by 1891, the Skiff Racing Association came along in 1901, the Thames Amateur Rowing Council in 1903, and in 1905 the ARA revised and published the rules of racing. In 1914 rowing was revived at Westminster School after a thirty-year lapse, when a coxed four stroked by Lyle Schlotel beat Haileybury from Beverley Brook to Harrod's Wharf. Both boated from London.

And by the turn of the century, the non-tidal Thames was a place of recreation as much as commercial highway, a place for regattas, weekends and day excursions by river and rail. In 1884 a letter in the *Field* complained of the nuisance of bathing from the banks of the river '...it is by no means an infrequent occurrence to find [bathers] in the main stream eye, and see them run along the towing path, seemingly devoid of all sense of decency. It is risky to enter the backwaters for a picnic with ladies in the party.' Another letter complained of white-trousered 'gentlemen' who infest the Thames about Weybridge. The use of the river for leisure was epitomised in Jerome K Jerome's Three Men in a Boat, published in 1899.

Nevertheless, in 1914 a heavy cloud hung over both British rowing and Henley Regatta in more ways than one. Almost a hundred London members were already on active service. Four British crews were obliterated in the first round of the Grand, making the semifinals an all-foreign affair. Harvard beat the Union Boat Club in an all-Boston final. E D P Pinks lost his heat of the Diamonds to the eventual winner, Giuseppe Sinigaglia of Lario, Como, who was later killed in action. After Henley, London won four events at Kingston, which turned out to be the last regatta before hostilities began. The First World War was about to take its toll.

Below: *Fish knife and fork set, prize for the twelve-oar race, 1871*

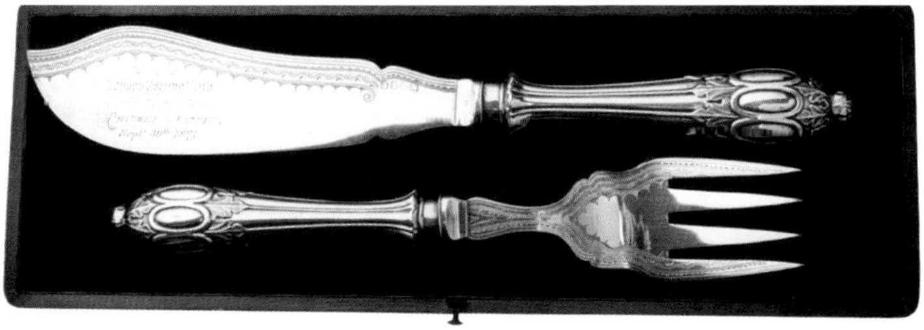

8 FOREIGN AFFAIRS

The London Rowing Club was more than a gentlemen's club; it was a gentlemen's club whose members wished to actively pursue rowing, many of whom had not passed through rowing schools nor attended university. There is no definition of 'gentleman'; the term encompasses the possession or aspiration to all or some of a list of vagaries, such as wealth (preferably unearned), profession, possession of land, success, style, status in the community and trust. It is all juicily vague. Most of the London oarsmen who owned up to an occupation worked in the stock exchange, in banks or trading companies, with a fair smattering of professions such as architects, doctors and lawyers. They lived in the most exciting city on earth in the mid-nineteenth century, a city driving a growing empire fuelled by trade, invention and great advances in engineering. Many of them had overseas connections. From its foundation, London had a large number of members who lived abroad, and names such as Monteuuis, Schlotel and Casamajor suggest either foreigners in their midst or family connections with other places.

Detail of J R K Fenning's certificate for winning the Olympic pairs, 1908

If the original aspiration of the club was to see off the universities at Henley, it is not surprising to find that taking on foreigners soon became a challenge to which the members warmed. Before London Rowing Club, rowing was established in Australia, Belgium, China, France, Germany, Hungary, Ireland, Russia, Spain, Sweden and the United States, though not in that order. Most of the pioneer clubs had some British involvement in getting them going, a good example being the first club in Budapest which involved Hungarians and British workers constructing the Chain bridge which was modelled on the old Hammersmith bridge and was the first to join Buda to Pest. The entrepreneur who built it, Count István Szécheny, was taught to row in London by Lord Jersey in the 1820s.

So it was not long before international aspirations were voiced at London. The club's first venture overseas was to the Cork Harbour Rowing Club Regatta in August 1860. Messrs Casamajor, George Sherriff, Boydell and Herbert Playford, with twelve-year-old Weston steering, manned the gig Blonde to take on the Sylph and the Mystery from the regatta quay at Glenbrook round a flag boat near Ringaskiddy and back, a distance of about three-and-a-half miles. The other two crews were from Cork Harbour RC and both were trained by Thomas Grant, the champion sculler of the Trent. The boats were matched gigs

J.B.CLOSE.

F.S.GULSTON.

A.De.L.LONG.

W.STOUT.

EDWARD SMITH

ALEXANDER HANDY

THEODORE VAN-RADEN

D.r RUSSELL WITHERS

THE INTERNATIONAL FOUR-OARED BOAT-RACE: THE ENGLISH CREW.

THE INTERNATIONAL FOUR-OARED BOAT-RACE: THE AMERICAN CREW.

by Wyld of Lambeth. It was a close race, London's *Blonde* losing an early lead to *Sylph* until, passing Glenbrook Hotel, they regained it, and were ahead by twelve seconds at the turn. The Cork crews closed up on the return leg at Monkstown Pier until London gained again at Glenbrook Pier and won by a length and a half. The *Cork Daily Herald* praised Weston for his skill on the currents of the harbour, and remarked that 'there was seldom a better contested race witnessed on the river'. Next year another London crew – Grubb, Boydell, Ryan, Stout and Weston – rowed in the *Vivid* for the Glenbrook Cup against Lee Harbour RC, Phoenix Club from Kilbogie and Cork Harbour RC, this time two-and-a-half miles round the flag. Lee ran out the winners, but London put up a good race, Weston gaining a couple of lengths at the turn which he executed as upon a pivot, aided by a nudge in the stern from the Cork Harbour boat.

In 1860 the club proposed an international regatta involving gentlemen rowers of the United States, France, Belgium, Sweden and Russia. Nothing came of it, but the real breakthrough came when London entered the senior fours at the Paris International Regatta in 1867. They were beaten by three lengths by the Western Club from St John, New Brunswick, a crew regarded with suspicion because they were fishermen and not, therefore, tainted with a gentlemanly hue.

Portraits of LRC and US crews 1872, LRC (left) and Atalanta (right)

More to the point, however, was that their heavy boat was lightened by the absence of a cox. They had fitted it with steering gear operated by the bow man's foot, and swept all before them. The man from the *Manchester Guardian*, Charles Prestwich Scott, gave them other attributes: 'Splendid condition and enormous grit, but also partly to the good qualities of their boats, which though much too heavy [200 pounds against the others' 60 pounds], are keel built, stand up well at the bows, and displace wonderfully little water.' R Gesling of Paris won the sculls after a foul with London's Stout was awarded in his favour. Eugene Monteuuis, another Londoner who on this occasion was sculling for Boulogne, was second, and Gibbons of London third. The third day of the Paris Regatta was run under British rules on a mile-and-a-half course between the bridges of St Cloud and Suremes on the Seine. It was organised by Edwin Brickwood of London RC who also acted as umpire with his fellow Londoner, James Ireland. Stout beat another Londoner, Ryan, to win the sculls, with 'Guts' Woodgate of Brasenose third.

This regatta, and the great match which took place on London's doorstep two years later when Oxford raced Harvard in fours, were to spark profound changes in rowing. The appearance of the St John crew without a cox sent reverberations through the rowing world, and caused Henley to drop coxswains from all four-oared events by 1874. This was brought about by Woodgate, who fitted self-steering wires to his foot stretcher in the Brasenose four at the 1868 regatta and won the Stewards' by a street. When Brasenose's intention of rowing without a cox was made known, the stewards hastily created a rule stating that all eights and fours should carry one. But the new rule did not specify that a cox must be on board at the finish line. Woodgate arranged for the Brasenose cox, Fred Weatherley, to jump overboard after the start. The crew was disqualified but the point was made. The St John crew, meanwhile, could not row at Henley, but they engaged in matches with world-class professional Tyneside crews during the next few years, contributing to the quest for the sliding seat.

The Oxford versus Harvard race was a huge affair. An American crew in London aroused the press on both sides of the Atlantic and provided a month-long saga of practice and testing boats before the two coxed fours lined up on the Boat Race course, on 27 August 1869, before a crowd alleged to be several hundred thousand strong. Both crews boated from London's shed. Many members were involved in hosting the Harvard men, finding them accommodation at the White House along the Lower Richmond Road, which was more suitable than the Star & Garter where they first stayed, and entertaining the stream of VIPs who visited them. Several were also involved in staging the race, notably

Frank Gulston, captain of London, who acted as Harvard's umpire, while London's Sir Aubrey Paul was in the flag boat at the finish line. Charles Dickens Jr was one of organisers of the concluding grand dinner hosted by London in the Western Avenue of the Crystal Palace, where his father, the novelist, was the main speaker. Thomas Hughes MP proposed the 'London Rowing Club', which he described as 'a sort of oasis for rowing men from the universities'. Hopes of repeating this fixture failed, but the impact it had on post-Civil War America, despite the fact that Harvard were defeated after leading by a length at Hammersmith bridge, was immense. Within the next few years dozens of colleges added rowing to their programmes right across the Midwest. The Harvard versus Yale race had started collegiate sport in 1852, and the trip to race Oxford seventeen years later opened a new chapter on the west side of the Atlantic.

The next thing that happened for London was an invitation from the Hudson River Boating Association in 1870, but the club could not raise a crew. Two years later, however, the Atalanta Boat Club of New York challenged London to a match on the Thames. The letter assured London that Atalanta had been strictly amateur since its inception in 1848, never racing professionals nor rowing for a money prize. 'The recent contests between the professional oarsmen of Europe and America, as well as the colleges of Oxford and Harvard, having proved of so much interest and benefit to rowing, we feel assured that a race between amateur oarsmen of England and the United States would not fail to create an interest in rowing never before felt.' In accepting the challenge, London rejected Atalanta's assertion that the club stood at the head of amateur oarsmen of Europe. 'Such a distinction we do not merit, or claim even in England, having been frequently defeated in our numerous contests,' wrote president Layton and captain Gulston.

The Americans sailed to Liverpool on the *Montreal Star* and were met by a delegation from London who took a tug out to meet their ship and bring them ashore. The party of

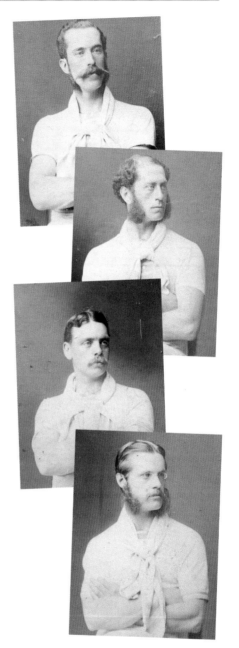

The men who beat Atalanta in 1872 Top to bottom: *A De Lande Long*, *F S Gulston*, *W Stout, John B Close*

five – the spare was named Leander Waterbury – brought a four and a single with them, and were entertained by Liverpool oarsmen for the evening that they spent at the Washington Hotel. The *Daily Telegraph* reporter who wrote of their arrival was at pains to distance Atalanta from professionals who row for stakes, and from students who come and go. 'Both [crews] consist of what we are obliged to call upper middle-class men, and both recruit largely from "the City".' The American crew was chosen from the club six-oar which had beaten both Harvard and Yale, eights being almost unknown there at this time, and they practised on the quiet tidal waters of the Passiac River. Their occupations were listed as physician, banker, ice merchant and two clerks in mercantile houses.

The London and North Western Railway did the party proud, giving them a special salon and a truck for the boats and routing it from Liverpool to Putney via Crewe, Willesden, Kensington and Clapham Junction. London decked out Putney station with bunting and conducted their guests to Mr Marshall's Fox and Hounds Hotel, and a reception at the club followed that evening. A salute was fired 'from several small pieces' and a statement made to the effect that the Americans would not appear on the river for three or four days to allow recuperation after a stormy voyage.

The Americans moved to Hammersmith, where their boats were housed at Biffens. The two boats by the New York builder Roahn that they brought with them had filled with water and warped on the voyage. Biffen made them a new, light, fixed seat pine boat in time for the race. The crew was Dr Russell Withers, stroke, Alexander Handy, Theodore van Raden and Edward Smith at bow. London picked Stout, Long, Gulston and Close, with Fred Fenner coaching. They were practising in an old Messenger fixed seat boat steered by a 'clever contrivance invented by Gulston', but had others on order from J H Clasper, now of Oxford, and Jewett of Dunstan. At the end of May they went for a long row to Kingston on the day before trying out the Clasper, built of cedar with pine fittings and sliding seats. 'The crew are, we believe, very impressed in favour of this new style of rowing,' said the *Times*, while publishing a leading article condemning it. London tried the Jewett before opting for the Clasper. The papers had failed to whip up much interest in the event outside the rowing fraternity, but on the day of the race a sizeable crowd assembled on a windy day. 'The river was crowded with rowing boats of all shapes and sizes,' said the *Standard*, 'steam pleasure boats and tugs panted and puffed everywhere; great barges floated up with masses of spectators, and a large number of steamers went up early and took up places of "vantage."' Although the wind dropped and the water was calmer, it remained rough above Hammersmith, and at the last moment the decision was taken to row the race down instead of up. This was because the American crew were known to be averse to rough water, and London, confident in their superiority, were anxious to give the visitors every advantage so that there should be no grounds for quibble afterwards. The decision made, the boats were each paddled up to Mortlake by two watermen, while the crews were taken up by the umpire's steamer.

London won the toss and chose Middlesex, giving them an advantage of the first bend. The starting point was the university boat race finish. A dozen strokes after the pistol shot that began the race, London were half a length in front, and clear in twenty strokes. Rating 39, they took Atalanta's stream and were five lengths to the good at Barnes bridge, according to the *Standard*, while the *Globe* put it at three. 'Gulston kept his boat in a capital course, in the full run of the tide, and at each stroke they gained.' Below Hammersmith bridge there was congestion. 'In spite of the exertions of the police and Conservancy boats, it looked a ticklish mass to thread,' said the *Standard*. 'By the soap works, unluck- ily, a couple of boats from below the bridge, with a full consignment of women, managed to foul the Atalanta for 6 secs... Free from these boats, the Atalanta kept on at 40 and 41 to the Point, where another near shave of a foul occurred, and they were eventually beaten by 46 seconds, London easing slightly at the end.' The *Globe* has the margin at 45 seconds, with London's time as 21 minutes 23 seconds.

Only four steamers were allowed to follow – one for the umpire, one for the press and one for each set of supporters. The day was a bit of a disaster for the American supporters' club, because they packed nearly three hundred people on to their boat, including the Coldstream band. Consequently the gaily-decorated vessel could not keep up, reaching Hammersmith when the crews were threading their way amongst a mass of rowing boats to the finish at Putney.

The verdict hardly lived up to the billing, and the *Standard* lamented: 'A more hollow affair was never witnessed upon the Thames, and the American crew, although they are the champions in their own country, would not be good enough to win an ordinary country river regatta here.' But in lecturing the 'plucky cousins' to 'take a leaf from the older country, and diligently mark, learn, and digest how we row in England, and why we do so,' the paper identified one of the reasons for the strength of rowing in what it referred to as the mother country. Rowing is now more than an art, it alleged: it is now a scientific art. 'For many years professional rowing in England has given occupation, on both Tyne and Thames, to men whose sole object in life became henceforth to learn theoretically the fastest way to propel a boat over the water, and practically to put into execution those ideas and to tone the two down to suit one another.' So innovation has been tested. The *Globe*, meanwhile, found that London's coxless crew for the contest opened a new era in English rowing. 'Hitherto we have held the opinion that the additional weight of a coxswain was fully counter-balanced by his usefulness in the boat. The Americans have held a different view, and the introduction yesterday of the American system is likely to strongly modify the previous notion,' it said. 'Besides the credit of having rowed a gallant race, the Atalanta crew deserve the thanks of English rowing men for having taught them the advantage of a new system.'

The ripples of this race, and the mysteries of rowing for the outsider, reached the leafy lanes of Devon in a curious way. Henry James, the novelist, was travel-ling by coach between Barnstaple and Ilfracombe enjoying the landscape, he said, in spite of two 'worthy aboriginals' who were reading about the facts of the race. 'It seemed to me, I remember, a sort of pledge and token of the invincibility of English muscle that a newspaper record of its prowess should have the power to divert my companions' eyes from the bosky flanks of Devonshire combes.'[1]

In August 1872 an invitation arrived to send a crew to Sydney to compete at Balmain Regatta in coxed four-oared gigs, Sydney RC offering hospitality, but London had to turn down the offer because captain Gulston could not find enough men able to take the required time off business to visit 'your colony', as London's letter put it.

The Anglo-Teuton Boat race took place on 24 June 1876 and resulted in a drubbing for a lightweight crew from Frankfurter Ruder-Gesellschaft, conquerors of the Continent, over the championship course from Putney to Mortlake. The *Illustrated Sporting and Dramatic News* had a great time sniping at all and sundry. The Frankfurt men, 'forgetful of the fate of the Atalanta Club, which, misled by ex-university reporters, found out too late the calibre of its opponents.' The reporter noted that they issued a challenge to London even though one of their crew, educated in England, had once been a member of another well-known London club, and ought, therefore, to have 'well understood the true nature of his countrymen's undertaking'.

Furthermore, they insisted on the 'forgotten practice of carrying a coxswain', so London had to use a new, 'and of course now practically useless', Clasper boat which was too light in the bows, causing her to 'suck under nastily forwards at every stroke'. London were seven pounds per man heavier and had more power and weight on stroke side. According to the club report, the Frankfurt crew insist-ed on the Londoners carrying extra weight because they were heavier, a contribu-tory factor to the performance of the boat. They also had the Surrey station with a strong wind blowing off the Middlesex shore, thus being impeded by rough water for the first mile. London had a bad start and took some distance to shake off their opponents, settling to 36 or 37 strokes to the minute and turning a half-length deficit into clear water at Craven Point before achieving an easy victory. The Germans reached well forward but put all their power into the finish of the stroke, leaning far back and ending with a jerk that 'quite buried the boat', at a rating of 29 to 30. The club reporter remarked that the difference in stroke was very deceptive to spectators, giving the appearance that London were rowing very fast and Frankfurt extraordinarily slowly. The man from the *Sporting and Dramatic News* noted that there was not much interest in the betting, either, the odds moving from 5 to 1 on London to 10 to 1 on London, and still with no takers. He clearly had a bilious day.

London's first competitive venture abroad took place in 1876 when the club sent a four consisting of Labat, Gulston, Trower and Howell to the Philadelphia Centennial Regatta on the Schuylkill River, a confluence of the Delaware. The Schuylkill Navy, as the clubs centred on Boathouse Row in Fairmont Park were known, staged a five-day meeting at the end of August, which went sour for London. The reporter from the London *Times* set the scene: 'In the first place, the climate affected them terribly, the heat being intense and trying to Europeans, the mosquitoes exasperating, the place enervating, the food utterly different from

London's crew at the Philadelphia Centennial Regatta, 1876 (left to right): Labat, Gulston, Trower, Howell

1. Struggle between the London and Yale Crews at the Finish, August 29th. 2. The Finish on August 30th—The Beaverwycks Victorious—Scene from the Grand Stand.

THE INTERNATIONAL FOUR-OARED REGATTA ON THE SCHUYLKILL RIVER.

Views of racing in Philadelphia, 1876

anything they had ever been accustomed to. Everyone became more or less ill within a few days after arrival in Philadelphia, want of sleep, diarrhoea, nausea, vomiting, sore throats etc, being prevalent.' First Trinity BC, Cambridge, and Dublin University RC were also affected. He described the course – captured brilliantly by the artist Thomas Eakins five years earlier in his painting of Max Schmitt in a single scull – as a mile and a half amid pretty scenery and wooded banks, with the start below the Pennsylvania and Reading Railroad Bridge, immediately bending to the right for half a mile before straightening out, with the finish being under another railway bridge. The current was scarcely perceptible, 'but the water is dirty and unwholesome, emits a faint, sickly odour, and produces malaria in the cool evenings', being one reason why the racing had to take place in the heat of the day. The status of American amateurs did not escape the eye of the *Times*, either. Still more objectionable than the weather and food, the reporter said, were the oarsmen of doubtful status with whom London and Co were expected to compete. They included 'coal whippies, glass blowers, hewers of wood, drawers of water, working mechanics, and other handicraftsmen, such as one is accustomed to see take part in the professional races at the Thames National Regatta, and who gain their living by manual labour.'

There were seven heats for the amateur fours. London were drawn against Atalanta, who did not start, and the powerful Northwestern from Chicago, whom they defeated after a struggle in the fastest time of the day. Dublin came second to Eureka, of Newark, New Jersey, while First Trinity won easily from Oneida of Burlington. Trinity lost their semi-final against New York's Watkins Glen crew when one of their men was ill and had to be transferred to a steamboat. London defeated Yale in a good race to earn a place in the final, but it was not without controversy. Robert J Cook, who was rowing bow in the Yale crew and enduring his first experience of steering, had spent time being coached by Gulston at London in 1872 when he visited Oxford and Cambridge to learn the English stroke and how it was taught.[2] The unprejudiced observer from the *Times*, on whose reports London relies in its records, described the race between master and pupil on the perfect amphitheatre formed by the high bluff on the western shore, the park and curve above the waterworks, thus: 'London, on the faster western station, took off at 44 to 46 strokes to the minute to Yale's 38 to 40, settled at 41, and went out to half-a-length lead. By the mile this was almost a length, with Yale rowing at least three strokes lower. Without open water London's Gulston began the first of his jockeying and edged Yale very close to the flags on the east shore. As the crews came into the last straightaway, he again edged Yale to the outside of the curve. Now three-quarters of a length down, Kennedy sprinted up to 40 and pulled London right back. The crews crossed the line with London the winner by five feet in 8:51.75.' Cook always maintained that Gulston had jockeyed him out of the race, even though he regarded Gulston's remark as they rowed back to the boathouses – 'Well, boys, this is a vindication of your English stroke even if you didn't win' – sincere rather than patronising.

In the final against Watkins Glen and Beaverwyck from Albany, London had the centre station and held their own for 300 yards. They were level with Beaverwyck at the half-mile but trailed Watkins by half a length. Here Watkins 'took a shot at them, although called upon by Mr Gulston to give way', according to the *Times*. Watkins's starboard oars clashed with London's ports, and London's stroke claimed a foul by raising his arm. With Watkins still leading, Beaverwyck now moved on London and a further clash took place. Entering the last half mile, London dumped Watkins by two lengths and, crossing towards the judges' box,

THE CENTENNIAL REGATTA—THE LONDON CREW WINNING THE SIXTH AND LAST HEAT OF THE FOUR-OARED SHELL RACE, AUGUST 29th, 1876.

London on the Schuylkill, Philadelphia, 1876

led Beaverwyck by half-a-length. Both crews spurted and London thought they crossed the line a quarter of a length ahead. The judge awarded the race to Beaverwyck by 18 inches, so London claimed the race on foul by both of their opponents or requested a re-row. The umpire's refusal on the grounds that he saw no infringement – his steamer being a long way behind – caused the London captain to give the race committee written notice of withdrawal from the rest of the regatta. The American version of the final refers to Beaverwyck's jockeying, gives them a verdict of three feet instead of 18 inches, and cites the slow time of more than nine minutes as evidence of both head wind and the damage Yale did on the previous day.[3] Dublin University won the international graduates' race by a row-over, and First Trinity lost the international undergraduates' race when they hit a shoal of weeds 'which should have been removed' before their number 2, Close, collapsed for the second time in the regatta, run out by drinking the water of the Schuylkill.

The *Times* reporter concluded that 'To the unprejudiced observer it was evident that the native style of rowing could not compare with the English.' He cited the victory of Yale over Harvard as testament to the fact that Bob Cook of Yale had spent time in England, particularly at London, studying the English stroke. 'To remedy the present objectionable state of affairs is the first duty of the universities of the New World, as it was the task of the Old in years gone by,' pronounced the *Times*.

Meanwhile, the *Field* issued a catalogue of accusations about the behaviour of the Americans. 'During the progress of the regatta an attempt was made to drug the drink of the London crew, but it was fortunately frustrated,' reported the paper.[4] 'But Yankee's cunning was not to be outwitted so easily.' Being on board the umpire's launch, the *Field*'s man Argonaut saw, from a few feet away, the 'miscreant who held the stern of the London boat' try to wrench the rudder with his right hand while holding the boat under water with his left. Fortunately he failed to get it off, but it was bent out of position, as verified after the race. Gulston wrote to the *Field* shortly afterwards alleging that the winning posts were positioned on the skew and not at right angles to the course, and said that he lost faith in the judge because his verdict was not given until several people had rushed into his box. Finally, Argonaut claimed evidence from an American newspaper that the American crews in the final against London were not true amateurs. Beaverwyck contained three plumbers and a foreman to a teamster, and Watkins Glen consisted of four iron-puddlers.

Two years after the Philadelphia excursion, the first American entries arrived at Henley Regatta. Columbia College's victory in the Visitors' and the very presence of the Shoe-wae-cae-mettes – French-speaking watermen who hardly passed the 'gentlemen' test – was fuel to both the argument over amateur status, and suspicion of anything foreign. London defeated the 'Shoes' in the final of the Stewards'. Whatever one's opinion, international contact in rowing was increasing. London men competed at Dublin Metropolitan Regatta in 1878, where C J White won the senior sculls under Pembroke RC colours and R H Labat won eights and fours with Dublin University RC. In 1879 White repeated his win and Labat and Gulston won two pots with University RC. The sculler Willoughby Grove was beaten in the French amateur championships in 1881. In 1883 London's tentacles were felt in Poona, where, reported the *Field*, 'Lieut. Grove, 61st Regiment, and Mr Croft, an Etonian, added much to the brilliancy of the meeting by their excellent rowing. They won the challenge fours after a very hard race. Croft rowed a fast stroke of 45 to the minute. They won the pairs easily and also the double sculls in outrigged gigs. Lieut. Grove won the sculls against Mr Croft after a very hard race. Grove rowed a much slower and longer stroke, as of old in the LRC at Putney, and jumped ahead with half a stroke at the first stroke, being two or three lengths ahead at halfway, gaining every stroke, and came in a winner. Grove also won the ladies' fours, a lady steered.'

The largest regatta on the Continent by now was Hamburg's, and London won the senior eights there in 1891, defeating Thames, Favorite Hammonia, Berliner Borussia, and Berliner Ruderclub, by nearly a length on a ten-abreast course on the Alster, '36 yards short of a mile and a quarter'. They used a Swaddle boat 'sent round by steamer'. Germans row short and bucket forward badly, despite English professional coaches, says the report. Thames won the Hammonia Cup for fours.

In 1892 an eight accepted a challenge to race the French in Paris. It was a disaster from London's point of view. The crew were suffering from seasickness, their swaddle was soaking wet and wouldn't dry out properly, and the bows were smashed during practice. On the Seine from Andresey to above the lock at Carrières-sous-Poissy, downstream, number 2's slide was faulty, and they lost by two lengths. The French crew used swivels, with unanimity of swing.

In 1895 A F G Everitt of London won the sculling championship of the Netherlands on the Amstel over 1900 metres, the first foreigner to win, beating J J Blussé of De Hoop, Amsterdam. By now, competition abroad and against foreigners at home was ceasing to be a novelty, and, of course, rowing clubs were proliferating in many countries, some with London influence, as in the case of T E Coulson, who won the Grand with London in 1890 and then took the Arrow Club of St Petersburg to the top of rowing in Russia.

The third modern Olympic games took place in London in 1908, and London had its first Olympian medallist at the regatta at Henley in the form of John Fenning, who won gold in the coxless pairs with G L Thomson from Leander, and a silver medal in the coxless fours with Thomson and two other Leander men. The club's second Olympic aspirant was the captain, R B Freeman, who unfortunately met with his death before the largely self-selected team to represent the 'United Kingdom' was formed. The absence of Freeman and Fenning disrupted the first eight and wrecked the chances of a good Henley. The Olympic regatta was stretched thinly over four days, the public took little interest, and the London barge was deserted except on the last day. The club report said that 'the English pairs were not up to the standard of the average winners of the Henley Goblets, but were quite fast enough to beat the foreign crews'. It went on: Fenning 'worthily represented the standard of oarsmanship which was once the marked characteristic of the London Rowing Club.'

The next London representation in the Olympics came in 1928 when Archie Nisbet and Terry O'Brien won silver in the coxless pairs and Denis Guye and Humphrey Boardman were unplaced in the double sculls. The regatta was on the Sloten canal in Amsterdam, and Nisbet and O'Brien reached the final by way of the new 'second chance' repêchage round, having beaten the Swiss but lost to the Americans in the opening heats. Their protest that the Americans cheated by starting on the 'Etes' and then washing the British down was rejected on the grounds that an 'international incident' might follow. Their defeat of the Italians admitted them to a final against the Germans, which they lost by two seconds. Despite finishing second, Nisbet remembered the final as their finest piece of rowing, and therefore the most enjoyable, together. 'I have always retained the clearest memory of Terry's stroking and rhythm and the way the boat travelled, which was as near perfect as anything in which I could have hoped to take part.'[5] Incidentally, Nisbet and O'Brien received their Olympic medals by post some time later. Nisbet's came in useful years later

The course at Lake Ontario, 1932

when his daughter Tilly had a part as a mayor in a school play. Archie drilled holes in his medal and attached it to her gilt chain of office with fuse wire.[6]

In June 1927 an eight went to Ostend for a grand challenge race and won in 5 minutes 6 seconds over a shortened course of 1,500 metres. At that time the start was given in French at international regattas, the routine being 'Etes vous prêt? Partez!' London got away smartly on the 'partez' only to find themselves a length behind the French, but went through them after a minute and won easily. At Whitsun in 1932 a hastily assembled crew flew to Cologne to race at Trier, where the German Olympic eight of 1928 beat them twice, but not dishonourably. Later in the year, the victorious Henley Grand eight and Stewards' four represented England at the British Empire games in Canada. They sailed on the Canadian Pacific line's *Empress of Australia* and survived a rough crossing to Quebec while keeping fit via deck games and skipping. The games were at Hamilton, Ontario, which they reached by overnight train, with accommodation at the Prince of Wales's School for the men and Hamilton Leander for the boats, situated on Hamilton Bay on Lake Ontario. The water conditions were atrocious, and the English team moved their boats to the basement of the Brandt Inn which was across the bay and close to the main lake, giving them options for practice. The downside was a forty-mile trek by lorry from their accommodation. The weather almost undid the regatta completely, but England won the eights in difficult conditions without the help of stake boats at the start. It was a neck-and-neck race with New Zealand requiring the stroke, Terry O'Brien, to call for three spurts from his crew. England won by three-quarters-of-a-length, with Canada third. There followed delays and stormy meetings with

Inside the certificate:

J. R. K. Fenning

MEMBER OF THE *London Rowing Club and Leander Boat Club.*

WINNER OF FIRST PRIZE FOR *Pair oared Race.*

AT·THE·OLYMPIC·GAMES·LONDON·1908·

Desborough

PRESIDENT OF THE
BRITISH OLYMPIC COUNCIL·

J R K Fenning's certificate for winning the Olympic pairs, with Leander's G L Thomson, 1908

officials before the fours race was staged on the old course on Hamilton Bay. London dismantled and transported all the boats to the venue, and then outclassed their opponents. But the day ended with the greatest tragedy of many, according to coach George Drinkwater's account.[7] 'The manager of the Brandt Inn had asked us to dinner, and had collected all the pretty girls of the district to dance with us. Alas! There was no alcohol.' The official dinner on the next evening was marred by tedium of interminable speeches but relieved by flasks of gin in the pockets of the crews.

The 1930s was a golden age for London at Henley, and a decade marked by expeditions to Paris, Copenhagen, Denmark, Portugal and Australia. In 1932 the sculler Tom Brocklebank and the London eight won their races at Surennes, the eight beating two French clubs and Mainz of Germany and enjoying great hospitality from their hosts, the Société de Regattes Internationales de Paris. They returned with a valuable Sèvres porcelain vase. They returned next year and won again, this time beating an allegedly fast and heavy crew from Yugoslavia. The social side was marked by presentation of a medal from the French government to London's Colonel Sankey. An admiral who gave a most complimentary address performed the ceremony in a restaurant but, 'to our disappointment, it was not crowned by any osculatory exhibition'. The colonel responded in eloquent fourth-form French. A third consecutive win by the eight was chalked up in Paris in the following year, the year in which London became the first English club to compete in Denmark. The eight lost there narrowly, but the four won.

An invitation to the centenary regatta of Henley-on-Yarra in Melbourne in 1934 was met at short notice, and seven men, a cox, their coach, Dermot St John Gogarty, and a new boat for the Victorian Rowing Association set sail from Tilbury on the RMS *Ormonde*. The eighth oarsman was Donald Wilson, an Australian, who was cabled to get fit. The crew entertained other passengers each morning and evening by displays of skipping and medicine ball exercises on the poop deck. Sight seeing and attempts at alcohol abuse in Gibraltar, Toulouse and Naples and romantic affliction in the moonlight and excruciating heat through the Suez Canal and Red Sea were capped by hospitality at Colombo Rowing Club, where chauffeur driven cars were supplied for trips to beauty spots. An outing in ancient fours in turtle-infested water was followed by pints of stout and tonic and a hasty departure aboard the harbour police launch because the *Ormonde*'s tender had already left. The ship stopped briefly at the Cocos Islands to drop provisions for the staff of the telegraph station, and then at Fremantle, where an outing in an eight was taken on the Swan River in Perth. Five weeks out from Tilbury, the crew arrived in Melbourne after a further stop in Adelaide and an outing on the Torrens estuary. After a welcoming lunch at the Melbourne Club, they unpacked the boat and, re-united with Wilson, began serious practice. The Australian press were much taken with the Fairbairn style of London, for there was little evidence of Fairbairnism among the Victorian crews. 'They appeared to neglect leg-drive, so the excitement the London style provoked was not without justification,' Gogarty reported. A programme of two outings a day was under-taken for most of the four weeks leading up to the regatta, and life was a constant battle between fitness and hospitality. The course on the Yarra was a measured mile downstream. London beat Hawthorn Rowing Club in their heat of the Grand Challenge Cup, and Richmond Rowing Club in the semifinal. They expected Wanganui of New Zealand to trail in the first half of the final before a customary strong finish. At halfway London were two lengths ahead and kept the pressure on. They continued to draw away and won by four lengths in 4 minutes 37 seconds, one second outside the record. Gogarty, who had entered the sculls, met with disaster in the first heat when his boat suddenly broke in half when he was in the lead. A week later, London won the seven-abreast two-and-a-half mile Victorian State Championships by thirteen lengths in 14 minutes 20 seconds. Second-placed Melbourne University were awarded the state title.[8]

Martin Bristow was the bow man in the GB coxless four at the Olympics at Grünau, Berlin, in 1936. He and two other London men, Alan Barrett and Jacko Jackson, with Oxford's Jan Sturrock in the stroke seat, went to the opening ceremony, which was performed by Adolf Hitler. When the Olympic flame was lit by the last runner in the torch relay, 30,000 pigeons were released at the same time, and Bristowe remarked that 'no one in my vicinity received a direct hit.'[9] The pigeons of peace were actually one basket under strength because members of the British eight, bored with waiting for the ceremony to begin, had discovered them stacked behind the stadium and liberated thirty birds before proceedings began. The crews were housed in a police academy and beat the inflexible transport system to the course on the Dahme Lange See by using their free bus passes. The near professional preparation of the German crews which led to gold medals in five of the seven events was recognised by Bristow as the sign of things to come after the Second World War, especially in the countries of central and eastern Europe. The German grip on gold was only broken by Jack Beresford and Dick Southwood in the double sculls and the University of Washington's eight. Messrs. Bristowe, Barrett, Jackson and Sturrock won the silver medal in the coxless fours.[10]

Several London men returned to Australia in 1938 for the British Empire games in Sydney. England's crew was a composite eight selected by London's Jacko Jackson and Thames's Jack Beresford after the Amateur Rowing Association had decided it was 'not practicable' to send a team. London University provided a new boat, and four London men were included in the eight, including Jackson who was also entered in the single sculls.[11] The multi-disciplined team sailed on the RMS *Ormond*, the same ship as had taken London to Melbourne in 1934. Beresford, the coach, had designed 'swinging boxes' for use on the poop deck, but they proved inadequate because the men found that they exhausted unexpected muscles such as triceps, neck and ankles, so they abandoned them in favour of two Lillywhite sculling machines which were fitted with dials to show them how far they had gone. They spent Christmas Day at Colombo Rowing Club by taking a middle-of-the-day outing on the stagnant waters and cooling off with stout and tonic. Six weeks on the *Ormond* brought them to the Empire village, next door to Sydney Cricket Ground, before the oarsman moved to a luxurious hotel on the edge of the Blue Mountains, close to the Nepean River where the regatta was to take place. Of their opponents, they observed that the New Zealanders were still and orthodox, while the Australians seemed to have worked towards a Fairbairn style under the close eye of Syd Raper since London's visit to Melbourne in 1934. After more than a week of practice, the English crew were going nowhere; although fit, they were not moving faster. Jackson eventually took matters out of

Beresford's hands by dropping Harman of Thames and bringing in London's Turner, who had been in Australia since 1934, at stroke. He shuffled the seating order completely. Their rhythm, rate of striking and confidence improved immediately, while the Australians interpreted the changes as weakness. The press and the public did not notice any improvement, and England went to the start as underdogs at 6–4, with Australia attracting odds of 4–6 and New Zealand at evens. The Aussies spent too much energy in blasting into the lead. The English reduced their lead to half-a-length after half-a-mile. Turner gave them a 'silent ten' to take them through, and they wound up to a rating of 40 strokes to the minute to win by three-quarters-of-a-length. 'Every credit is due to Turner, who rowed a perfect race on only twelve days training after not having rowed at all for three years; also to Jackson for his bold and farseeing action in bringing him into the crew in such circumstances,' Sturrock said. Jackson was second in the sculls. Ten days later they sailed for home on the *Stratheden*. 'With our pipes in our mouths and our glasses in our hands, we watched the Australian coast fade away behind us, leaving us with the pleasantest memories of a delightful country, a good race, and hospitality the like of which few of us will ever see again.'[12]

The 1930s were also marked by a series of visits to Figueira da Foz International Regatta on the river Mondego in Portugal. On the first occasion in 1935, London's coxless four encountered conditions 'rarely seen on the tideway at

The London 'style' on the Yarra, Melbourne, 1934

its worst', once having to disembark on one of the half-submerged sandbanks scattered over the course to empty their boat. They beat the Portuguese in a heat and a crew from the Marne in the final to win the Taça da Victoria.[13] A London four retained the trophy next year, beating the crews from Brussels and the Marne by three lengths over the one-and-a-auarter-mile course. The voyage from Southampton to Lisbon included a stop at the Spanish port of Vigo, which had been taken by General Franco's forces a few days beforehand, one of the first engagements in the Spanish Civil War.[14]

An ill-assorted four returned in 1937, composed of two men each from the first and second eights. Peter Lee reported that the journey out was not enlivened on this occasion by any Spanish interludes, agonising bus rides or affairs of the heart. They went on a long outing, the equivalent of Putney to Kew, but 'though mileage may make champions, this journey made no champions of us. It may have been due to the indifferent boat or the exceptionally rough conditions, but the effect was rather demoralising on a crew whose morale was never of the highest.' They scraped home in their heat to beat virtually the same Belgian crew as the year before and two Portuguese challengers. They came up against Caminha of Portugal and Njord (Leiden University) in the final. The Portuguese crew raced with immense spirit but 'little regard for the more essential features of non-syncopated rowing.' The Dutch crew was the best encountered by London in three visits to Portugal, rowing in the Fairbairn style of the German Wiking crew who had won the Grand at Henley earlier in the year. They set up a lead of two lengths while London floundered deplorably, but nevertheless London made up a length when the Dutch faltered. 'But at the critical moment, when a spurt might have brought us on terms, we elected to stage a most monumental shipwreck, and that decided the race.' The trophy was lost by two-and-a-half lengths.

If the aquatic performances left something to be desired, the three days of post-race junketing, enjoyed by all save some Dutchmen engaged in 'chasing the mouses out of their heads', did not. A charabanc tour of belvederes in forests led to a long walk through trees in answer to the question of whether the party would like a drink. 'Just when the whole proceeding of searching for a drink in the midst of a dense wood in the mountains was beginning to seem particularly farcical, we suddenly emerged into a clearing and were confronted by such a spectacle as must have inspired the hymnologist to declare "Thou spreadst a table in my sight..." for there, all alone in the forest glade, were two waiters in white coats and black bow ties guarding two very large tables, the one loaded with plates of sandwiches and the other groaning under cases and cases of bottled beer and red and white wine.' Fifteen bottles of vintage port arrived some time later, and the party eventually 'dispersed in considerable disorder'. Once more, thanks were conveyed to A F Fawcus for arranging the invitation through his friend Eduardo Pinto Basto.

The lesson Lee drew from the escapade was that 'it is a very great mistake to visit a foreign regatta, whether the standard is likely to be high or otherwise, except with the very best crew available'. He observed that national prestige in sporting events had become important, 'and for this reason it might be said that a bad entry is worse than no entry at all.'[15] Evidence for this argument followed in 1938 when the ambassador in Lisbon, through the British Council, urged London to send a crew to Estoril as well as to Figueira, an opportunity for a display of British culture and sporting prowess. The club answered the call with alacrity, although the Estoril Regatta never took place. A strong four consisting of a thirteen-and-a-half-stone bow man Guy Morris, Peter Lee, Harold 'Tootles' Carter and a sixteen-stone stroke, Dick Parker, with Guy Harris coxing at ten stone, had an adventurous journey to Figueira. They sensed the British Council's instructions to win in the invitation, and accordingly interrupted practice in Lisbon harbour with visits to the embassy, various ministries and newspapers. On the first day of the regatta they won the Taça da Victoria by a length and three-quarters after shipping gallons of water. This was a straight final against the universities of Brussels and Leiden and the Portuguese national champions. The crew from Wansee in Berlin were barred from entry because the trophy had been instituted to celebrate the victory of the Allies in the First World War. However, Wansee were a serious contender for the new and magnificent Taça Salazar, the most prestigious trophy of the Iberian peninsula.

On board
RMS Ormond *to*
Melbourne, 1938

England crews in Sydney, 1938

Commemorative rudder for winning the Centenary Grand Challenge Cup at Australian Henley, Melbourne, 1934

There were shenanigans with the draw, but eventually London, Wansee, Njord and Portugal's Associação Naval de Primeiro Maio lined up for the final. 'Our start was not all that could have been desired. It is regretted that bow-side beat the starter in disgraceful fashion and were already rowing hard on the "Are you ready?" Number 2 decided to wait for the "Go", and stroke caught a magnificent crab. In the next twenty strokes a further seven mini-crabs were caught.' They pulled themselves from last to second after 1,100 yards, a length behind the Germans. A prolonged spurt created a neck-and-neck race for the line, and in the last 165 yards London drew ahead to win by a bare length, while the pro-English crowd 'palpitated with emotion'. Lee sympathised with the German oarsmen, who could not let their hair down because of frostiness between the politicians of Germany and Portugal, when he recorded that the four remaining days 'are not likely to be forgotten'.[16] We can only guess at what he meant. This visit closed an era of overseas adventures for London, for developments in transport after the Second World War, in particular roll-on-roll-off ferries and air travel, eventually made training and competition abroad part of the rowing season for club and national crews alike.

HOME AFFAIRS

There were several attempts during the nineteenth century to set up a grand regatta in the capital that would rival Henley. Pollution, traffic, lack of funds and lack of organisation conspired against several events aimed at amateurs and professionals until, as much by luck as inspiration, the Metropolitan Amateur Regatta got started in 1866. At a dinner for the rowing clubs of the metropolis at the London Tavern in May 1866, the novelist Charles Dickens, president of Nautilus Club, said that he 'could not avoid the remembrance of what poor things the amateur rowing clubs of the Thames were in the days of his noviciate', and he called for a really great national regatta, and hoped that the committee selected for the purpose 'would carry on its labours to a triumphant result'. His son, Charles junior of London, had called a meeting in the previous year to organise a procession of boats to open the season, and more than twenty clubs had responded. Races for pairs and junior eights followed in August 1865, and in April 1866 the committee to which Dickens senior referred met for the first time, with London's Herbert Playford in the chair and Dickens junior as secretary. On 14 August the first Metropolitan Amateur Regatta took place, aiming to be a 'meeting of real importance and national interest in the metropolis itself'. Six events were 'open to the world' and the Lord Mayor gave away the prizes. Next year a proposal to include a river fête to impress Belgian visitors, with the Prince of Wales in attendance, never came off, 'partly perhaps through lack of cooperation from Leander Club'.[17] The regatta was soon in trouble, having lashed out on medals and trophies – £350 for the Champion Cup – and having in Dickens a secretary notable for his lack of business acumen. There were many discussions about paying jewellers' bills, and in 1868 insurance of trophies was abandoned, but later restored. In 1869 a dramatic entertainment at the Lyceum Theatre reduced the deficit, and London Rowing Club, by far the largest club involved, took over responsibility for running the regatta. Thus the Met became the club's prestigious open meeting, and from now on the same names would be associated with its operation as were running the club. They set about the task in customary fashion. An annual pattern was established for arrangements, a collector collected funds on commission, and in 1874 the Met shakily entered the black.

In 1869 there were entries from John O'Gaunt in Lancaster, and the west of Scotland. In 1879 some events were opened to foreigners, and the assembled

Metropolitan Regatta medal

crowd listening to the military band on the spectator steamer must have looked on in alarm when the first foreigner arrived. Monsieur Bidault from Lyons was a 'theme of wonderment to the Putney folk, standing, as he did, 7ft 1in and weighing 17 stone. He is a very fine man, but looked ill before the race, and was unable to go farther in his heat than the upper end of the boathouses, at which much sympathy was expressed for him. He sculls a very slow stroke, but is a good waterman...' In 1880 the Cercle Nautique de France appeared, and in the next few years they were followed by Frankfurter Ruderverein, Cornell Navy and the Argonauts of Toronto. In 1884 there was a dead heat between London and Thames in the Champion Cup, and in 1885 a gargantuan struggle for the London Cup took place between Guy Nickalls, Vivian 'The Major' Nickalls, the Canadian E A Thomson, Harry Blackstaffe and Rupert Guinness, the winner. The Met – or any other regatta – has never achieved the social cachet of Henley, but it has enjoyed prestige and success on the water. During the 1920s, for example, London and Thames struggled mightily for the Champion Cup, and Jack Beresford won the London Cup in the same years that he won the Diamonds and the Wingfields, so setting up his unique record of being thrice-holder of the scullers' 'triple crown'.

The course was generally over a mile and three-quarters between Putney and Hammersmith bridges, held on one day until the 1930s, when it was split over three consecutive evenings. In the 1960s it was shortened to 2,187 yards with stake boats. In 1966 the regatta daringly moved to Sunday, one of the first to do so, and became a one-day event again. This lasted until 1977, when it gave way to the demand for multi-lane racing and moved to Thorpe Water Park in Surrey, re-opening in 1980 using four lanes of 1,640 yards This allowed the introduction of women's events and was popular with competitors, but spectator interest and revenue declined, so a subscribers' enclosure was re-introduced. The regatta moved again in 1988 to the London Regatta Centre on Royal Albert Dock, now enjoying seven lanes of 1,914 yards. Increasing interest caused it to expand to two days in 1990, and in 2001 it moved venue for the third time, to the 2,187-yard Eton Rowing Lake at Dorney. While at the docks, the Met became the first English regatta to use FISA's (Fédération Internationale des Sociétés d'Aviron) new starting system of red and green lights, achieved by hiring nine real traffic lights and rigging them up on the starting pontoons. Solid silver medals were re-introduced for premier events in 1991, and a new regatta medal offered for others. Five years later John Pinches's medal factory reproduced the original Layton Cup medal from its original.

Four of the eight original challenge trophies are still offered – the Metropolitan Champion Cup for elite men's eights, the Thames Cup for men's elite coxless fours, the London Cup for elite men's single scullers and the Metropolitan Challenge Cup for men's senior 3 eights. The first three are 'open to the world'. There are fifteen other trophies, among them several with London connections – the Ampthill for men's elite coxless pairs, the Layton, now for men's elite coxed fours, the Freeman for men's senior 3 singles, the Peter Coni for men's lightweight eights, and the Charles Dimont for men's junior eights. In 1998 Putney Town Regatta made eight further fine old trophies available to the Met. With in excess of 750 entries these days, the regatta is a testament to good management that seems customary in the world of blue-and-white. One who made a lasting impression on the Met is Charles Dimont, the driving force – usually wearing a duffle coat – behind its move from the unpredictable waters of the tideway to the multilane courses of first Thorpe and then London Docks. His sharp wit, mischievous chuckle and endless fund of anecdotes enlivened every committee meeting, just as it did the club bar and any conversation you ever had with him. Teacher, journalist, historian, coach and storyteller, Dimont was a sparkling diamond among glittering company. He was one of many who make the Met a success story. Paul Reedy, the current London coach, rates it next to Henley in importance, seeing the Met, and to a lesser extent Marlow Regatta, as vital measures of how the season is building.

HEAR THE BOATS SING 1919–1939

HEAR THE BOATS
SING 1919—1939

WHEN THE 1920S TURNED INTO THE 1930S, London Rowing Club basked in a glorious aquatic revival brought about by an evangelist and his disciples. 'The regatta was a triumph for Metropolitan oarsmanship and in particular for Mr Fairbairn, for crews influenced by his teaching won every single event except the Diamond Sculls,' reported the *Times* of Henley in 1931.

Yet the first few years of revival after the armistice with Germany in 1918 had revealed nothing of what was to come. More than ninety members had joined the forces by December 1914 and, says the report of the war years, 'not a single member was affected when the Government brought in conscription in 1917.' Fifty members, including the 1914 captain, Herbert Lumb, lost their lives. The premises were requisitioned for the Welsh Guards, and when the 1919 annual meeting took place on 29 April, Australian and Canadian military crews were using the boats and premises. Attendance at the meeting was poor because demobilisation was not advanced. The veteran Percy Adcock was elected captain, and Vivian Nickalls coached an eight for the Fawley Cup at the Peace Regatta organised by the Henley stewards in July 1919. W T Raikes, who succeeded Adcock as captain in the autumn, stroked both the eight and a four in the Wargrave Manor Cup. The eight lost to Oxford University and the four conquered the 1st Battalion Coldstream Guards before going out to Jesus College, Cambridge – the *alma mater* of Mr Fairbairn.

The club gradually put its house in order. The annual subscription, set at two guineas in 1872, was raised to three guineas and life membership to twenty guineas, and the life members responded generously to an appeal. Fifty new members were attracted, and subs owing from the war years trickled into the coffers. London's own Victory Regatta on 27 September was hailed as 'a most enjoyable day, although the committee's arrangements were upset to some extent by the great railway strike which had commenced that morning'. December's Christmas Eights produced four crews in a close race from Walden's

Overleaf:
*London winning
the Grand against
Berliner Ruderclub,
1933*

Winners - Silver Goblets and Nickalls Challenge Cup
R. A. Nisbet 11.7.   *T. N. O'Brien 11.9*

Archie Nisbet and Terry O'Brien, winners of the Silver Goblets in 1927, and silver medallists in the Olympic pairs, 1928

Wharf to the Putney dummy (a barge for short-stop mooring, probably situated off Beverly Brook).

In 1920 the full programme of club races was revived. Under the captaincy of Jock Wise, the Thames Cup eight beat Marlow and then Kingston before going down to Caius College, Cambridge, at Henley – all in atrocious weather. The Grand eight was no match for the eventual winners, Magdalen College, Oxford, and the scratch Wyfold four was beaten by Thames in their first race. The rest of the season was undistinguished, but more than eighty new full members

London Rowing Club in 1920

*London's Thames
Cup crew, 1925,
resplendent in
Henley blazers*

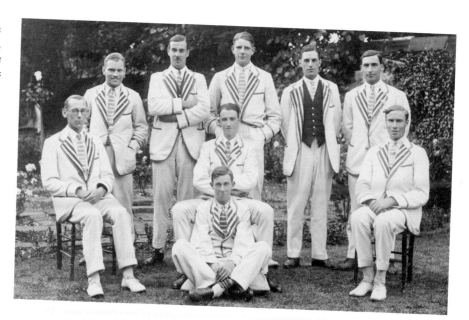

presented themselves. A new category of undergraduate membership started at a reduced rate –
a leaf out of Leander's book, perhaps. The war
memorial and special repairs fund realised
£1,386, enough to provide a spacious new balcony
and leave £380 for the memorial tablet and general repairs. The royal princes, Albert and Henry,
were entertained by president Ampthill – another
who had done sterling war work – for the first
post-war Boat Race, won by Cambridge. The club
dance was held for the first time since 1914 at
Princes Galleries, Piccadilly.

You can sense the angst pushing the pen
which drafted the annual report for 1921. The
outstanding event was identified as H R H the
Prince of Wales becoming a member, a judgement
possibly influenced by the second paragraph:
'It is regrettable that the year should have been
the most unsuccessful rowing season the club has ever known.' Neither a four
nor an eight gained success at any regatta. The blame was placed, as far as
possible, on outside forces: 'Regular practice had hardly started, when the
country was faced by the dangerous national crisis caused by the miners' strike,
which, owing to the anticipated action of other powerful trade unions, caused the
Government to take the drastic step of calling up the army reserves and forming
a defence force.' Mobilisation caused the trial eights to be brought forward by
two days in April at short notice. The captain and vice-captain joined the colours,
and 'following their example,' so did a large number of active members, thus
depleting the crews. Many were to idle the early summer away in camp on
Wimbledon Common. Both the dance and the AGM were wrecked by influenza.
Recruiting was the only strength at a moribund time for rowing.

The next two years were bad, too. The 1923 report says that club events and
winter training were good, but 'hopes entertained that good crews would be
available from the largely increased membership were not realised... It was
found that many of the men rowing during the winter and early part of the
season were again not available for the Henley crews. It was only with extreme
difficulty that a very moderate eight was got together for the Grand.' The one
outstanding feature was M K 'Geoffrey' Morris's win in the Diamonds, the first
London member to do so in forty-seven years. He narrowly beat the deaf and

Letter from Lord Ampthill, president, 1920

Trailing Thames in the Wyfold in the rain, 1920

dumb Donald Gollan, and was so exhausted that he fell out of his boat. In addition, a young man from Pembroke College, Cambridge, who also appeared for Twickenham RC, Archie Nisbet, was beginning to make a mark at London. And in the outside world, Benito Mussolini's Blackshirts marched on Rome, and one Adolf Hitler failed to overthrow the Bavarian government in the 'beer hall putsch'. Lloyd George's coalition was ousted and Bonar Law became Tory prime minister. Vladimir Lenin denounced Stalin and suffered a major heart attack. The first Cup Final was held at Wembley.

Nisbet became captain in 1924 and covered four seasons. He had had a brief association with Thames, being drawn there by Steve Fairbairn, who took on the captaincy of London's rivals in 1919, with the veteran oarsman Julius Beresford as his vice-captain. Fairbairn was from Melbourne. He rowed for Cambridge four times while at Jesus College, and in the early years of the century he brought his college – numerically small in rowing terms – to prominence on the Cam and the Thames. His methods were controversial and outspoken, and Pembroke College, where Nisbet was an undergraduate, was an early conversion to Fairbairnism. The Australian who adopted England as his home also had a long association with Thames, and his mission after the war was to inject the methods which empowered small colleges like Jesus to outgun big players like St John's and Trinity on the Cam into the heart of metropolitan rowing. Nisbet, quiet and methodical, was also on a mission to turn London's fortunes round, and he, sensing tension at Thames, issued a standing invitation to Fairbairn – universally known in the rowing world as Steve – to come to London to coach should he ever be free. In 1923 Nisbet was bow man in the Pembroke eight in the Grand, beaten by Thames in the final. Thames were coached by Steve and stroked by his son Ian.

This victory put Thames into the limelight once more while London was in the doldrums. But earlier in the year, Fairbairn had almost brought his sojourn at Thames to an end. He had threatened to resign before Marlow Regatta because the second eight rejected his replacement for a man who was unavailable for Henley and appointed a choice of their own, thus also disrupting the club's junior crew. Steve wrote two letters of resignation, the first citing illness as his reason but the second, mutiny.[1] His son eventually helped to smooth things over on the committee, but there was clearly bad blood. Meanwhile, Nisbet's move from Thames to London was attributed by some to his desire to take revenge for the blow dealt to Pembroke, but Nisbet himself said he took offence one day when members of the Thames first eight had used up all the hot water in the showers after rowing.[2]

At any rate, Nisbet was made captain at short notice in 1924. In May 1925, ill health caused Fairbairn to resign the Thames captaincy, with 'Bones' Long taking over and Jack Beresford, son of *éminence grise* Julius and with two of his eventual five Olympic medals already round his neck, as deputy. Then in the autumn there was a contested election for the captaincy between Steve's man, Long, and Beresford's candidate, his father. The Beresford camp won by forty-one votes to thirty-three. The cause of the bad blood between these two brilliant coaches has been lost, but their rift was never repaired.

Steve had other reasons to stop. He was by now writing down his coaching tips and his philosophy, and answering the 'orthodox' critics who had been sniping at him.[3] He was also troubled by an old back injury caused by a collision on the river while a student at Cambridge and suffered from jaundice. But it was that crucial election that caused him to walk along the embankment and knock on Nisbet's door, and on Sunday 18 April 1926 he began to coach at London. On that day he took the first eight down to Westminster. On arriving back at the club, he asked whether the crew would like to go a little further. Not liking to confess how tired he was, the captain replied in the affirmative. 'Mr Fairbairn thereupon took the crew up to Mortlake and back!' From that date untll Henley Royal Regatta, the first eight rowed 245 miles. 'Mileage makes champions' is one of Steve's best-known adages. He also introduced 28-inch slides for the first eight, and 12-foot oars with $6^1/_2$-inch blades instead of the customary 12 foot 2 inch oars with 6-inch blades.

Thus began a period at the helm which,

Trophies won by London crews in 1930, including the Head of the River Race, the Wingfield Sculls, and the fours and eights under the English flag at the Empire games

although short-lived on the towpath because ailments increasingly kept him away, brought a long period of success for Steve's crews, and influenced the club profoundly long after he had died. By 1935 London had notched up three wins in the Grand, two in the Stewards', three in the Thames, four in the Wyfold, one in the Goblets by Nisbet himself, with Terry O'Brien in 1927, and five in the Wingfield Sculls (three by Denis Guye and one each by C K Buckle, and Peter 'Jacko' Jackson). The editor of club reports from 1924 to 1937, Frank Ward, wrote: 'There is not the slightest doubt that Mr Fairbairn's coaching is chiefly responsible for the eventual pre-eminent position gained by the LRC, and every member who has the success of the club at heart owes him a great debt of gratitude.' He also noted that Nisbet laid the foundations. 'When he took on the captaincy in 1924 the fortunes of the club were at their very lowest ebb. He succeeded in breathing a new energy and enthusiasm into the club; he introduced new methods and had the courage to follow his convictions. We did not achieve our greatest triumphs until after Nisbet had resigned the captaincy in September 1927, but it was primarily due to his efforts that the London Rowing Club became once more in fact, as we have always claimed it to be in name, the Premier Amateur Rowing Club of the World.'

Half of the Grand eight won the Wyfold in Fairbairn's first season, the other half losing in the Stewards' and the eight itself bowing out of the first round to Lady Margaret Boat Club. The Wyfold win was the first Henley pot for the club since the war, and was a narrow squeak after London 'crashed and caught a crab' at the mile with a length-and-a-half lead over Lady Margaret, only to recover and win by four feet. Whether Steve himself knew of the antics of this crew in Sussex on the Saturday before the regatta, involving 'mild horror and a good deal of anxiety', is not recorded. More of that later. Meanwhile, the Fairbairn revolution continued. Regular rowing for next season began on 20 September, and a week later swivel rowlocks were fitted to all the eights. There were four eights, two fours and a pair on the water, and each weekend the eights rowed the boat race course on a handicap system, leading up to a momentous event on 12 December, when three London crews were among twenty-one starters in the first Head of the River Race, initiated by Steve and covering the Mortlake to Putney course. The three finished first, fifth and tenth respectively. The third and fourth London eights were coached by Thames's R F 'Reevo' Reeve, an ex-Jesus man and friend of Steve's who was outstanding with beginners. Reevo became the first honorary secretary of the Head, the second of which took place on 27 March next, with forty starters, half of them in cutters and

Letter from the Duke of York, 1922

BUCKINGHAM PALACE

3rd April, 1922.

Dear Lord Ampthill,

The Duke of York desires me to thank through you The London Rowing Club for their kind hospitality to him on Saturday last.

His Royal Highness greatly enjoyed the day, and was naturally delighted at the result.

Yours very sincerely,

Louis Greig

The Lord Ampthill, G.C.S.I., G.C.I.E.

half in clinkers. London retained the headship, as it was to do for ten years, though on this occasion equal with Thames. After the Head the line-up was three eights, four fours and a pair. The first eight covered 960 miles to get to Henley and were beaten there by Thames, stroked by the publisher Hamish Hamilton, by three-quarters of a length in the final of the Grand, having knocked Jesus out on the way. This was London's first Grand final since 1899. Six hours later, bow man Nisbet and stroke O'Brien won the Goblets easily against Gully Nickalls and H O C Boret of Leander, having defeated the European champions Siegenthaler and Reinhard of Luzern Reuss and 'Bean' Vernon and Douglas of Thames on the way.

Next year Steve's ailments forced him to stop coaching from launch or bank, and the main burden fell on Charles Rew who, as an oarsman, had followed Nisbet and Fairbairn along the way. Rew was training master, and from October to Easter there were twice-weekly sessions of skipping, weightlifting and rope climbing at the club, plus strenuous rowing at the weekends. The first two crews rowed to Weybridge and back on two occasions. The head was won by 23 seconds in 18 minutes 41.5 seconds. A young Oxford oarsman called Hugh 'Jumbo'

London leading Leander in the Henley Grand, 1930

Edwards, notorious for blacking out in the Boat Race in 1926, took over the coaching after Marlow, where under the colours of Old Westminster BC he won the single sculls on a foul from London's Denis Guye.

The Grand eight once more had Nisbet and O'Brien at either end of the sandwich, but Henley was a close call for O'Brien because he cut his hand very badly two days before the regatta, and could do no practice until the races began. With Edwards at three, they beat Union Boat Club of Boston but lost to Thames by a length in the final. In a desperately close Stewards' final, three of the eight with Rew at stroke lost by two feet to half of the Thames eight. O'Brien's injury was very likely a factor in the holders' poor showing in the Goblets, where Nisbet and O'Brien were beaten by G C 'Bill' Killick and Jack Beresford. But all four of these men went on to win silver medals at the Olympic games in Amsterdam – the Thames pair in the eight, picked after their Grand victory (Beresford's third consecutive Olympic medal), and the Londoners as Great Britain's pair. London's Denis Guye and Humphrey Boardman represented Britain in the double sculls, but were unplaced.

I do not know what is the outlook of the present generation, but certainly as regards Terry [O'Brien] and myself are concerned, printed records and medals meant very little. The former gather dust in a bookshelf while the latter repose in a drawer or cabinet and only come to light if and when their receptacle is spring-cleaned.
— Archie Nisbet, 1928 Olympic medallist reminiscing in 1984

Progress on the water was threatened in 1929, caused by an annoying sequence of injuries which brought about changes in coaches and crew. New members included a strong contingent from Cambridge, where the Light Blues were half way through the longest run of wins in the Boat Race to date (thirteen), but London's Oxford tyro, Edwards, was available only at weekends. The first eight were rowing with three substitutes a week before Marlow Regatta, the important curtain raiser to Henley. Alfred Peppercorn, captain in the previous year, coached until he 'left for India', to be replaced after Christmas by the stroke, O'Brien, who was ill and had to interrupt his rowing. Harby went down with jaundice and his replacement, Long, was not fit. Crawford retired with injury and Long developed a poisoned hand. Nisbet, who was in charge of the coaching after Easter, thought the crew unfit, and consequently worked them hard. There was lightning improvement as the halt and lame returned, but they went stale. In the Grand they dead-heated in a head wind with the Argonauts of Canada in 7 minutes 13 seconds. They won the re-row by three-quarters of a length, which knocked the stuffing out of them for a gruelling encounter against Leander on the next day. London lost this by a length, and Leander went on to beat Thames in the final. The stern four lost the Stewards' to First Trinity by a length, and the Wyfold four – Nisbet and three others out of the eight – beat Sidney Sussex but lost to another Cambridge college, Jesus, in the final. The Thames Cup eight beat Trinity Hall before losing to Thames. The club extended largesse in 1929 by voting to give temporary membership to members of foreign clubs when they found themselves in London. The rowers of Shanghai, Hong Kong, Calcutta, Singapore, Rangoon, Manila, Calicut and Miri found at LRC a home from home.

London's major breakthrough at Henley came in 1930, but before then, there occurred an experiment more entertaining, if less successful, than Francis Gulston's tests on the sliding seat in the 1870s. It was conducted by Squadron-

London defeating Leander in the Stewards', Henley, 1930

Leader F E Hellyer, a Cambridge coach and dubbed, in this age of jazz, 'syncopat-ed rowing'. Hellyer's observation was that the light construction of boats had increased the check on their progress during the recovery phase of the stroke, and his theoretical cure was to have pairs of men in an eight rowing in sequence instead of ensemble. He set out his conclusions in a newspaper article:[4]

'The time-honoured way of moving a boat along is to swing forward togeth-er and grip the water together. The drawback is that a modern racing boat is of such light construction that oarsmen swinging forward check the boat considerably – in each successive stroke the craft has to be restarted. Thus it is necessary to accelerate it during the stroke and at the finish propel it faster than its average speed in order to make up for the amount by which it has been stopped at the beginning.' And, Hellyer said, power is wasted in trying to outdo average speed because doubling the speed requires eight times the power.

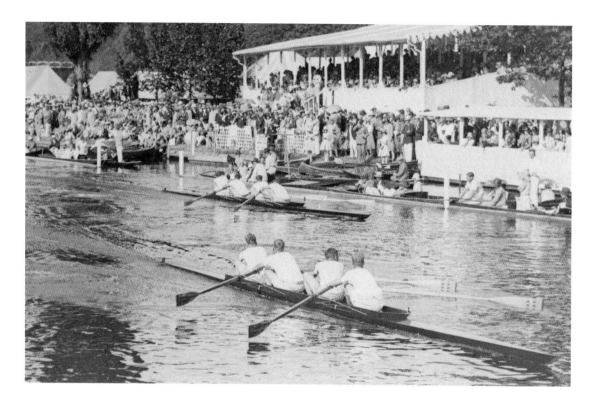

London winning the Wyfold against Vesta, Henley, 1930

'The object of 'syncopated' rowing is to keep the craft moving at a speed as constant as possible, effected for an eight by dividing the stroke into four equal intervals and the crew into four pairs, each of them a quarter of a stroke later than the pair in front. It will be understood that by this system there will always be men swinging back while others are swinging forward, and never a time when there are no blades in the water pushing the boat along. It is difficult to master at first as it offends the oarsmen's instinct to row together, and also because the thrust of men going back upsets the rhythm of others who are swinging forward.' Three weeks of experiments using an eight rigged for six to allow enough room between the pairs were deemed so successful that 'a special boat is being constructed which will be ready for use in a few days' time, in which it is hoped to prove by the end of the year whether the syncopated style is an improvement upon the orthodox.'

The six produced a 'weird and wonderful effect upon eyes accustomed to seeing an eight going well together,' reported one newspaper. 'Its appearance brought forth some amusing comments from the uninitiated spectators on the towing path, who noted a crew, accompanied by a coach complete with mega-phone, behaving in a seemingly eccentric manner, and considered there was

something radically wrong with it.' Criticism was heard that it was tough work on the pair that had to start the boat. 'As a matter of fact the crew... set off in the normal manner for the first stroke and broke time afterwards. The 'syncopaters' admit it is not an easy job, but they appeared to be getting on with it fairly well, and certainly the boat ran without check.'

London crews at Henley, 1930

The eight was built and tried out with Phelps coxing from the centre of the boat. Evidently the experiment was inconclusive, and there was further interest in syncopated rowing. Philip Carpmael, who rowed for Jesus in the Grand in 1929 and 1930 and for Cambridge University in the races of 1930 and 1931, was singled out in an article on jazz rowing by Conrad Skinner. Pointing out that Jesus had initiated seventeen-mile rows from their boathouse to Ely with jolly lunches en route and lock-to-lock races on the Cam, he says: 'It is not surprising to find that Carpmael was venturesome enough to investigate recently the claims of "jazz rowing". He still feels, I think, that in theory the innovation is defensible, in that it avoids the spasms of high speed at the beginning of the stroke, whereby water resistance is disproportionately increased; for by allowing men to make eight separate beginnings the boat would tend to preserve a steady evenness of speed, like a caterpillar, and thereby incur less total resistance from the water.' Conrad then puts his finger on the real difficulty, the snag that probably ended Hellyer's experiment. 'The difficulties consist in expense (the boats would need to be longer and proportionately stronger), also greater length produces greater weight and greater resistance.' All existing craft would be rendered obsolete, to say nothing of the racking and transportation implications, for boats were not yet sectional. Also obsolete would be 'the whole corpus

On the way to winning the Grand at Henley, 1931

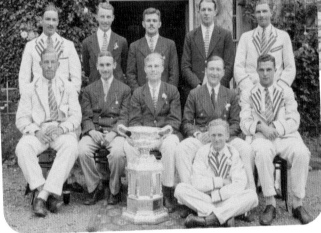

Winners of the Grand, 1931

of coaching experience built laboriously during a century.'

That seems to be the end of syncopated rowing in Britain, although it emerged again in the Soviet Union in 1979. The women's coxed four from Pskov in Russia held secret trials before the Moscow Olympics of 1980 in a boat designed by their coach, Valeri Prokopenko, which had the cox seated in the centre. They succeeded in perfecting asymmetrical, or syncopated, rowing, but concluded that they gained no speed advantage. They rowed the boat conventionally to win world gold medals in 1979 and 1981 and Olympic bronze in 1980. Their boat is now in the River & Rowing Museum's collection at Henley-on-Thames. The second boat to the design had the cox's seat sliced out of it when women's fours went coxless in 1989.

Winners of the Thames Cup, 1931

In 1930 London won the Grand, the Stewards' and the Wyfold, but syncopated they were not. There were some comings and goings, notably Donald Gollan arriving from Thames and Edwards going back to Oxford, but after a first eight trip to Trier where they suffered air sickness and were beaten by Mannheim, Germany's Olympic eight of two years before, coach Rew finished up with the same crew as in 1929 for the Grand. They dismissed Jesus, stroked by Carpmael, in the first round and Leander in the final. In the Stewards', half of the eight beat the stern half of Jesus's eight at a paddle, before pulping Third Trinity and beating half of Leander's eight to the trophy in the final. The Wyfold four beat Sidney Sussex, followed by Thames in a six-foot verdict, followed by their other neighbour Vesta more easily in the final. All but Crawford from the eight rowed in the Stewards' or the Wyfold, so nine men and a cox did all the damage. The commentators

Winners of the Stewards', 1931

were ecstatic. 'London gave a superb exhibition of oarsmanship, and demonstrated the perfection to which Steve Fairbairn's teaching can be brought,' said the club report on the first Grand win since 1890. 'They were undoubtedly a classic eight.' Rew received plenty of credit, but the *Times* lauded the crew and the inspirator. 'In the Grand Challenge Cup London rowed off at 11, 21 and 41 to the 10^1/$_2$, 20 and 39 of Leander. With scarcely a splash they led at the sixth stroke, and then went away amazingly fast. At the top of the island they were clear.' They reached the Barrier three and a half seconds inside two minutes and equalled the record to Fawley, where they were two lengths ahead. Edwards, and Leander's Graham, were singled out as the men of the match. There was perfect weather, the only untoward incident being a small whirlwind which 'sucked balloons, sunshades and coats from the punts opposite the Stewards' enclosure. Conditions were fairly fast, with the lightest of light head breezes, but not so fast as the London crews made them appear...'

The *Times*'s triumphal verdict was that 'at no regatta has the preponderance of the Fairbairn style and swivel-rowlock rowing generally been so marked, nor have the crews rowing in that style ever been better. Orthodox crews have much to learn from London, Jesus and Pembroke in the matter of wristwork, and until Leander and the universities put their house in order in this respect they must expect to see such fine crews as London triumph with the swivel rowlock. But the Fairbairn crews had a lesson too in the Ladies' Plate in which Lady Margaret proved the importance of swinging. London needed no such lesson...'

London's reward was to go off to Hamilton, Ontario, a week later to represent England in the British Empire games. Recruits for 1931's first eight included Carpmael of Jesus and Dermot St John Gogarty of Pembroke, son of the great Irish surgeon and writer Oliver St John Gogarty. The newcomers had some difficulty at first, Carpmael having rowed 'too recently in the Cambridge crew to have re-found his old loose easy style' and Gogarty 'handicapped by lack of winter practice in our methods'. Besides, much of the effort was going into the second eight, which consequently was the best club crew until Marlow Regatta had passed. The club won both eights and both fours events at Marlow. At Henley they made an indelible mark on the *Daily Telegraph*'s George 'Drinkers' Drinkwater: 'Without hesitation I can say that their Stewards' four (Fitzwilliams, Carpmael, Edwards, Harby) was the finest coxwainless boat which has raced at Henley since I first went there thirty years ago. They were so perfectly together that only twice in their race with the Italians did I see the rudder on, once when they gave way soon after the start to their opponents who were out of their water, and once when towards the finish a gust of wind threw them out of their course. Their length, their rhythm, and their power were superb. Again, their Thames Cup crew was certainly the finest which has ever won that race.' The *Times* joined in: 'It was a pity there were no fast days, for the London Stewards' Cup four plainly were likely to make a new record. Unlike the eight, they had improved on their form and power of last year.' Turning to individuals, 'Drinkers' singled out Edwards, the first man to win three Henley medals since Guy Nickalls in 1904. Beside the Grand and the Stewards', he won the Goblets with Lewis Clive under Christ Church colours.

Winners of the Wyfold and friends, 1933

A curiosity of the Grand was that Archie Nisbet occupied the bow seat of the Pembroke crew, beaten by Thames who booked their place in the final. London easily defeated Harvard and then had a humdinger against Berliner Ruderclub. Berlin led at the island, London at the Barrier, Berlin at the mile and headed London to the grandstand by three-quarters of a length. There the Germans went to pieces and the exhausted London crew won by a third of a length. In the final London turned Thames's canvas lead to their advantage by the same distance at the Barrier. London went clear some time after Fawley, but Thames spurted to within half a length at the enclosures before London got home by a third of a length. Compared with the previous year, said the *Times*, they did not swing so well and they shot their slides more.

This was the regatta at which the *Times* noted that every event except the Diamonds showed Fairbairn influence at work. 'Indeed, Cambridge orthodox rowing suffered an eclipse that was only overshadowed by that of Oxford rowing as a whole.' Edwards, the Oxford exception, was given credit for allowing Clive to get

Winners of the Grand, 1933

the best results from his strength in the Goblets. After Henley, Gogarty went into the seven seat of the second eight for Kingston Regatta, where they beat Thames again in the Grand, and an eight made up from the first and second crews dealt Thames a third defeat at Molesey. The juniors, however, who started the season with an eight made up of the heaviest remaining regulars after the first two crews were picked and were known as the Sea Elephants, faded away.

Next year began well on paper but not in

Jack Phelps,
succeeded by his
brother Tom as
boatman in 1935

motivation. All but one of the previous first eight and five of the second eight were available for Henley, but many seemed to expect their successes of the last two years could be repeated where they left off. There was an early-season interlude when a scratch eight visited Curlew Rowing Club at Greenwich, a round trip of thirty miles. After rowing from the club to Blackfriars, cox Jack Phelps allowed each member half a glass of beer, except Colonel Sankey, who received full measure. The return row was taken in easy stages after Curlew's excellent lunch and hospitality. At the more serious end of things, the squad appeared to adopt as their motto 'Good oars need not train' and take beer as their training medium. 'In this cheery, carefree atmosphere, delightful to all except the coach and captain, the season progressed, and were it not for the untimely illness of the stroke, just prior to Henley, that gave the crew a justifiable excuse for their defeat, it might well have ended in a genuine "bitter" disappointment.'[5] Consequently they were kept in clinker boats until Christmas, after which optimism but not skill returned. 'Flu then hit the head crew and Terry O'Brien was reluctantly co-opted to stroke it, and the Head was won. They then won an invitation race at Surennes on the Seine, before being beaten by Thames at Marlow. Defeating the Société Nautique de la Marne in the first round of the Grand at Henley, they led Leander by half-a-length at the barrier in the second round before the latter went through, the eventual winners. The eight was divided into two for the fours events, the Wyfold half winning against Nottingham and Union Rowing Club in the final after taking out National Provincial Bank, Thames and Jesus College, Cambridge. The Stewards' half lost the first heat by a length to Berliner Ruderclub. This was the last time that oarsmen in the Grand were permitted to compete in the Wyfold. The second eight were uncompetitive until two weeks before Henley when E D Wetton, a previous stroke who had returned from India, was put in the stroke seat. They went through four rounds of the Thames Cup to face Imperial College in the final, their scalps being University College (Oxford), Peterhouse (Cambridge), First Trinity (Cambridge) and Reading Rowing Club. Imperial repeatedly attacked London's early lead and forced a four-feet verdict, but in London's favour.

The junior crews had a good year in 1932: exemplary in their training and attendance, they had but one failing. At the end of the season it was discovered that the most promising had not paid their subscriptions. The action taken by the secretary is not recorded, but one hopes that the tactics of Herbert Playford almost eighty years before had not been forgotten.

London had a minimal part to play in the Olympics in Los Angeles, but

'Jumbo' Edwards once more distinguished himself by winning two golds on the same day. He won the pairs with Clive, his Christ Church partner, and subbed into the Thames Stewards'-winning coxless four in place of 'flu sufferer 'Tig' Tyler for his second. The others in that crew were Rowland George, Jack Beresford and Felix Badcock, Beresford now having two Olympic golds and two silvers.

In 1933 the first and second eights and the junior and junior-senior crews were levelled and mixed for the winter, with nine boats entered for the Head. 'Equal' crews continued until mid-May, when the first eight won again in Paris. While there, Colonel Sankey, the honorary secretary, was presented with a medal of honour in physical education awarded by the minister of education and fine arts. The crews had a pre-Henley camp at Molesey, and the first eight won every first-class event for senior eights on the river, including the Grand. They beat Thames by a length, Pembroke by a length, and Berliner in a closely fought final by a quarter-of-a-length. In the Wyfold, London beat National Provincial Bank, Vesta and Westminster Bank in the final. The Thames Cup almost came the way of the club as well. There was an easy win against Eton Excelsior and a hard one against Reading Rowing Club. Then came a tussle with the American school, Hun. Hun led up the island, London advanced by a few feet at the Barrier, and this did not change until Hun dead-heated at the finish. The re-row was similar, London having a slightly greater lead for most of the distance until Hun charged and were beaten by a foot. London then lost to Bedford Rowing Club fairly easily in the semifinal, Kent School of the United States being the eventual winner.

This year was not the end of London's roll at Henley, but the next was empty handed – unfortunately so in the case of the Stewards' when, leading in the final against Pembroke, stroke Edgar Howitt suddenly caught so violent a crab near Fawley that he was thrown out of the boat. Jackson, the three man, jumped in to rescue him, and the boat completed the course rowed only by Carpmael and Wood. Pembroke responded by cutting the records to Fawley and the finish by three seconds each. In the Grand, London were beaten in the first heat by Leander, pushing the pinks to a record at all markers. The Thames Cup crew lost their final to Thames.

Steve Fairbairn had not been driving the London crews on a daily basis for a number of years, but there was no doubt that his influence dominated the age. The newspapers relished the style wars, with particular reference to the Boat Race, and vitriol was not unknown between the headstrong men who coached the blues. For years Oxford had been under the influence of the high priests of the ramrod back at Eton, whose crews made Henley's Ladies' Plate their own from 1893 to 1914. At Cambridge the 'Lady Margaret' orthodox style at its best could match the Fairbairn adherents, and it was predominant in the university crews who were enjoying a winning streak. Conrad Skinner, writing in 1931, detected an uneasy truce between the Cambridge coach Haig-Thomas and Fairbairn to desist from influencing each other's stylists. 'This only serves to show what for years one has believed... that a synthesis of these two was absolutely within the bounds of possibility and that it had to be pursued for sanity's sake... The coaching of the leading authorities of the two [styles] is mutually indistinguishable on the main points. It is only in their diction that they differ. Their ends are identical.' Skinner's analysis was right.

Denis Guye, three times winner of the Wingfield Sculls

Fairbairn's influence penetrated through his pen, both in books and prolific letter writing, and in chats to the stream of oarsmen who beat a path to his door. For example, Arthur 'Truri' Dreyfus, the coach of Zürich Football Club's rowing division, made his crew watch slow-motion footage of the Pembroke four that set a Henley record in 1934 as part of their preparation for the 1936 Olympics. His inquiries led him to Steve, and correspondence ensued, undoubtedly contributing to Zürich winning the Grand in 1936. Steve's influence was felt also in Germany where Karl-Heinz Schulz's Wiking eight represented their country in the Olympics in 1936. Schulz, a newspaper proprietor and head of sport at Berlin Radio, was a Fairbairn coach. In Australia, Bill Sambell and Donald 'Clapper' Wilson, two old boys of Melbourne Grammar School in London's crew which went to Melbourne's Centennial Regatta in 1934, took time out to teach the boys Fairbairnism.

London got back to winning ways at Henley in 1935, despite a late start to the season because many of the men who had travelled to Henley-on-Yarra did not get home until Christmas. Nevertheless, the Thames Cup was secured, followed by the Wyfold for the next three years, and the Grand again in 1938. The 1935 Thames crew had a hard slog to a hard final, beating Pembroke by a quarter-of-a-length. The scalps taken on the way were Bedford, First Trinity, Quintin and Thames. Pembroke's first crew stopped London in the first heat of the Grand, and went on to win it. The Stewards' four lost the final to Zürich, who lowered the record by an incredible ten seconds. Lord Ampthill, president since 1893, died, and Stewart Bradshaw was elected in his place. Ampthill's Goblets partner of 1891 and 1892, Guy Nickalls, also died. So did the last living honorary member, J Tetley. The club's waterman, Jack Phelps, took a job on the training ship *Conway*, and his brother Tom replaced him. The boat clubs of Guy's Hospital and King's College, London, moved out of the premises.

The next year was notable for the loss of the headship of the river for the first time since Fairbairn set the race up in 1926. At Henley, the Wyfold four beat Thames, Walton and then Reading in the final. The Stewards' four were beaten by Zürich again, once more the winners. But Messrs Martin Bristow, Alan Barrett, Jacko Jackson and Edgar Howitt were selected to represent Britain at the Berlin Olympics. Unhappily the stroke, Howitt, was unable to go because his employer refused him extra leave despite pleas from high places.[6] After considerable difficulties which involved a farcical trial against half of Leander's Olympic eight, the Oxford oarsman J D Sturrock joined the crew. They won the coxless fours silver medal behind Germany and ahead of Switzerland, but Jackson's account of the regatta points out that the Swiss were doubling up on the day, so that the reversal of the Henley result did not look quite so good. The Germans, some of whom were coached by British professionals, were hoping to achieve a clean sweep in the presence of chancellor Hitler, but the Thames double scullers Beresford and

At Henley in 1920 (left to right): Thorn, Pile, Trotter, Bremner, Seward, Sturgis and Semple

Southwood messed this up with a lightning start and tactics taught to them by Eric Phelps, sculling coach to Maurice von Opel.[7] The Americans then made mayhem of the Germans in the eights final with a fine win by the University of Washington. Jackson is critical of the British selection system. 'Every effort should be made to ensure that each member of the crew is chosen on his rowing merits alone... It is not difficult to visualise that this would inevitably produce not an eight from any one club...'[8] Although Jackson got his own way when selecting for the British Empire games two years later, his voice was to remain in the wilderness for many years as far as the Amateur Rowing Association was concerned. This was the year of the abdication of Edward VIII, who ceased to be patron of the club.

In 1937 there was no Head of the River Race because a suitable tide could not be found on a Saturday, and the Amateur Rowing Association refused permission for the race to be held on the Sabbath. London arranged a race with Thames instead. The annual report bemoaned the twin evils of bad health and marriage for making oarsmen inactive. Four level crews were operated, and 'each Saturday and Sunday the London flotilla would set out, two by two, and all four crews would race each other home — it being hoped that by this method a

Medal winner's certificate, Olympic games, Berlin, 1936

XI. OLYMPIADE BERLIN 1936
EHRENURKUNDE
GROSSBRITANNIEN
ZWEITER
VIERER OHNE STEUERMANN

ORGANISATIONSKOMITEE FÜR DIE XI. OLYMPIADE BERLIN 1936   INTERNATIONALES OLYMPISCHES KOMITEE

PRÄSIDENT   PRÄSIDENT

fighting spirit and the principle of rowing hardest when behind would be instilled into all members.' As far as possible each crew kept the same personnel throughout, coached by George Harby and Derek Mays-Smith. Trial eights were on 19 December. But there was mutiny in the air. The second eight was 'rather depleted owing to three members preferring to make up a Wyfold four and go out when they felt like it. Since they won they must be forgiven their revolutionary tendencies, and it is interesting to note that the following year three of them were rowing regularly and pulling their weight as club members,' says the annual report. This crew consisted of Jack Ormiston, 'Tootles' Carter, John Pinches and Cyril Morris and became known as the Umbrage Four, beating Walton in the final. The incident is a good example of London's inclination to go with the flow instead of being dictatorial, although if the result had been different, such tolerance might not have been forthcoming. The Grand eight lost to Wiking of Berlin, and the Thames eight to the American schoolboys from Tabor Academy in the final. Pinches from the Umbrage crew also competed in the Diamond Sculls. A special review committee recommended that the subscription be raised to £4 4s. Cadet members became shareholders of the London Boat House company but were not required to pay an annual

Three cheers for London's Fred Fenner, born 1839, who gave the prizes away at Henley in 1930

subscription until they ceased to be cadets.

London won the Grand again in 1938, a feat hailed as a revival for the club in the year of Steve Fairbairn's death. Thames went quietly in the first race, but in the second Jesus was leading along the enclosures before London nosed ahead by three feet. In the final London went clear of Trinity Hall after three-quarters of a mile. Three of this crew had learned to row at London and, said the club report: 'Condolence is due to G A Morris and J E G Wardrop who would have rowed in the Grand if they hadn't turned a car on themselves.' The Wyfold

London leads Royal Chester in the final of the Wyfold, Henley, 1938

victory, the third in succession, was down to the captain, Arthur Fraser, rowing with a Rhodesian, Tom Hendrie, and two Australians, Bill Robertson and Ian Esplin. Three of them were Oxford students, so they only began training at the end of the spring term, and almost all of it was in the boat. They had easy wins against Durham School and Lady Margaret and a tough semifinal against Clifton Rowing Club, winning by four feet. Royal Chester were their victims in the final. Meanwhile, the fierceness of the argument over style petered out with Fairbairn's death. But captains and oarsmen continued to visit him for chats on rowing at his flat at the Moyston Hotel, near Marble Arch, to the end of his life, emerging with confidence and determination.[9] His disciples were by now legion, and his influence remains with us in the twenty-first century, not least at London.

In 1939 there was a new threat to membership. 'In the captain's report for 1937 marriage and medicine are cited as robbers, stealing from innocent rowing clubs their aquatic talent both maiden and otherwise, and in fact to the rowing captain marriage and medicine can be regarded only as twin afflictions, that, like the poor, must always be with us,' wrote captain Lee in his report. 'But when in 1939, to these two was added a third, the Territorial Army, a fearsome trinity was formed which made heavy and serious calls upon the active membership of the club. The effect of these counter-attractions was to reduce still further the already dwindling quantity of juniors, and although we started off the season with almost an *embarras de richesses* of ready-made oarsmen of high repute and many promises of help at a later date, these gradually thinned out until eventually the active membership stabilised itself at the low level of an A and B crew and a rather scratchy spasmodic junior eight.' There were regular weekday outings in the dark. Before Christmas, crews visited Jesus and First Trinity in Cambridge and the A crew met Brasenose of Oxford. On another visit to Oxford in February the first crew hit the pier of Folly bridge on the flood. Then Territorial Army recruiting coincided with the summer programme and made holes in the junior and second eights.

Before the war brought this period to an abrupt end, we will paraphrase Charles Mellor's account of the incident which contained elements of 'mild horror and anxiety' at Henley in 1926, Steve's first year as coach at London. The members of the Grand eight were staying at Blandy House in Hart Street, famous because Mary Blandy was hanged for poisoning her father there in 1752. The current owner, a dentist, had taken a holiday, so Dodo Carswell, Alfred Peppercorn, Gerry Block, 'Wee' Webb, Jack Rofe, Archie Nisbet, Terry O'Brien, cox C W Bellerby and Mellor had the run of the place. All except Block and Bellerby decided to go to Bracklesham Bay in Sussex for the weekend after

*The Umbrage Four,
winners of the
Wyfold in 1937 (left
to right): Harold
'Tootles' Carter, John
Pinches, Cyril
Morris, Jack
Ormiston*

their morning outing on the Saturday before the regatta. They had only a four-seater Talbot between them, so Peppercorn hired a Ford delivery van from a local butcher. It had double doors at the back with oval portholes in them. They put one of the dentist's armchairs in the back, and Rofe, Webb and Peppercorn set off, with the rest in the Talbot. They stopped for dinner in Chichester, a dinner which included port. 'Whether this had more than the normal effect on men in strict training, I don't know, but at any rate, after starting up again, a curious inclination to race came over the drivers, possibly helped on by a desire to reach Bracklesham before dark. We tore along those Sussex roads in what was certainly a manner dangerous,' Mellor wrote. Sometimes the Talbot was ahead, sometimes the Ford, and in between they were abreast. 'Henry Ford, after having its bonnet removed and taken inboard just before it rattled off, was, after half-an-hour of this treatment, showing signs of packing up, with its cylinders literally glowing red.'

The Talbot led into a sharp left-hander, and O'Brien got round on three wheels without hitting anything. The Ford, however, flipped over into a hedge and landed on its roof, headlights on, minus a wheel. Rofe emerged from the back doors still wearing his London cap. O'Brien was unscathed, but Webb had a nasty cut on the middle finger of his right hand, undergoing temporary repairs at a nearby cottage.

Next day the van was taken to a repairer by a breakdown wagon. Two of the party then took the dentist's chair by train to London and on to Henley.

Blade commemorating Grand Challenge Cup, 1931

'I remember being told by them of the impressive figure they must have cut, trundling an armchair on its castors off the Underground train at Paddington, and up on to the main line station. I also remember sitting reading a paper in the dining room at Blandy House on the Sunday after the regatta and, on getting up, suddenly noticing – pasted to a leg of the chair – a smallish white label bearing the words "GWR Paddington to Henley". Greatly concerned for the good dentist's peace of mind on his return from his holiday, I carefully, yet regretfully, removed the tell-tale piece of paper.' 'Wee' Webb, by the way, recovered from his cut in time to row in the Grand.

On 30 August 1939, the London committee appointed an emergency board to assume responsibilities for the club and the boathouse company in event of national emergency. On 7 September the emergency board closed the club for duration of war. Four days later, a stretcher party occupied the first floor and changing rooms.

IO FOUNDERS, FIREBRANDS AND FAIRBAIRN

The founders of London Rowing Club were a remarkable bunch of resolute men, as the early chapters of this book make clear. Their fortitude and sense of purpose was picked up by subsequent generations, some with more success than others. While success or failure is usually attributed to aspirants and heroes in boats, others also serve in a variety of capacities, and this chapter acknowledges some of them.

Stephen Fairbairn was the coach who had the most profound effect on London's rowing in the twentieth century. Indeed, the man from Melbourne is, arguably, that century's most influential rowing coach in Britain. His teaching was felt far beyond Jesus College, Cambridge, where it started, Thames Rowing Club where it continued to develop during his captaincy from 1919, and London, where it settled in 1926. An epic argument with Julius Beresford caused him to walk along the embankment to take up Archie Nisbet's open offer at London, and Steve, as he was universally known, never looked back.[1]

His coaching brought an array of trophies to the small boat club of a small Cambridge college, continued to do so with Thames, and then gave London a golden age during the 1930s. The tall, portly figure spent thirty-three years on the riverbank, 'in an old blue blazer, with back as straight as when he rowed in '82, chest thrown out, head slightly on one side, and eyes fixed immovably on the crews racing past'.[2] Oarsmen continuously beat a path to his door when illness prevented him getting to the towpath, and he also taught by correspondence. Among his disciples were Arthur Dreyfus of Zürich, Karl-Heinz Schulz of Wiking, Berlin, and Bert Haines of Harvard, all coaches of successful clubs in the 1930s.[3] He exhibited a genuine love of rowing, boundless enthusiasm, kindliness, and a genius for coaching, willingness to experiment and, above all, the ability to impart his enthusiasm to others. He did much to make rowing popular, particularly at London, and his lasting memorial is the Head of the River Race on the Boat Race course, which he instituted in 1920. The concept of a long-distance time trial operated as a ladder from year to year spawned such events the length and breadth of Britain, and brought a new dimension to winter rowing and training.

Fairbairn was a good all-round sportsman in his schooldays, and remained an agile skipper and light-footed dancer until his advanced years. He learned

Steve Fairbairn by James Quinn

rowing from pulling boats on the Yarra and listening to the arguments of the professionals and amateurs of Melbourne. His was not so much a creed or a style as an approach to rowing, psychological as well as physical. He described the Jesus or Fairbairn style as 'concentrating on working the oar, and natural body action.' His son Ian described the difference between orthodoxy and Fairbairnism: 'The orthodox ideas started from fixed seat rowing and a consequent veneration of 'swing', and they thought of the slide as only an extension of fixed-seat rowing; to Steve, slide and leg-drive were the source of power which fixed seats only served to dam.' Steve taught that the slide should be driven evenly, that looking at your blade occasionally helped you to control it, and that the arms were best elastic as the stroke took off. Orthodox crews were well drilled, whereas Fairbairn crews were taught that the only uniformity that mattered was togetherness of bladework. Steve said, often, 'Teach the crews to work their oars. Never teach them to do anything with their bodies.' Hence Fairbairn crews may look sloppy, but appearances were deceptive. Hard work and discipline were required. Steve got the best out of people of any age, shape or size. He did not merely seek to put together only the best men. Above all, he was passionate about rowing, and fanatical in pursuing the elusive perfect stroke.[4]

G E Fairbairn, killed in action in the First World War

Fairbairn was born at Toorak, Melbourne, on 25 August 1862, the fifth of the six sons of George Fairbairn and his wife Virginia, youngest daughter of George Armytage of Geelong, who was a native of Derbyshire. George Fairbairn emigrated to Australia from Berwickshire in 1839 and owned a large sheep station. In the 1870s he started the first canning and meat-freezing works in Australia. Steve was a spirited and unruly child who passed through several schools before settling at Geelong Grammar. He was tall and handsome, and earned distinction in all forms of sport, but also performed well academically. Like his brothers before him, he was sent to Jesus College, where he rowed in the losing Cambridge crews of 1882 and 1883 and in the victorious crews of 1886 and 1887. Among many other successes, he won the Grand, the Stewards' and the Wyfold at

2nd.Lieut.G.E.Fairbairn

Henley. He graduated in law in 1884, and was called to the bar two years later but did not practise. From 1884 he worked at the family's farming interests in Victoria and western Queensland. He married Ellen Sharwood in 1891 and they had two sons. During this time in Australia he spent two intervals in England before moving permanently to the old country in 1904. Thereafter he devoted himself almost exclusively to coaching various rowing clubs, both in Cambridge and in London, where he worked as a director of the merchants Dalgety & Company.

Steve's fame rests on his methods of coaching and the success of the crews that he coached. In an era of competing styles, with their emphasis on differing body positions during the stroke, some tried to attribute to Fairbairn a new style, 'Fairbairnism'. That, however, came from a complete misunderstanding of the man. Steve had no desire to invent a style, and nor did he. He wrote: 'There are certain principles underlying rowing, and what is called style is the endeavour to carry them out. Variations are merely failures to carry out the principles. There can be only one true style.' He emphasised above all a powerful leg drive and a relaxed recovery to maximize boat speed, and he cared little for the aesthetic effect that this produced. He turned the pupil's mind to the oar in the water and to moving the boat, regardless of the angle of the head or the straightness of the back, whereas the orthodox coach would concentrate on positioning the body in order to produce certain results on the oar and the passage of the boat.[5] Fairbairn summed up the debate over style as '"pretty pretty" versus honest hard work' and wrote: 'Never sacrifice work to appearance; but of course style is effect, and honest hard work will give true style eventually'.[6] What Fairbairn's crews lost in aesthetics they often gained in speed.

Steve was ahead of his time in recognising the importance of the subconscious mind in the development of technique, and his famous phrase 'Mileage makes champions' resonates still. He coached for looseness and ease. The key was to be positive in coaching and encourage rather than criticise. A favourite remark was: 'If you can't do it easily, you can't do it at all'.

Steve died at his residence, the Mostyn Hotel, Portman Square, London, on 16 May 1938, a year when Jesus retained the headship of the Cam. His name endures on the Fairbairn Cup races in Cambridge; his bust by George Drinkwater is the trophy presented to the winning crew in the Head of the River Race; his memorial stone on the tideway marks one mile from the start of the boat race course at Putney, and one mile to the finish of the head course. A trust was set up in his name which supports the advancement of physical fitness and improvement of health for young people by providing rowing facilities. Fairbairn's teaching has also endured; London named its new lounge after him

Steve Fairbairn

in 1972, thirty years after his death. The fact that, in the twenty-first century, his name is known and frequently invoked both at London Rowing Club and in rowing circles generally is testament to his intelligence, his thinking and the attention he gave to anybody who asked, from star performer to humble novice. His writing still lifts off the page, and in any hall of fame, his name would appear in the highest echelon.[7]

George Drinkwater's 1931 bust of Steve Fairbairn, the trophy for the Head of the River Race

Before the First World War and before Steve made his mark at Putney, the founders and the early generation of London men were dying out. Among them was Francis Playford, who was secretary, captain and vice-president of London in his time, and a keen patron of professional rowing. He won the Grand at Henley and the Gold Challenge Cup at the Thames Regatta in 1846, rowing for a club called Thames. This club died long before City of London, founded in 1861,

adopted the moribund Thames name in 1862, having sought Playford's permission to do so as the last survivor of the old Thames. In 1849 he won the
Wingfields by half-a-length over T R Bone from Westminster to Kew bridge, a
distance of six miles, and he won the pairs at Henley with E G Peacock. In 1855
he wrote a key text in the stock exchange's case for professional status, Practical
Hints for Investing Money, and he died in 1896, aged 72.[8]

James Sprent Virtue was London's first treasurer, jointly with John Ireland
from 1856 to 1864. He was born in 1829 and apprenticed to his father's firm –
printers, engravers, bookbinders and publishers of lavish illustrated books, part-
works and the Arts Journal. In 1848 he was sent to New York and three years later
was head of a firm with branches across North America. He returned home in
1855 to succeed his father George. Virtue founded the monthly magazine St
Paul's in 1867, with the journalist and novelist Anthony Trollope as editor. He
continued to publish illustrated books of distinction, particularly editions of the
Bible, Shakespeare, and topographical works. He became a founder member of
LRC in 1856, and for several years donated the annual prize of a sculling boat for
novices. He was vice-president from 1865 to 1870, and died of heart disease in
1892.[9] John Ireland, Virtue's co-treasurer, was one of best-known figures in the
rowing world at a time when 'Thames and Tyne were frequently the scenes of
regattas in which both amateurs and professionals took part,' said his obituary.
He was an acknowledged authority on the sport and an experienced umpire and
referee, especially of watermen's matches. He occupied the bow seat in the
winning Grand crew of 1857. In 1872 he helped to revise the laws of boat racing,
the major change being that taking your opponent's water was prohibited.

Leeds Paine was a prominent member of the Argonauts, many of whom were
founder members of London. He won the Visitors' at Henley twice before
London existed, and perhaps his main claim to fame is winning a sculling match
in 1851 from Hammersmith to Putney against Herbert Playford, H C Smith and
Charles Schlotel, all of Argonauts. He was of comparatively short stature, but 'a
good man in the forepart of a rowing boat and a sculler of more than average
merit' according to his obituary. He worked on the stock exchange and died in
1898. Eugène Monteuuis, French by birth, died the following year. He was a
founder member who donated a prize for junior sculls and was the first editor
of the club's annual records, a mine of information which continued until 1953.

Tom Nickalls, another founder member, was a jobber on the stock exchange
known as the 'Erie King' because of his prominence in the competitive world of
American railroad financing. He was born in 1828 and accompanied his
corn-dealing father to Chicago when he was five, returning to England in

1845. He was a burly, popular man on the exchange, credited with integrity and independence of thought. He married a farmer's daughter, Emily Quihampton, who became the first woman to climb Mont Blanc and Monta Rosa in the same week. They had twelve children, all but one of whom survived infancy – rare for a Victorian family. The brood included Guy and Vivian who became great oarsmen despite their father's discouragement when he famously said, 'Cricket, my boy, will take you round the world, and rowing, up and down the Thames'.[10] Tom ensured that his children learned to shoot, ride to hounds, box and play billiards and cricket, and he satisfied his own field-sporting interests by purchasing a large estate in Sweden and a neighbouring estate in Norway. His sons' dominance of the Goblets at Henley[11] resulted in their father presenting the stewards with a silver peg cup, the Nickalls Challenge Cup, which has been awarded with the silver goblets since 1895. Nickalls became master of the Surrey staghounds in 1879, and he died in 1899.[12]

John B Close-Brooks was known as John B Close at Cambridge, where he was the eldest of three brothers who rowed for First Trinity. A Cambridge blue, he was bow in the 'finest four-oar ever manned' – the crew containing Gulston, de Lande Long and Stout who beat Atalanta in 1872. Close-Brooks was described as a 'stylish and strong oar for a middleweight with a straight-backed, stylish open-chest finish'. He won the Diamonds for First Trinity in 1870 and the Stewards' and Grand for London in 1872 and 1873. After that he retired from rowing and settled to banking, becoming a partner in Cunliffe, Brooks and Co and a director of the Lancashire and Yorkshire Railway. He was High Sheriff of Cheshire in 1911 and died in 1914.

William Stout, one of Gulston's chief contemporaries, expired at his home in Gloucester in June 1900, aged fifty-eight, from a complication of ailments.[13] His rowing career was bisected by some time spent in China, but that did not prevent him from winning all the chief prizes on the Thames. These included the Grand and Wyfold in 1862; the amateur sculls at the Paris International Regatta in 1867; the Stewards', Diamonds, London Cup, Wingfields and Metropolitan pairs in 1868, and in 1869 the Stewards' and the Goblets. His pairs partner was Alfred de Lande Long. Stout stroked the London four who beat Atalanta on the Thames in 1872.[14]

G B James, stroke of the winning 1885 Thames Cup and the 1890 Grand crews, died in 1899. In 1892 he was a member of the crew beaten by the Union

Eugène Monteuuis, first keeper of LRC records, vice-president from 1892 to 1898, and first master of the Argonauts lodge of the Freemasons

James Layton, first president, by R Barraud

des Sociétés Françaises de Sports Athlétiques in Paris. The union was formed to purify sport in France by doing away with money prizes for amateurs, and its invitation to London followed recognition by the Amateur Rowing Association. R S Farran was also in that crew, killed in action at the battle of Elands Langte as a trooper in the Imperial Light Horse in 1899. James was also a first class rugby football forward. H M Agnew was killed at Tweefontein in 1901. Edwin Brickwood, who spent forty years as aquatic editor of the *Field*, died in 1905. R B Freeman expired while he was captain after a distinguished record since he joined London from Staines in 1905. But for his illness and subsequent death in 1908, he would probably have been chosen to row in one of the Olympic crews that year. W W Hewitt, who was a rugby international as well as an oarsman, died in 1909.

George Alfred Henty, war correspondent, historian and novelist, made up in character what he lacked in presence at the clubhouse. He was the son of a stockbroker and mine manager who studied classics at Westminster and Caius College, Cambridge. A delicate child, he boxed and rowed at both places of education, and retained sufficient interest in rowing to join the club, although in his mature years his sport was yachting. He left Cambridge prematurely in 1854 when he and his younger brother joined the army commissariat on the outbreak of the Crimean war. Henty's letters home were published by the *Morning Advertiser*, including a description of Florence Nightingale's arrival in Scutari. His brother died of cholera in the Crimea; Henty returned home, and the combination of boredom at the Army office and the premature death of his wife of tuberculosis in 1865 led him to seek work as a foreign correspondent. The *Standard* took him on. He began by joining Garibaldi's advance on Milan and was arrested as a spy, but escaped by subterfuge. The *Standard* then sent him to Abyssinia, and some of his reports were syndicated to the *Illustrated London News*. His dispatches were published as a book, and in 1868 he published his second three-decker novel. In the same year he wrote a story for his children, Out on the Pampas, followed by The Young Franc-tireurs that was the forerunner of a great series of historical adventure stories for boys in which the author insisted on historical accuracy. His reporting took him to the Anglo-Asante war, the Spanish civil war of 1874, a royal tour of India and the Turco-Serbian war of 1876. He edited the boys' magazine *Union Jack*, wrote adult novels, and Redskin and Cowboy (1892), possibly the first western. He wrote over 120 books, contributed to many more, and was a prolific contributor to newspapers and

The Thirties Club
29th September 1959

The Thirties Club
dinner in 1959

magazines. In his later years he was physically robust and spent six months of the year writing and six months yachting on the *Egrit*, which he kept at Weymouth, and on which he often entertained fellow members of London Rowing Club. His biographer quotes friends' descriptions of Henty as 'one of warmest-hearted shortest-tempered men in the world' and 'a rough diamond of the first water, sometimes boisterous, genial, generous, sympathetic and simple-minded as a child.' His suffering from 'gouty diabetes' is offered as an explanation of his irritable outbursts.[15] He died in 1902.

London Rowing Club's first president was James Layton, donor of the Layton Pairs, who died in 1875. He was succeeded by the Earl of Londesborough, who resigned in 1893. Lord Ampthill, who was forging a career in the colonial service, succeeded him next year. Oliver Russell became the second Lord Ampthill when he was fifteen. He was born in Rome in 1869 and educated at Eton, where he was captain of boats and president of the Eton society Pop. While at New College he rowed for Oxford in three boat races, winning in 1890 and 1891. In those two years he won the Goblets at Henley with Guy Nickalls, and was extremely busy in 1891, when he was president of both the university boat club and the Oxford union, won the Grand with Leander, and graduated with third-class honours in modern history.[16]

Ampthill presided over the club until 1935, during which period London's results at Henley were frustratingly at low ebb until the Fairbairn revolution set in during the late 1920s.[17] In the same year as he took up the presidency he became Britain's first representative on Baron de Coubertin's newly formed International Olympic Committee. Indeed, London, together with Leander and Thames, received a mention in dispatches in the *Olympic Review* of October 1894 as shining examples of the great sporting revival in the nineteenth century. Ampthill resigned from the IOC in 1898, possibly because his career was taking off. In 1895 he was appointed assistant secretary to Joseph Chamberlain at the Colonial Office, with elevation to private secretary in 1897. His instinctive liberalism was gradually subsumed by an appreciation of empire, especially after 1900, when he was appointed governor of Madras. The viceroy, Lord Curzon, found the young Ampthill arrogant, allergic to criticism, and addicted to pomp and ceremony – flaws that many contemporaries thought Curzon's own. The two men disagreed over Curzon's attempts to curb the racism of British soldiers, and when Ampthill reacted with insufficient outrage to the killing of an Indian by one of his aides (by 'a push with the foot'), Curzon forced the man's resignation. Nevertheless, Ampthill proved himself a loyal deputy in covering for Curzon when the latter went on leave in 1904. Upon returning to England in 1906 he took up the cause of Indians in South Africa, and chaired an advisory committee on Indian students in Britain convened by John Morley, the Liberals' Indian secretary, but had little sympathy with Morley's proposals for Indian political reform, an attitude which may have cost him the viceroyalty. Until his death in 1935 he persisted in his argument that it was Britain's failure to treat Indians throughout the empire equally that had encouraged them to repudiate British suzerainty.

Ampthill also took an active interest in affairs at home. In 1895 he contested the Fulham seat on London County Council as a moderate, unsuccessfully. In 1908 he became pro-grand master of English freemasonry, and in the run-up to the First World War he fostered the Territorial Army in Bedfordshire. He was an active president, his speech at the dinner in 1912 typically rousing the troops and setting out his stall on patriotism and sport. 'It seems all wrong that the LRC should have gone for over twenty years without winning the Grand Challenge Cup,' he said. He pinpointed an increased number of pleasures and the stress of business as factors, but 'notwithstanding these, our superiority ought to be unchallenged and unchallengeable. We need more time and better training.' He went on: 'We should remember that our sport is one of the primary sports. No game can compare with those sports which are connected with the various means of locomotion, in which men have striven to excel in all ages – I mean rowing, running and swimming. They call out the best quali- ties of manhood, they are essential for our supremacy, for the supremacy of our race, and are therefore imperative. Patriotism demands that we should do all in our power to secure that supremacy. I am sure that the end we all have in view, the safety of our country, will, when the day comes, be secured by the superiority of our race in self-denial and discipline, the finest features of our rowing.' When the day came, Ampthill himself commanded the 13th battalion of the Leicestershire regiment in France and subsequently the 3rd and 8th battalions of the Bedfordshire regiment, and was twice mentioned in dispatches. After the war, he became a JP and sometime chairman of Bedfordshire county council, and died of pneumonia at the Bath Club in Dover Street, London, on 7 July 1935.

Dr W F Sheard coxed twenty-one consecutive Grand crews from 1877 to 1897, and won five of them

The war, however, took a terrible toll of the members. Ninety had joined the forces by December 1914, and fifty lost their lives, many of them on the Somme. The memorial book in the committee room tells moving and tragic stories, like these plucked at random: Lieutenant P F A Cocks, Royal West Surrey Regiment, died on a hospital ship approaching Bombay; Lieutenant Cecil Crosley, killed at Gallipoli; Captain Walter Fawcus MC, Northumberland Fusiliers, decorated for gallant service on the Somme 1917, killed 25 March 1918; Captain M B Higgins, Australian Light Horse in Gallipoli, Egypt and Sinai, killed in action at El Magdhada; Lieutenant Thomas McKenny Hughes, Artists Rifles, killed in France in February 1918 while flying over German lines north east of Bailleul, after acquiring intimate knowledge of Front in that sector as observer and as intelli- gence officer with the Royal Army Flying Corps; Captain Frank P Lacy, Royal Engineers, killed 13 Aug 1915 in Flanders, 'a young mining and metallurgical engineer of great promise', awarded MC and promoted to captain five days before being killed. There were also notable natural deaths during the war, including F W Lowenadler and W E Green who were donors of club prizes, W H Lowe, the last surviving founder member, and Frank Gulston and his team- mate Alfred de Lande Long, standard bearers of the 1870s. The architect of the

Left: Lord Ampthill, president from 1894 to 1935 and first Briton on the International Olympic Committee. Cartoon by Spy (Sir Leslie Ward) in Vanity Fair

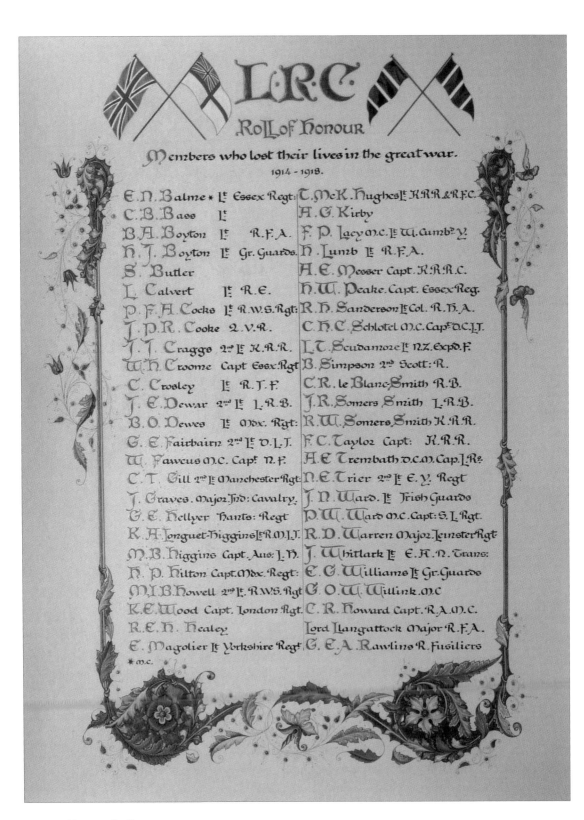

L.R.C.

Roll of Honour

Members who lost their lives in the great war.

1914 - 1918.

E.N. Balme ∗ Lt Essex Regt.	T. McK. Hughes Lt K.R.R. & R.F.C.
C.B. Bass Lt	A.G. Kirby
B.A. Boyton Lt R.F.A.	F.P. Lacy M.C. Lt W. Cumb.d Y.
H.J. Boyton Lt Gr. Guards.	H. Lumb Lt R.F.A.
S. Butler	A.E. Messer Capt. K.R.R.C.
L. Calvert Lt R.E.	H.W. Peake. Capt. Essex Reg.
P.F.H. Cocks Lt R.W.S. Rgt.	R.H. Sanderson Lt Col. R.H.A.
J.P.R. Cooke 2. V.R.	C.H.C. Schlotel M.C. Capt. D.L.I.
J.J. Craggs 2nd Lt K.R.R.	L.T. Scudamore Lt N.Z. Expd. F.
W.H. Croome Capt Essex. Rgt	B. Simpson 2nd Scott: R.
C. Crosley Lt R.J.F.	C.R. le Blanc-Smith R.B.
J.E. Dewar 2nd Lt L.R.B.	J.R. Somers Smith L.R.B.
B.O. Dewes Lt Mxx. Rgt.	R.W. Somers Smith K.R.R.
G.E. Fairbairn 2nd Lt D.L.I.	F.C. Taylor Capt. K.R.R.
W. Fawcus M.C. Capt. N.F.	A.E. Trembath D.C.M. Cap. J.Rt.
C.J. Gill 2nd Lt Manchester Rgt.	N.E. Trier 2nd Lt E.Y. Regt
J. Graves. Major. Ind: Cavalry.	J.N. Ward. Lt Irish Guards
G.E. Hellyer Hants: Regt	P.W. Ward M.C. Capt: S.L. Rgt.
K.H. Longuet-Higgins Lt R.M.L.I.	R.D. Warren Major Leinster Rgt
M.B. Higgins Capt. Aus: J.H.	J. Whitlark Lt E.A.N. Trans:
H.P. Hilton Capt. Mxx. Regt.	E.G. Williams Lt Gr. Guards
M.I.B. Howell 2nd Lt R.W.S. Rgt	G.O.W. Willink. M.C
K.E. Wood Capt. London Rgt.	C.R. Howard Capt. R.A.M.C.
R.E.H. Healey	Lord Llangattock Major R.F.A.
E. Magolier Lt Yorkshire Regt	G.E.A. Rawlins R. Fusiliers
∗ m.c.	

First World War roll of honour

building, George Alchin Dunnage, died in April 1915, aged 75. He was nineteen when he won the Grand, the last survivor of famous 1859 crew who beat Oxford in the heat and Cambridge in the final.[19]

Robert Hamilton 'Pat' Labat, the genial skipper of the speedy launch *Hibernia*, also expired during the First World War. He was conspicuous in aquatics for about forty years after a rowing career with Dublin University (Trinity College) and Thames before joining Gulston's crew in Philadelphia in 1876. It was there that Labat lent a pair of sculls to the young Canadian Edward Hanlan and prophesied that he would be a phenomenon. It took only two years for the professional sculler to prove him right. Labat won the Goblets with Gulston in 1879, and was a sound judge of form and prospects. He was driver for umpires at Henley, and the king and queen were aboard *Hibernia* for their visit to the regatta in 1912.

Notable deaths between the world wars included James 'Jack' Farrell, who won the Thames Cup in the bow seat in 1880, one of his six appearances for London in fours and eights at Henley. He also attempted the Diamonds three times, reaching the final in 1884, and later in life found success as a coach in Sweden. He went to Malmö in May 1911 and was asked to select and train rowers for the next year's Olympic games in Stockholm in 1912. Malmö Roddklubb paid him three pounds a week and gave him free board and lodging, probably something that violated the Amateur Rowing Association's amateur status rules back home in England. He found that the oarsmen in Malmö had already adopted the same rowing style as used by London. He banned hard liquor, tobacco and dancing, the latter on the grounds that it uses muscles that are not used in rowing, which will disturb your rowing muscles. After training sessions the 'Old Man', as Farrell was known, used to go to the Hotel Savoy with the oarsmen for supper. He recommended a pint or two of beer with the meal for the men, disliking milk, which he thought useless for a powerful athlete who had to keep his weight. Farrell himself would have a Scotch. His inrigged four – a wide boat type mainly used in the Nordic countries – won the Olympic silver medal for Sweden. His eight won the Nordic championships on the same course after the Olympics, and Farrell was back in Malmö the following year to conduct a coaching course. His Malmö Roddklubb eights became Nordic champions in 1914, 1915, and 1916. He died in 1923.[20]

Ebenezer Cobb Morley had reached 93 years when he died in 1924. He was an accomplished oarsman and honorary solicitor to the club for many years, founder of the Football Association, and an able administrator in the Victorian sporting world. F H C Boutell, who gave his address succinctly in the life members' list as 'South America', died in the 1920s. Lachlan Maclean, Thames Cup winner in

1883 and 1885, treasurer from 1896 to 1909, and designer of the first London one-man tank, died in 1922. Stuart 'Sleb' LeBlanc-Smith, who followed Gulston as captain in 1879, died in 1923. Major C V Fox DSO, a London member who won the Wingfields in 1900 and the Diamonds for the Guards Brigade in 1901, died in 1928. He made three attempts to escape from Germany during the First World War, the third being successful. Dr W F Sheard, cox of twenty-one consecutive Grand crews from 1877 to 1897, died in 1930. He won five of his Grands. The great sculler and oarsman Francis L Playford expired a year later.

Guy Nickalls, son of founder member Tom, died of injuries at Leeds general infirmary after a car accident in 1935. He was considered to have a delicate constitution as a youth, but developed an extraordinary physique and stamina through rowing at Eton, Magdalen College, Oxford, London and Leander. For these clubs he rowed eighty-one races at Henley, winning sixty-seven of them, including the Olympic regatta in 1908 when, at the age of forty-one, he was in the victorious British eight. Away from the river, Nickalls was on the stock exchange for thirty years. He then forced his way into the army in 1914 with no previous military experience and spent the war in France supervising physical training and bayonet training for three divisions. He also established an endowment fund for the Worcester College for the blind. His record of medals at Henley stood until

Lieut Herbert Lumb, captain of LRC 1910 to 1915, stroked Grand eights four times and won the Wyfold 1914, barrister, died of sickness at Gallipoli, 1915

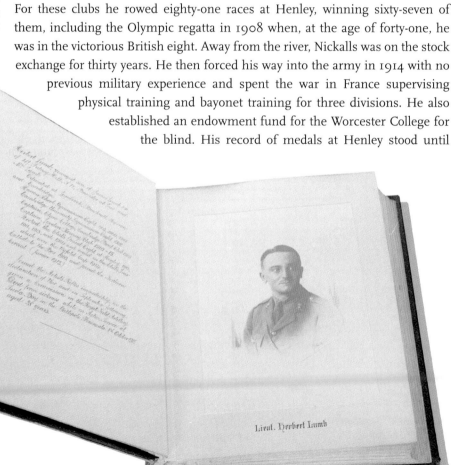

Lieut. Herbert Lumb

Sir Steve Redgrave overtook it during the 1990s. An example of Nickalls's toughness came at the regatta in 1895, when he and his brother Vivian joined Little and Stout in London's Stewards' four. The event began with what Nickalls described as 'the hardest race I ever rowed to that date, and I never recovered from it for weeks afterwards.' Against the Argonauts of Toronto, the race was one continual spurt at 36 to 38 strokes to the minute all up the course. 'When they spurted they got four feet; we replied and got two feet ahead. We must have changed places six times before the mile with neither boat ever leading more than three or four feet. At the mile I made what I hoped was my last spurt, I was now rowing blind, and we got half a length up at the Isthmian enclosure, but they came with an outstanding rush and were half-a-length up opposite the grandstand. It was do or die, and I felt much more like dying than doing.

George Dunnage, Grand winner in 1859, who was the architect of the clubhouse

I had one more go, and, magnificently backed by Vivian, we lifted the boat over the line winners by two feet.'[21] Next day they 'came out very stiff and sore' to row New College, but beat them comfortably. The final was a close race against a hot Thames four, London leading by a trifle to the mile before creeping ahead and winning by a length-and-a-quarter. The Nickalls brothers won the pairs at the same regatta, receiving the Nickalls Challenge Cup presented by their father on the first occasion that it was offered, and Guy lost the final of the Diamonds to Rupert Guinness, Vivian having withdrawn.

NEW WORLD, LITTLE BRITAIN 1945–1970

New World, Little Britain 1945–1970

SIXTY MEMBERS OF LONDON TURNED UP at the Great Western Hotel, Paddington, to begin rowing again on 19 December 1945. The meeting elected Tommy Langton as captain and the Australian Bill Robertson vice-captain. Robertson had an astonishing war, fighting with Australian and British forces in North Africa, Greece, Crete, New Guinea, France, Belgium, and the Netherlands before joining the staff of Australia House in London. There was a vote of thanks to Thames for wartime hospitality, and London accepted an invitation from next-door neighbours Barclays Bank Rowing Club to use their premises until their own was available. The first post-war annual general meeting took place at Barclay's on 16 March, with president Stewart 'Bradders' Bradshaw unable to attend because he had broken his arm. He died shortly afterwards.

The building had been requisitioned and used by several bodies, including the river fire service from 1941 to 1945, and the Royal Electrical and Mechanical Engineers after that. Tom Phelps had looked after the boats (and would be presented with a tankard for his trouble four years later). Thirty-one members lost their lives on active service, and Captain George Drinkwater MC, a civilian, was also killed by enemy action. Notable among the survivors was Oliver Philpot, an RAF pilot who escaped from the German prisoner of war camp Stalag Luft III by tunnelling out from the famous 'wooden horse'. He, and both of those who escaped with him, were among the very few prisoners of war not to be re-captured. Philpot disguised himself as a Norwegian margarine salesman and endured a hair-raising journey to Danzig (now Gdansk), where he stowed away on a Swedish collier. The club's only material loss was three paintings, including de Prades's portrait of the founders, which were destroyed by a bomb while stored in Chiswick for safekeeping.

Initially London had only about ten oarsmen and a chronic shortage of coaches and coxes in 1945, but a crew was put together for the Head of the River Race,

Overleaf: London Rowing Club by Cosmo Clark, RA, painted for the club's centenary in 1956. On the hard with sculls: Tony Fox. In the launch (left to right): 'Jumbo' Edwards, Archie Nisbet, Jock Wise, Charles Rew. In the shell (left to right): Farn Carpmael, John Pinches, 'Bunjie' Langton. Tom Phelps is standing in the centre

run over a short course from Barnes to Putney bridges. Not surprisingly, Imperial College won it, having kept boats on the water throughout the war. Kingston were second, Jesus third and London fourth. There followed an expedition to the Dublin Head, a visit notable for its steaks, Guinness and good fellowship rather than for rowing success. The crew had to carry an archaic, borrowed boat over a weir at the start, and almost lost their cox, 'Winky' Winkworth, in a minor whirlpool – 'adding to our hilarity if not our proficiency'. This turned out to be a good move for the first post-war Henley, because London, resigned like everyone else in Britain to lean, rationed times, arranged to share Dublin University's camp at Remenham Rectory, with meals provided in the village school. 'Our diet improved considerably thereby,' said Langton's report. There was a downside, however, when they lost to Thames in the Grand and the Stewards' after a night of holding down tents in a tropical storm. With entries in every open event except the Goblets, London came away empty-handed, including John Pinches in the Diamond Sculls, who had returned to the fold during the season. Jack Kelly Jr of the US Navy beat him in the Diamonds. Nevertheless, there were pots to put on the table from successes at post-Henley regattas.

The next few years were taken up with recovery in austerity. In the rowing world and the real world, new factors came into play for captains and selectors, the most notable being two years of compulsory military service for all men

London on the Liffey: the Dublin Head in 1946 was notable for steak and Guinness

Grand eight practises at Henley, 1958

reaching the age of eighteen. Added to that, demobilisation of the wartime armed forces took some time. The voters elected a Labour government under Clem Attlee to reconstruct the country. But as radical policies changed the social and political map of Britain, as nationalisation changed industry, and as health and welfare services were born, traditional ways of life lingered on in many areas which were less concerned with the wealth of the nation – rowing being one. This is illustrated by surveying what happened during the next twenty-five years.

London's record at Henley to 1939 was seventy-nine wins (sixteen in the Grand, seventeen in the Stewards', ten in the Thames, sixteen in the Wyfold, twelve in the Goblets and eight in the Diamonds – not including the Argonaut victories in the founding year of 1856). Fifteen of these were during the 1930s. In 1947 John Pinches and Edward Sturges got things back on track by winning the Goblets. The international scene recovered in the following year at the London Olympics, when two golds and a silver were added to the ten Olympic medals which British crews had won between the two world wars.

Henley's post-war statistics also make interesting reading. After the war, the Grand stayed at home, with one exception, until 1953 (won by Leander four times, and once each by Thames, Lady Margaret Boat Club and Jesus College, Cambridge). The exception was Harvard's win in 1950. But British crews won it only three times during the next twenty years. The Stewards' followed a similar pattern, although home crews were more successful in this event than in the

Grand. The Thames Cup went to America every year between Imperial's win in 1946 and London University's in 1961. Antony Rowe (Leander), Tony Fox (London, twice) and Hugh Wardell-Yerburgh (Eton Vikings) were the only home grown scullers to win the Diamonds until 1977. The new Double Sculls event, started in 1946, was won fifteen times by foreigners in its first twenty-five years, and the Goblets ten times over the same period. The Wyfold was largely kept at home, but the names on it were new – names like King's College London, Burton Leander, Royal Engineers, Royal Air Force, and National Provincial Bank.

Blade commemorating Grand Challenge Cup crew, stroked by Graham Hill, Henley 1953

For the blazerati and those with an uncritical eye, rowing's recovery was a slow but sure return to 'business as usual'. But the Henley results tell a different story about the standard of domestic rowing, and results at the next four Olympics dismally reinforced the decline of British rowing in the international arena. London was fortunate in that a group of exceptional scullers emerged in the 1950s, but the enthusiasm and talent of individuals and crews produced little business for the scribe of the club's honours board. Between 1945 and 1970, when the Amateur Rowing Association appointed Britain's first professional full-time national coach, the governing body in England was forced to reform itself and its selection procedure radically. This process was initiated by frustrated, rebel oarsmen and carried through by the captains of the big clubs, London included. A lot of blood was spilt on the way, and London's alter ego, Thames Rowing Club, virtually imploded.

The first important change was the completion of a process which had started in 1936, when the Australian eight, on its way to the Berlin Olympics, was refused entry at Henley on the grounds that, being policemen, the oarsmen were not true amateurs. It is said that the palace hinted at the withdrawal of royal patronage unless the stewards put their house in order. At any rate, before the London Olympics in 1948, the Amateur Rowing Association and the National Amateur

Rowing Association merged, accepting the NARA's view of the amateur, which barred from amateur status only those who competed for money prizes or were in paid employment in rowing occupations. Henley followed suit, and this is why the royal regatta's entries included many clubs not seen there before the war.

This merger made possible the next change. The new, combined ARA now had an acceptable definition of an amateur for affiliation to FISA, the international rowing federation. Britain had always participated in the Olympic games, but affiliation to FISA put the mother country of the sport into the arena of international competition fifty years after the ARA was first encouraged to join. This was important for several reasons, one of which was that the international federation was now responsible for running the competition at the Olympic games.

The third change was the gradual introduction of new events and additions to the national calendar, although this did not amount to a national strategy. On 15 March 1947 London raced Thames over the Boat Race course for one of these, the Boustead Cup, presented by Guy Boustead in memory of his father who rowed for Oxford in the dead-heat Boat Race of 1877. London won by two-and-a-half lengths after their cox, Guy Harris, ordered 'a silent twenty' when the crews were level at Barnes bridge, with London on the outside Surrey station. This fixture was intended to be a 'Boat Race' between the two leading tideway clubs. In its early years it was fiercely fought, and remains on the calendar, but it has not enjoyed a continuous presence, nor reached the prestige that it might have done.

My involvement with the club started in 1948 as a small boy in Norwich watching the large contingent from LRC taking part annually in the Norfolk long distance sculling race. It attracted the great men of the day.
— Nick Cooper, Wyfold, Wingfield and Britannia winner

More important developments occurred in 1951 when the Norfolk Long Distance Sculls came along, the first time trial for scullers. The top four were Tony Fox, John Pinches, Archie Nisbet and Farn Carpmael, all of London. The Scullers' Head of the River Race for the Blackstaffe Trophy started in 1954, and was organised – and won – by John Marsden, who was a London member but who wore Vesta's colours in this event. The trophy is a silver model of Harry Blackstaffe, the Olympic champion in 1908, presented to him by the City of London. A third scullers' head started at Weybridge in 1956 and was won by Doug Melvin of London, although he always sculled in the colours of his Lancaster club, John O'Gaunt.

Melvin turned up on the Thames in 1953 after his boss and patron, Sir Harold Parkinson, sent him to compete at Reading and Marlow regattas. He won the first and was beaten by Sid Rand at the second, which was good enough for Parkinson to arrange a transfer for his young electrician from the North Western Electricity Board to the London Electricity Board at Wandsworth. Melvin was sent to the tideway to be coached by Eric Phelps, then with the Midland Bank at Putney, who had coached Jack Beresford and Dick Southwood of Thames to their famous double sculling victory in the Berlin Olympics. Phelps encouraged Melvin to join London Rowing Club because several of the best scullers in the country were there, and thus Melvin became part of the group which included Fox, Marsden, Pinches, Sturges and Carpmael, some of whom were ducking and diving in and out of crews as well as sculling. Melvin found Phelps to be an excellent coach, and the company competitive, inspirational and congenial. They leapfrogged each other's careers, and spurred each other on. There was tea and fruitcake for the crews in the long room after rowing, and he trained all through the winter with outings on Saturday afternoons and Sunday mornings and Tuesday and Thursday lunchtimes, when he was allowed extended breaks by his employer. 'There was a feeling of real friendship,' Melvin recalls. 'Every time we sculled past Thames we would chant "FT".'

The process began in 1948 when Carpmael, by now qualifying as a veteran, won the Wingfields, and won it again in 1949. Next year Edward Sturges won it. In 1951, the year of the Norfolk sculls, Fox, a London member studying medicine at Cambridge, won the Diamonds wearing Pembroke College colours, and followed this up with the Wingfields and a silver medal at the European championships in Macon, France. One of his victims there was Robbie van Mesdag of Dublin University, representing Eire (now Ireland). This was, incidentally, the year when Oxford launched their *Leviathan* to the accompaniment of fireworks and a band playing Canal Street Blues, a sixteen-oar monster enabling 'Jumbo' Edwards to coach his whole squad in the same boat. At London's dinner James Crowden, president of CUBC, replied for the guests by announcing that he hoped 'to put a girdle round the earth before the *Leviathan* could move a league.'

In 1952 at May's Vesta Dashes, Pinches, Fox and Carpmael won a heat of the senior sculls each, and finished the final in that order. Pinches was captain, and he put together a scratch eight of scullers for the Head which finished fourth, much to the delight, but more significantly to the surprise, of everybody. Fox was beaten in the Diamonds by Merv Wood, the Australian policeman who had won the Olympics in 1948, but he won the Wingfields for the second time and finished fourth in the Helsinki Olympics, having beaten Wood in a heat. Sturges and

Carpmael also tried for the Olympics but lost the double sculling trials to the young bloods MacMillan and Brandt of First and Third Trinity (London's four and the pair of Pulman and O'Brien also lost Olympic trials). Next year, Fox won the Dashes, the Diamonds, the Wingfields, the Metropolitan, and the Norfolk Sculls, and represented Britain again at the European championships in Copenhagen, where van Mesdag, now sculling for the Netherlands, beat him in a heat. In 1954, the first year of the Scullers' Head, Fox was second to Marsden, with Melvin fourth, Pinches ninth, Nisbet tenth and Carpmael sixteenth. Fox was second in the Wingfields to Sid Rand of the RAF, and he and Marsden entered the Double Sculls at Henley and went to the European championships in Amsterdam, finishing fourth. Fox then won the Norfolk sculls again.

Melvin was a rising London star, although he remained faithful to John O'Gaunt in the big events. He finished second in the Scullers' Head to Fox in 1955 and 1956 before winning it himself in 1957 and 1958. His regatta season went through Chiswick, Walton, Vesta Dashes, Reading and Marlow to get to Henley, after which the season was more relaxed. In the Diamonds he lost to the eventual winner P Vlasik of Morna Club, Yugoslavia, in 1954 and Teodor Kocerka of Bydgoszcz, Poland, in 1955. Kocerka won for a second time in 1956 and then the Australian Stuart Mackenzie made the Diamonds his own for six consecutive years. The next Briton to win was Wardell-Yerburgh in 1968, whose career and life ended in a car crash. After him came Leander's Tim Crooks in 1977.

While all this was going on, there was a lot of rowing activity at London as well. The Head was a calamity in 1947 when, on a bitterly cold and windy day, it was decided to tow the boat up to the start, and the crew were not warmed up. They started favourites but were trounced by a Jesus crew coached by Derek Mays-Smith, a former London oarsman, by twenty seconds. Next year they were second to Thames before winning the next two. A London crew lost the 1948 Olympic coxed fours trials to Oxford. In 1950 the annual record recorded that things were improving at Henley, but the club was yet to win an eight-oared or four-oared event since the Second World War. It also noted the shortage of young recruits, the active oarsmen being mostly pre-war stalwarts or those returning from National Service. A new category of membership for non-rowing members was announced. The first new eight was purchased since the war, and a visit was made to a regatta in Antwerp as guests of Antwerp Sculling Club. This was repeated next year, although 'much of the time was spent arguing about appalling accommodation and boats'. The highlight of this year was the aforementioned domination of the first Norfolk Sculls. Thick fog and floods contributed to a rotten season in which the club was ousted to third in the Head. There was a row to Windsor and back at Whitsun, and a new, fun event in August to end the season – the Festival of Britain Regatta on the Serpentine in Hyde Park. A big effort was being made at this time to introduce social events which would raise money. Among the new functions were a children's party and a New Year's Eve dance at the clubhouse.

Before Christmas in 1951 the club invited college crews from Oxford and Cambridge to a regatta at Putney which turned out to be a most enjoyable affair, and was added to the calendar for several years. Its introduction followed the practice of visiting both universities during the autumn to race college crews, notably Jesus at Cambridge and Brasenose at Oxford. It was won by a scullers' eight formed by Fox and Carpmael, battling in a gale which opposed the stream and kicked up rough water, in spite of the low tide. London's first eight were second, and Jesus third. As we have seen, the scullers' eight persevered into the Head and finished fourth. Although Pinches was happy with the numbers of men to man the boats, he was not happy with the results. The eight was second to Jesus in the Head, losing

CLUB DINNER

Held at the "Star and Garter" on 15th May, 1956 to commemorate the first meeting of the London Rowing Club held in the original "Star and Garter" on 15th May, 1856.

Centenary dinner at the Star & Garter, 1956

Invitation to a banquet at the Worshipful Company of Grocers to celebrate the LRC centenary, 1956

form due to 'conflicting views on methods of teaching and training', according to the captain. Although the conflict between orthodoxy and Fairbairnism had seemed to die out in the late thirties when the former Cambridge oarsman and former premier of Australia, Stanley Bruce, had written to the *Times* to suggest that there was little discernible difference between various crews he had enjoyed watching at Henley, it was alive and well in some quarters. In the autumn, reported Pinches, 'some ground was covered by long outings and at this stage the controversy for and against Meldrum[1] or Fairbairn teaching remained comparatively dormant.'

The fostering of relations with the old enemies, Oxford and Cambridge, was shrewd for future membership and for the good of rowing. While London's 'Jumbo' Edwards was coaching at Oxford, the club's list of coaches now included Dr David Jennens, a recent Cambridge blue, and Ran Laurie, the Olympic pairs champion of 1948 who also rowed for Cambridge in the 1930s, and who had given up being a civil servant in Sudan to study medicine at the London Hospital. There were problems when 'Push' Pulman dropped out of the eight with job trouble before Henley. He returned to row in the Goblets with Mike O'Brien, and his 'humour and clowning were a great asset in happily balancing the more serious moments of Henley training'. The crews stayed at Shiplake House on the river, where a member kept a launch at the bottom of the hill below the garden 'which gave vast amusement to us and caused considerable terror in the surrounding reaches.' The best they achieved at the regatta was the final of Stewards', which they lost to Thames.

Pinches's captaincy saw several innovations off the water, too. The Duke of Edinburgh agreed to become the club's patron. A notable new member was Field Marshal Lord Montgomery of Alamein who was entertained to tea at the club by Charles Rew after starting the Head of the River Race, and he was so taken with rowing that he joined up and, proposing the guests at the annual dinner, said that 'rowing appealed because it demanded leadership and discipline'. The duties of the officers of the club were de-centralised by forming committees to look after finance, entertainment and the building. 'In view of our financial position it seemed necessary to take steps to raise money in various ways which we had hitherto preferred to avoid. Jack Ormiston successfully ran a Christmas draw and a Derby sweep. I ran several dances with financial gain. Efforts were made in the house steward's department which were not successful until later when we were able to install an entirely new team.' The annual subscription was raised to six guineas. The season ended on a low note when the college

Metropolitan Rowing Club first appeared at Henley in 1967. A properly constituted club, it is a London flag of convenience for events where entries are restricted to one per club

LONDON
ROWING
CLUB

EMBANKMENT
PUTNEY
S W 15

The FiFTH oF NoVEMBER
FireworkS ✶ BarBecue
DANCE
6.00pm – 11.30pm

FireworkS

A £100 SPECTACULAR DISPLAY (BRING YOUR OWN BANGERS
TO ADD TO THE FUN)

START at 7.00pm

BonFire

TO MAKE THIS AS BIG AS POSSIBLE, COME
ALONG DURING THE AFTERNOON AND HELP COLLECT
DRIFTWOOD

BarBecue

SAUSAGES TO NIBBLE WHILE YOU WATCH THE FIREWORKS . . . STEAKS AND SALAD FROM 6.00pm
ONWARDS - IN CASE YOU WANT TO GET AWAY EARLY WITH THE CHILDREN

BAR

OPEN DURING THE EVENING AT NORMAL PRICES

DANCE

FOR A CHANGE FROM THE INEVITABLE DISCOTHEQUE, DANCE TO A
JUKE BOX - FIXED TO GIVE FREE PLAYS THROUGHOUT THE EVENING

PriCe

£1.20 ALL INCLUSIVE
ACCOMPANIED CHILDREN UNDER 14 FREE IF THEY BRING
A BOX OF FIREWORKS TO ADD TO THE SHOW

BooKiNG

BOOK IN ADVANCE OR PAY AT THE DOOR. BRING AS MANY FRIENDS AS POSSIBLE -
NON CLUB MEMBERS ESPECIALLY WELCOME. IF YOU ARE LIKELY TO COME, PLEASE
COMPLETE AND RETURN THE BOOKING SLIP TO GIVE US AN IDEA OF NUMBERS

- CUT HERE

LONDON ROWING CLUB   BOOKING SLIP   THE FIFTH OF NOVEMBER

Please send me...........tickets @ £1.20.   I enclose £................

I hope to come with ....friends and pay at the door

I will be bringing .... children under 14

Cheques/postal orders payable to "London Rowing Club" and send with this slip to D.G.AINSLI
LONDON ROWING CLUB, EMBANKMENT, PUTNEY, LONDON S W 15 as soon as possible

regatta in early December was called off because of very thick fog which, unfortunately, had not prevented the crews from making the journey.

In December 1953 a porpoise breaking the surface at the Crab-Tree preceded the Boustead Cup race. London lost by two-and-a-half lengths. Monty proposed the guests at the dinner for the second time and, in an unusual speech for such a gathering, warned those present to beware of the rise of the power of Germany which, he predicted, 'would lead us into war with Russia' in 1963 to 1968. 'I would say that you people have about ten or fifteen years peaceful rowing on the Thames before the next "party".'[2] One doubts whether he had rowing in mind, but he was close to the mark in that respect. Karl Adam was already shaking things up in Federal Germany by creating a centre of excellence based at Ratzeburg,[3] and at Henley a few months hence, Club Krylia Sovetov would win

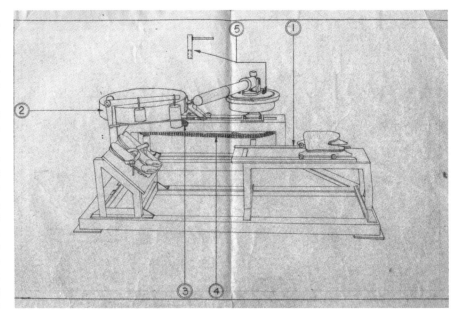

Design for rowing machine by Kennedy and Kempe Ltd, 1961. Key to maintenance notes: 1 Grease sliding gear. 2 Remove rust on flywheel with emory paper. 3 Ensure arm on rev counter registers when tripped by flywheel pin. 4 Oil chain once a week. 5 Adjust top brake shoes with spanner. 6 Oil all moving parts weekly

the Grand. But Gully Nickalls, the chairman of the Amateur Rowing Association, who replied for the guests, did not realise the full significance of what had happened at the Henley just past, where the Royal Air Force won both the Thames and Wyfold cups, setting records in the latter. One 'service' was ready for the gloom-ridden forecast made by Monty in his dinner speech, but it wasn't the ARA, as Gully was to find out a decade later.

In 1954 London were second in the Head to RAF Benson and winners of the first Vernon trophy for the fastest tideway crew, donated by Thames's Karl 'Bean'

Vernon, who had it made from an amalgam of all the trophies he had won. A new attraction on Boat Race day was the installation of a television set at the club to watch it on. At Henley the Grand eight became one of Krylia's victims. London invited the Soviet crew to a training supper at their Henley house, but they either couldn't or weren't allowed to come. Later, the president and the first eight attended a reception at the Soviet embassy for the Soviet rowing and chess teams and those who had competed against them. Ambassador Malik presented pewter goblets to the captains of London, Thames, Leander and the RAF. It was a most pleasant and enjoyable evening, said the London report. 'Vodka was tested by many for the first time... the effect on those who had been training over a very long period of time was quite startling.' Later that day there was an outing at Putney. 'Our coach, Archie Nisbet, seeing the state of the crew, quietly retired into the background and made off home, thinking that discretion was the better part of valour.' The captain diplomatically ordered a row from the mile to the flag post.

Tony Fox, winner of the Diamond Sculls at Henley in 1951 and 1953

By 1960 London had a Russian member, Lt Cmdr Paul Shevyrew of the Soviet embassy, who showed a film on his country at one of the club's functions. Colin Porter introduced a film of the Rome Olympics, and copies of Rowing Notes by Fairbairn were recommended to all members at a reasonable price. During the 1960s there were programmes of Charlie Chaplin movies, talks by Jumbo Edwards on moving boats, on sailing round Britain and on the Olympics in Japan. Graham Hill, the Formula One champion and stroke of the eight in 1953, came to talk on fast motoring, and the premier of a curious production called the Chelworth Houseparty (cert X) was staged, the plot of which is lost in the mysteries of time. Profits accrued from the annual Boat Race ball at the Dorchester, organised by Archie Nisbet with proceeds shared by London and Pembroke, Cambridge. Edward Sturges welcomed London oarsmen to his gym in a mews behind Sloane Square, where the heir to the throne was among the young clientele. Circuit training and weights 'transformed us physically' according to Owen 'Tubby' Bryant. Chris Woodall, from a slightly earlier generation, remembered eating after gym sessions in the restaurant upstairs run by Mrs Jean Sturges, first wife of Edward's rowing partner, Farn Carpmael. It was the sort of place where you would run into Farn as well as Merv Wood, the Australian Olympian. Weight training may have transformed men physically, but it did not help them with psychology. Bryant recalls sitting on the start in the number 5 seat of the Grand eight in 1958 and, foolishly and against all advice, looking across at his opposite number in the Trud Leningrad crew. 'He was built like a block of flats, bigger than Pinsent,'[4] he says. Bryant rowed three times in the Grand, and recognised that the club was pretending to be what it wasn't.

The membership reached nearly 650 by 1961 and was busy on the water, with the second eight often giving the first eight a hard time. The club regatta offered scratch eights, handicap sculls, whiff races for juniors and the Green Fours. The bar was buzzing after outings on most evenings, while at the cutting edge of competition there was a frustrating lack of success at the regattas that mattered, despite moments of fun glory such as the defeat of Thames's Olympic-designate eight of 1960 at the Vesta Dashes in front of a packed Thames balcony. Some promising new scullers came on the scene, such as Bobby Carpmael, who won the Wingfields in 1961 (the twelfth London win in thirteen years), George Justicz who won the Scullers Head in 1960 wearing a Birmingham shirt, and another Brummie, Graham Beech, who won at Bedford, Henley Town and the Serpentine that year and 'endeared himself to us by his single minded Zátopekian determination to punish himself into fitness to win, and to take on anyone, anywhere, anytime.'[5]

This was from the pen of Farn Carpmael who was attempting to record the club's activities after the printing of annual reports ceased in 1953. He described the Grand winners in 1960 as 'Molesey Cottage', a reference to the activities of Porter's mavericks – see below – and noted that after eight hundred miles of rowing before the 1961 Head, London finished fifth, only twenty-seven seconds behind Barn Cottage, which was an improvement of twenty seconds on the year before. It wasn't enough to defeat the USSR Navy in the Grand. The fleet was being updated in the early sixties, with a Pocock eight bought from Yale and the purchase of a new George Sims eight and two sculling boats by Edwin Phelps. The club reverted to pre-war oar dimensions of 12 feet 1 inch instead of 12 feet 6 inches, with barrel blades tapering from $6^3/_4$ inches at the middle to $6^1/_4$ at the tip. Most boats were rigged to slide $1^1/_2$ inches past the pin. Lt Col D H E McCowen DSO presented bow- and stroke-side ergometers modelled on Professor Harrison's Australian designs. 'Jumbo' Edwards's tenure as chief coach in 1962 was cut short at Marlow next year when, the worse for wear after the eight lost, he took a swipe at Charlie Dearsley for not wearing correct kit. Dearsley hit back, and that was the last the crew saw of their coach.

Monty's membership application

To appreciate what happened in British rowing after Peter Coni became captain for 1963, we must now backtrack to that moment in 1953 when Bomber Command exploded onto Henley Regatta's honours board. Rowing at six in the RAF's eight was Colin Porter, a national serviceman who had rowed for The King's School, Canterbury, and then London University while studying engineering at Chelsea Polytechnic. He found himself at Bomber Command's Benson base near Wallingford, where Wing Commander Jack Hay, a fanatical rowing man, had engineered to attract the most able rowers passing through their military service. Porter was the chief mover. His approach was that if the Americans kept on winning the Olympic eights, then they must know something that we didn't. His maxim was that strength, stamina and skill lead to speed. The Benson men studied a film of the 1947 Harvard crew and enlisted the help of American oarsmen studying at Oxford. They set themselves a punishing, seven-days-a-week training regime. They ran to and from the Nissen hut which they shared with Wallingford Rowing Club, and they conducted long, steady state rows as well as gruelling sessions in the gym.[6]

The RAF four was sent to the European championships with Christopher Davidge, a remarkable former Oxford stroke, as coach, and they won a bronze medal. Next year they won the Head of the River Race, lost the final of the Stewards' to Krylia Sovetov, and won the silver medal at the European championships in Amsterdam, trailing the Italian crew, Moto Guzzi, from the motorcycle manufacturing company. When he left the air force, Porter moved to Thames Rowing Club. His assessment of the eight he rowed with there in 1955 was that it was the best in Britain, but not good enough. Although strengthened for the European championships by the inclusion of Sid Rand and Mike Beresford from the 1954 RAF four, the crew did not reach the final. As an Olympic year approached, Porter concluded that there should be radical changes if British rowing was to meet the professionalism of the Soviet Union and other East European countries and the pockets of semi-professionalism now to be found in such places as Federal Germany and Italy – not to mention the Canadians from British Columbia and the still-powerful Americans. He wanted to see a proper system of composite crews and selection so that international representation was open to oarsmen from all

Molesey Boat Club, with London's John Vigurs at seat number 3 and Simon Crosse at 4, won the Grand in 1960, beating LRC in the first round, Lady Margaret in the semifinal and Oxford in the final. This marked a vital step in the changing scene of British rowing

clubs instead of the back-door composites of Leander and the universities. He saw clearly that British rowing was standing still, if not declining.

For 1956, Porter decided to put together a four to try for the Melbourne Olympics. He recruited Maurice Legg, Alistair Davidson and Mike Beresford, all of Thames, but the Thames committee would not hear of it. For the Head he added the Rand brothers, Gavin Sorrell and Ted Field, all ex-RAF oarsmen, and Thames reluctantly gave them a starting slot as Thames III. They won the head by ten seconds and showed up the paucity of eight-oared rowing. 'Goodness knows how the Thames committee and coaches handled that result,' Porter said. 'I avoided contact with all the officials, but the annual almanac failed to record the names of the winning crew for the first and only time.'[7] The club continued its hostility, but could not refuse to endorse the four's entry for the Stewards' at Henley. The draw brought Porter's crew and the official Thames crew together in the first round, and Porter's crew won by three feet. Then they trounced a strong Leander boat stroked by Davidge, and London in the final. The Rand brothers won the Double Sculls, and the RAF lost the final of the Thames Cup to Princeton.

Porter's four completed an undefeated season, but they never went to the Olympics in Melbourne. The selectors – all successful pre-war oarsmen – picked an eight for the European championships in Bled, Yugoslavia, from men beaten by Porter's four. When it failed to get to the final, it was strengthened by the inclusion of Davidge before it was sent to Melbourne, where it finished ninth. The only other British crews were Fox in the single sculls and the Rand brothers in the double sculls. London's Doug Melvin, named as spare man, was withdrawn from the team without explanation after his boat had been shipped to Australia. The decision prompted a withering editorial in *Rowing* magazine. The British team in Melbourne was, said Porter, the worst ever sent abroad. Even the team members petitioned the selectors to hold trials in future. Porter wrote to Rowing magazine saying so. At the end of the season, the British Rowing Almanack commented that the disbandment of the club at RAF Benson was the worst news for British rowing. As for Thames Rowing Club, it did not win a Henley trophy during the next forty years.

In 1957 Porter coached National Provincial Bank to become the first business house to win the Wyfold. Their eight reached the final of the Thames Cup, and the four then reached the final of the European championships in Duisburg, Germany, where Davidge and a former Cambridge oarsmen, Tony Leadley, won gold in the pairs. Home grown eights had again been a disaster in the Grand. In the autumn Porter carted his boat from Thames to Molesey, a club with some strong like-minded men. Meanwhile, Davidge and the new

Diamond sculling sensation, Stuart Mackenzie, took digs with Teddy Selwyn at Barn Cottage in Remenham, across the bridge from Henley-on-Thames, and formed an eight under that name for the Head. Next year a formidable Barn Cottage crew won it, and Porter was coaching Oxford at the invitation of the OUBC president, Sorrell. After the Head, Davidge suggested that Porter and Beresford got together with John Vigurs and Simon

Colin Porter's 1958 Barn Cottage four, with Mike Beresford of Thames and London's Simon Crosse and John Vigurs, won the Stewards' at Henley and then, taking a cox on board, set a record as they won the gold medal for England at the Empire games on Llyn Padarn, Wales

Crosse who had been stalwarts of London crews for four or five years to have a go at the Empire games in Wales. Rowing as Barn Cottage, they beat Porter's 1957 National Provincial crew in the final of the Stewards', and then won the Empire coxed fours on Llyn Padarn in record time. National Provincial won the coxless fours at the same regatta. The location was beautiful but the conditions were atrocious, the crew only surviving by being at the start half an hour early to give themselves time to bail out. They followed this by bitter disappointment at the European championships in Poznan, where the whole team suffered food poisoning, described in the report as 'D and V'. At the end of the year, Porter's book Rowing to Win was published.

In 1960 Barn Cottage won the Head by fifteen seconds and Molesey won the Grand. The Molesey eight was sent to the Rome Olympics in two fours. Beresford, Porter, Vigurs and Davidge set a record in a heat before finishing fifth in the coxless event, while the coxed four was unplaced. In 1961 Cottage won the Head for the third time, but internationally there was little progress. George Justicz and Nick Birkmyre achieved the best result for years when they won the European silver medal in double sculls in Prague, following negotiation with the Czech government over Justicz's status because he had migrated to Britain from Czechoslovakia before the war. Justicz and Birkmyre were the only British crew to reach a final at the first world championships in Lucerne in 1962. England sent five boats to the Commonwealth games in Perth, Australia, later that year. The coxless four, pair and double scullers won gold medals, with bronzes for the eight and coxed four. Some years later, Porter was to emigrate to New South Wales to work at the state's hydraulic research plant, but after the Perth games he determined to stop rowing and take a year off to decorate his new house. Meanwhile, back at London, Peter Coni had issued a manifesto as soon as he was elected captain for the 1963 season. His thoughts about what a serious Henley crew should do echoed Porter's thoughts of what a serious national crew should do, and is worth quoting at length.

'There are three necessary things for a fast crew: technique, strength and fitness,' he wrote, 'and I think we should go for strength and basic stamina up until the Head, with technique being dealt with all the time, of course, but with a real blitz on technique at racing pressure in April and early May, so that by mid-May, instead of still wondering who ought to be in the crew, the eights are ready to race. It seems to me that the traditional LRC style of Fairbairnism seen through a sculler's viewpoint is very easy to learn, very pleasant as well as economical and efficient to row, and is admirably suited to tideway conditions. I do not think that it is chiefly on technique that British crews lose to foreigners; it is far more because of their lackadaisical approach to improving their physical strength and fitness and I am sure we will do better to concentrate on raising our standard in these before wondering whether we should copy German technique or anybody else's. What we ought to learn from the Germans is the way in which they train, and that I hope we will emulate this year. There is no doubt that weight training, seriously done, is the quickest and easiest way to increase your muscle size (and therefore power). Because of this, I think it should be the kingpin of evening training from October until the end of January, during which time everyone should do at least three circuits a week. I don't believe that the tank improves technique when it is used for long patches of hard work – though it is splendid if an oarsman wants to practice technique quietly, or if a coach wants to explain criticisms in detail. Instead I think we should use the tub pair much more than we have done, especially on winter evenings, when it is perfectly easy to use it beside the Putney hard. Technique is better dealt with in the tub and in the eight, and the sculling boat for watermanship in early training, and in crew selection. My intention is that only those who have trained right through the year will be considered for Henley crews. If you do this sort of work from October, you can be quite sure you won't lose your place to someone who turns up only semi-fit in January, however brilliant his previous rowing record may be.'

Porter's house decorating was interrupted by an invitation to a meeting at the home of Peter Sutherland, an architect who knew Coni from Cambridge and was now captain of Leander. When he arrived he found several captains of his generation – Coni the barrister from London, Geoffrey Page the art teacher and journalist from Thames and Dick Knight the builder from Molesey. Together they resolved to confront the Amateur Rowing Association to demand the appointment of a professional trainer, proper trials for the formation of truly composite

Peter Beale, chief cashier of the Bank of England, served as London's treasurer from 1946 to 1954 and 1959 to 1966

crews, and reform of the selection board by nominating its members from the clubs. Gully Nickalls, seven times a Grand winner and chairman of the ARA, resisted until it became apparent that the major clubs supported the initiative. London's Doug Melvin became a selector along with Page and Porter, while 'Jumbo' Edwards, now retired from the RAF, was appointed chief coach to raise the standard of coaching in the country. A former junior GB sprinter, Jim Railton, was hired as trainer.

By 1964 Porter was chairman of the selectors and the members included Edwards, Davidge, Roger Pope of National Provincial and the charismatic professional coach Lou Barry. There was new blood on the ARA council, and a national squad system called Nautilus was in place and attracting talented men in London and the Midlands. There was Nautilus training twice a week at a school at Tulse Hill, and London's hierarchy and oarsmen were enthusiastic participants. The club followed where the likes of Crosse and Vigurs, its strong men, had gone of their own accord.

The strong tradition of British rowing – the deep base of large clubs, schools and colleges, the exacting demands of style and the conflicts between styles – had had its weakness exposed. There was, of course, still suspicion and disagreement, as illustrated by Jumbo's definition of Porterism: 'The cult of hard work and fitness to the exclusion of almost everything else.'[8] The new scheme did not win universal support; many of the best oarsmen hedged their bets and stayed with their clubs. A new nomadic club called Tideway Scullers' School grew up around Lou Barry. Its first home was at Barclays Bank, next door to London, and the emphasis was on sculling. Tideway Scullers was soon to dominate the Head for a decade, forming eights and eventually getting three of them to the top three

'Jumbo' Edwards
by Feliks Topolski

slots. After two years, Nautilus Midlands was doing well, but the scheme on the Thames foundered because it failed to became a truly national squad.

Julian Ebsworth was one among seven London men who joined Nautilus in its first year after a remarkable season when he first arrived at the club from Trinity Hall in the autumn of 1963. He joined a super eight which won a junior pot, three junior-senior pots and a senior pot in quick succession, and then reached the final of Thames Cup, the first London eight to reach a Henley final since the Second World War. They beat Molesey, Nottingham University, Twickenham and Thames before losing to Eliot House, a college of Harvard University. At the same regatta there was a travesty in the first round of the Grand, according to the report in London's newsletter. The London account, probably written by Coni, number 4 in the crew and a future chairman of the regatta, says: 'We reckon we had a chance of winning. In fact the race was a fiasco as the University of London deliberately began rowing on the "Are you ready?"

and had a good half length before either the umpire said "Row" or we had our blades in the water, and when we did go, we were sufficiently demoralised to be easy meat. It is easy to be wise after the event and say a crew should be prepared: one does not expect English Grand entries at Henley to copy the cheating of minor continental regattas, nor that the Henley umpires should let such flagrant breaches of rules go unobserved or unrestrained. Perhaps it was as well the superb Russian crew made the result of our heat look unimportant.' The official regatta record simply says: 'University of London won by three lengths.'

At the end of that season Coni tried to persuade Ebsworth to stand for captain, but he grasped the opportunity to join Nautilus instead, along with Simon Rippon, Peter Fraser, Roger Hughes, Graham Baldock, Ken Usher and Bob Potter. 'Jumbo' Edwards coached Nautilus, and his crews made a promising start with fifth, eighth and twelfth places in the Head of the River Race, having started among the new entries. But things went wrong when they lost the national trials to the University of London, whom, ironically, the London first eight had beaten at St Neots Centenary Regatta, with Rippon subbing into it.[9] One of the problems facing the selectors was that clubs such as London University and Tideway Scullers were not signed up with Nautilus, and after the trials they declined to send an eight to the world championships. Edwards fell out with his crew because some of them did not dress correctly for dinner. Bernd Kruse, a German, was appointed coach but never took up the post, and Edwards was replaced by Dicky Wheadon, a former London international. Ebsworth stayed on for another year during which the Nautilus coxless four more or less coached itself; Rippon returned to London. In January 1967, *Rowing* magazine printed Porter's eleven-point resignation statement as chairman of the selectors, which included the sentiment that 'our biggest need is for the alchemist who can turn our raw material into international gold'. The magazine also published George Plumtree's manifesto as the incoming chairman of Nautilus, a position which the 1964 captain of London was persuaded to accept after Lou Barry rejected the ARA's offer.

When Rippon was elected captain for 1966, he observed that 'tougher training has still not produced results.' By next year fifteen London men were training at the ARA's classes at Staveley Road gym (and a year later the club itself was using the gym at Elliot School under Roger Vincett). Meanwhile, members in the City met at lunchtime on Tuesdays for beer and sandwiches in the cellar of the Jamaica Wine Shop at St Michael's Alley, off Cornhill. Tom Phelps retired as the club's waterman on Easter Saturday in 1967, the day of both the Head and the Boat Race. The first eight won four regattas before Henley and four after, but nothing at Henley itself. There was tragedy when their cox, Michael Manning, drowned while swimming the river at Goring on the Sunday before Henley. The coroner commended Jonathan Steel and John Medhurst for their efforts to save him. The second eight drew National Provincial Bank in no less than six regattas, beating them only at Molesey. Two fours that went to the Exe Head sank, while the other survived by bailing. There was an unsuccessful move to revive the Boustead Cup. It failed because Thames refused to race before the Head, so it was decided that the Boustead would be settled by positions in the Head. A regatta for schools was organised by Peter Hilditch.

At Henley, Rippon put his best eight into the Thames Cup, and it survived into the second round where it was beaten by Vesta, while the Grand crew in which he rowed himself lost to the French in the first round. His decision was an answer to the growing but painful realisation that the Grand, which the club was formed to win, was no longer within its grasp. The club, as Bryant had found out when rowing in the Grand in the 1950s, was pretending to be what it wasn't. Rippon suggested to the Stewards that they introduce an invitation international event to preserve the trophy for club crews, but this idea fell on deaf ears. Next year, no entry for the Grand was made, the first time that London had not started in Henley's top event since 1857.

There were twenty London crews in the Head in 1969, the top place being seventeenth. Familiar names were still winning in the Scullers' Head – Melvin the over forties pennant, Marsden the over fifties, and Carpmael the over sixties. Rowing started for 'irregulars' who turned up on Wednesdays, and later on Sundays, and the club acquired two bicycles for coaches. Then came the long-awaited breakthrough, the first four-oared win at Henley since the second world war. Dan Topolski, Nick Cooper, Peter Harrison and Chris Blackwall won the Wyfold, Topolski being described as a masterful steersman and Blackwall as a great find at stroke. Cooper and Harrison provided the power. They also won at Marlow and were sent to the European championships at Klagenfurt, the first London crew to gain representation since 1955. Harrison's analysis in October's club newsletter concluded that Britain's problems of preparation and facilities were no greater than others, but while 'they overcome theirs, we hang ours round our necks.' He noted that many of the crews beating him had been together for two years or more. He advocated that taking part in international competition was essential, and that London should be one of several centres aspiring to temper club pride by working with others in the final shakedown of forming national crews. Robert Rakison, a spectator under canvas on the Worthersee, reported that 'a professional attitude is needed in

Graham Hill's blue and white racing driver's helmet. Hill stroked London's eight in 1953

Britain if we are to win, and plenty of experience of rowing on six lane 2000 metre [2,187-yard] courses' – reflecting Harrison's conclusion that side-by-side rowing has little relevance to the multi-lane business. Harrison also became accustomed to 'a towering Russian oarsman approaching one with a "you swap" and pointing menacingly to one's ARA lapel badge with one hand while clutching a polythene bag with badges portraying members of the Soviet Top Squad, such as K Marx, F Engels and V I Lenin.'

Daniel Topolski, Nick Cooper, Peter Harrison and Chris Blackwall won the Wyfold at Henley in 1969 and represented GB in the European Championships in Klagenfurt

Klagenfurt was another British disaster, but Guy Harris, a London pre-war cox who was the boat transport manager for the GB team, witnessed a significant event there. He was present when a Czech coach, Bohumil Janousek, made it known that he was looking for employment outside his home country. Janousek arrived in London before Christmas in 1969 to take up a post as Britain's first national coach. By now Jim Railton was rowing correspondent for the *Times* and coaching at Thames Tradesmen, a long-established club in Kew. Meanwhile, Lou Barry was helping Cambridge achieve a run of victories in the Boat Race. A small group of Oxbridge oarsmen and juniors who cut their teeth at Tradesmen became the core of Janousek's 1976 Olympic team which went head-to-head with the East Germans. The eight narrowly missed gold, and the double scullers also won silver.

During the period under review, timber swept up by the tide from the docks and the dumping of unwanted items such as bedsteads and motor cycles in the Thames was making the tideway dangerous for small boats, and expensive for clubs' repairs accounts. London Rowing Club took the initiative in solving this by calling a meeting of interested parties on 2 December 1965. In short, it was found that nobody was in charge, and the meeting set up a committee, with Farn Carpmael in the chair, to press for action.[10]

12 A CLUBHOUSE WITH A GRANDSTAND

From the start, much energy was spent on finding premises for members and their boats. Rooms were initially rented at the Star & Garter on the Putney waterside, followed in November 1856 by negotiation to rent a new extension at the suggestion of the landlord, Mr Heath. By the end of the year, agreement was reached to construct additional rooms after considerable haggling over whether the rent should be £50 per annum as requested or £40 as offered by the club, guaranteed for a minimum of six years. Meanwhile, part of Searle's yard, further west along the Surrey shore, was rented for boats for a minimum of two years, with undertakings to conduct no boat building work except small maintenance jobs on club boats. Any furniture 'now in the rooms' was to belong to the club during the time of the occupancy. The terms said that the club was 'not to be bound to leave the buildings in the same position as they now stand. You will be expected to have the place cleared at once of all your boats which now stand there.'

Herbert Playford's drawing of London's first shed for boats, 1857

The stay at Searles was short-lived. London built a shed of its own in June of the following year on Finches Field, site of the present clubhouse. It was described as a 'sort of box on the ground which can be taken in pieces and removed at any moment', 70 by 39 feet, made of wood with a felt roof, three doors to the boat bays and a side door and a barred window at each end. By May 1858 there was a causeway from the boathouse to the water, which gave cause for concern. In October the secretary, Herbert Playford, wrote to the contractor 'to request you to enforce Mr Green to set in repair the club causeway... it being now in most useless condition, the cause of which is, in the opinion of the committee, the very inferior quality of the (so-called) gravel laid down'.

By 1868, complaints were being made about the want of accommodation, and a sub-committee was appointed in the next year to look into what could be done. This led to the most momentous development in the establishment of the club. At the end of May 1869 members received a circular setting out a 'very simple' plan: while the London Rowing Club remained unaltered, a limited liability company would be set up to erect premises with a nominal capital divided into shares which would revert to the company on death, resignation or forfeiture. The estimated

cost of a building incorporating boathouse, club rooms, dressing room and washing facilities was £1,700, to be paid for by raising a loan through £5 debentures bearing an interest rate of five per cent. The London Boat House Company Limited (registered number 4711) was incorporated on 22 January 1870 with a capital of £2,000 divided into 1,000 shares of £2 each, with the object of leasing or purchasing land on which to erect a boathouse and rooms 'for the use and accommodation of an association of gentlemen now known as The London Rowing Club'. Four days later a meeting vested ownership of all the property of the London Rowing Club in the company.

The aims of the company included the purchasing, hiring and selling of boats, appliances and equipment for use by amateur oarsmen and scullers, and the encouragement of rowing on the river Thames amongst gentlemen amateurs. Of the nineteen original directors, only five admitted to occupations – a

The clubhouse in 2006, and an engraving of the new building in 1872 from the Illustrated London News

The Star & Garter, London's clubroom from 1857. Boats were housed at Searle's yard until a shed was built in July 1859

stockbroker, a ship broker, a manufacturer and two merchants. Eleven described themselves as 'gentlemen', two as 'esquire' and one as 'baronet'. Seven of these are named as the original subscribers: Herbert Harlee Playford, shipbroker; Frederick Fenner, stockbroker; William Moxon, decorator; Eugène Monteuuis, surveyor, Chas Edward Innes, architect, Robert Davis Price, merchant, and Henry Neville Custace, who gives his address as Middlesex Hospital, which may be a clue to how he made ends meet. Ebenezer Cobb Morley, solicitor, was witness to the signatures.

Company No 4711 is now one of the oldest surviving in England, and very little has changed in its memorandum and articles. The archaic 'association of gentlemen' remains despite the deletion of 'amongst gentlemen amateurs' after 'encouragement of rowing on the River Thames'. Reference to 'amateur' has been removed when referring to oarsmen, and oarswomen have been added. An interpretation clause at the end of the document now states that 'the singular shall include the plural and vice versa, the masculine shall include the feminine, and rowing shall include sculling'. Other small changes in 2004 are mainly concerning procedural matters.

The new premises, designed by the architect and club member George Dunnage, opened in January 1871, although the general meeting at the Guildhall Tavern was informed that severe weather had delayed the laying down of gas-pipes. Thus Mr Groombridge of the Star & Garter 'has kindly consented to allow us to make use of our old clubroom on Saturdays'. But clothes must be transferred from the Star & Garter at once. A life membership scheme topped up the sum raised by the debentures and also paid for the furniture, while the annual subscription was doubled to two guineas from 1872 to pay off the debentures. The building was fully operational before the end of March, with 'all necessary refreshments obtainable'. The newly elected secretary, T Rouse Ebbetts, begged members 'to distinctly understand that these can be ordered and paid for by members only'. They should make out a bill and put it in the box provided for that purpose in the clubroom. Money making facilities were an important part of the new premises. Lockers for rent came in three sizes, the largest being 16 by 13 inches, and 3 feet 9 inches high with a shelf and two pegs for 10 shillings,

Share certificate in London Boat House Company Limited

Certificate of Incorporation

OF THE

LONDON BOAT HOUSE COMPANY,

LIMITED.

No. 4,711. C.

I HEREBY CERTIFY that the LONDON BOAT HOUSE COMPANY, LIMITED, is this day incorporated under the "Companies Act, 1862," and that this Company is Limited.

Given under my hand, at London, this twenty-second day of January, One thousand eight hundred and seventy.

E. C. CURZON,

Registrar of Joint Stock Companies.

Fee, £2 0 0

Company No 4,711

The clubhouse in 1910

and the smallest – 14 by 16 by 16 inches – were half the price. The roof was specially designed as a grand stand, and seats were advertised for the 1871 boat race at a cost of half a crown (two shillings and six pence) for members and ladies, or five shillings for gentlemen visitors. A cold lunch cost 2s 6d afterwards, and strangers were not permitted on the premises until after the race. Ebbetts also announced that the heap of clothes remaining at the Star & Garter would be cleared out shortly.

The London Boat House Company Limited was a huge step forward, but it was clear that the new premises were too small from the first day. In 1873 plans for an extension designed by Dunnage were under consideration. They were apparently approved by the directors but shelved on the grounds of cost. A meeting in June 1875 – timed at 9pm to allow for oarsmen to come off the water — proposed raising £600 in debentures to meet the estimate of £576 to extend the premises on the east side to provide an additional boat bay of 26 feet by 26 feet with a dressing room of the same size and two WCs and urinals above.

The boathouse in 1869, when London hosted Harvard in their race against Oxford. Leander Club is on the right

A hundred lockers were included, estimated to produce a profit of £30. A month later half the money had been promised, and the extension was erected during the winter of 1875–76 at a cost of £839, the balance being found from the company's income account. Membership had reached almost 500, and finances as well as activity flourished.

Nine years on, further expansion took place with the addition of ten bedrooms, a sitting room and two bedrooms for servants. Adamson and Sons took on the work in 1884 for £1,372, to include repairs and improvements. Debentures for £1,600 were issued to pay for it, and loans were raised from Eugène Monteuuis and the architect himself to bridge the gap between the estimate and final bill, which amounted to £1,797 17s 11d. Building work was completed on 14 March 1885, but a lot remained to be done to make the place comfortable. 'Thanks to the exertions of several members who have occupied bedrooms for the last twelve months, they are now in a fit state for occupation... The new club room, which has been handsomely furnished and tastefully decorated, has been much frequented by members, especially on Wednesday and Saturday evenings, and the expectation which had been formed as to its usefulness have been fully realised. In fact, we think the members may now congratulate themselves upon possessing one of the best and most convenient clubhouses in existence.'

The annual report for 1890 was the most satisfactory for years. Not only had the oarsman deposed Thames from the top trophies by winning the Grand at Henley, the Champion Cup at the Metropolitan and the senior eights at Kingston, but also 'a distinct epoch in the history of the club' was marked, financially speaking. The A debentures, raised to build the boathouse in 1870, were paid off, to the tune of £1,665 plus accrued interest of £744 12s 3d. There remained £90 capital and approximately £66 interest to pay on the B debentures issued in 1875, and the whole of the C debentures issued in 1884. But the loans from Monteuuis and Dunnage had been paid off, and the C debentures were converted from a five per cent to a four per cent loan, thus enabling the directors to forecast that they would be paid off by 1900.

There were further developments in 1891 when a new washing room was constructed at the back of the premises, the old one being converted into an office for the secretary and a small lavatory. The old committee room became a lobby, and the original entrance – at the upstream end of the building – was enlarged and enhanced by a broader flight of stone steps. The roof was also thoroughly repaired and D debentures to the tune of £650 were issued, together with loans of £50 from three members, to pay the bill. Furthermore, after some years of unsatisfactory results, the food and wine account was a success.

Geoffrey Fletcher's drawing of LRC, 1968

Profit and loss, membership numbers and participation in the numerous regattas and activities at Putney waxed and waned, but there is no question that the building and the facilities which it offered – refreshments and bar, smoking concerts, social functions – were a tremendous asset to London Rowing Club. House managers often come in for praise in the annual reports, such as Mr Nevile in 1900, when 'the general accounts for the year are very satisfactory in spite of the war in South Africa, which so largely affected the Henley house boat'. The first tank, accommodating only one oarsman, was constructed in 1910 to a design by Lachlan Maclean, a former Thames Cup winner who spent many years on the coaching committee and was treasurer from 1896 to 1909, guiding the company through some difficult times. The tank is described as an addition, but it is unclear where it was situated. Its construction was a bold move considering that the freehold of the site was not obtained until 1913, when it was purchased from Lord Westbury for £3,000. When rowing activities resumed after the First World War, repairs could be delayed no longer, and an appeal which coupled a war memorial to a special maintenance fund was generously answered by the membership, raising £1,386. This was enough for a memorial tablet and a spacious new balcony with change for general repairs, all supervised by Charles Schlotel and completed in 1921. The club's claim against the War Office for requisition of premises was paid a year later. Electric light was installed in 1925, and by 1927 attention had turned to the desire for an eight-oared tank for indoor training and coaching. An appeal for £1,000 enabled it to open a year later to a design by Colonel Sankey – the first tank in Britain which could accommodate eight rowers. In the same year, standing committees were created to supervise the house, finance, repairs, the boat bays and membership.

In 1939 an emergency board was appointed to look after the club and the premises in the event of hostilities. The Second World War duly took place, and the club emerged with a small credit balance. The post-war world was marked by much do-it-yourself maintenance by the members, and in 1952 a new committee structure came into being under the headings of finance, building and entertainment. John Pinches energetically organised a social programme which included dances, Christmas draws and sweeps on the Derby to add to more traditional social events such as the Head of the River Race and Boat Race weekends. The report for 1961 remarked that the young man who re-painted the flagpole

The Hanlan versus Trickett match for the world professional sculling championships, 1882, showing LRC on the left and Thames RC on the right

using a bosun's chair 'certainly did not value his life highly and, being young, we pray for his future.'

In October 1961 the boathouse was repainted for the first time in sixty years, and George Plumtree supervised sterling work on cleaning and refurbishing the tank, including replacement of riggers. Tiles designed by Michael Hickey and fired at Chelsea Pottery were added to the fireplace in the long room. By the late 1960s, however, it was apparent that the boathouse was in urgent need of structural attention and modernisation. Symptomatic of problems were grey-green fingers of dry and wet rot creeping through the timbers of the old loo down the walls and into the boats. Simon Crosse, the architect who was put in charge of the first works since 1891, recalled the changing conditions which members were then suffering: showers consisting of two zinc troughs and a bucket of cold water; a floor of wet decayed linoleum; icy blasts from ill-fitting windows; a jumbo wicker basket of abandoned kit festering unpleasantly in the middle of the floor, and lockers assigned to people long-since dead. The entrance to the club was via a stone staircase at the west, upstream end of the building, leading directly into a lobby littered with last week's discarded barrels and bottles, a small lounge and a corridor where the present bar is, which led to the members' room and the changing room. There was an inadequate second-floor kitchen with a manual dumb waiter linking it to the dining area. The bar was in the upstream end of the main clubroom, and there was a hatch to the lobby through which pints for boatmen and their ilk

Map showing causeway, 1858

could be passed; heaven forbade them to drink with gentlemen. The descent from the changing room was down a rickety timber staircase to a lean-to with a leaking roof and a solitary light bulb. The dark cavernous boathouse had a floor permanently pitted with pools of dirty mud, where Old Tom Phelps, the club's waterman, tried to look after a fleet of mostly pre-war boats in conditions that would have made Fagin's flesh creep.[1]

Peter Coni summarised the committee's deliberations on solutions in a typically succinct 'Conigram'. There were four choices: selling the site to a developer and leasing back part of the new building; retaining ownership and re-building the site to include residential accommodation to finance the rebuilding; sell the site and move to another; stay put and modernise. A guide to the last two options was the recent re-building of the Barclays Bank three-bay premises next door for about £65,000. Hard decisions had to be made in the complex finances of the enterprise. While Coni recognised that the club's competitive record was bad at this time, Crosse maintained that its superb Victorian pile was its best asset. They saw that good performance and attractive facilities were linked. Crosse's vision was to turn London into the finest clubhouse in the land, boasting a glass-covered roof-top lounge and restaurant, the brain child of Joyce

Conwy-Evans, overlooking the river. Coni's view was more pragmatic; he asked if it was realistic to keep 'open house' for the bar and catering. His priorities included a basic plan to house sufficient good boats and launch effective crews, to run social activities and entertain members and, not least, to be a money-spinner.

Happily the membership chose the option of extension and refurbishment. The modernisation appeal was launched in November 1968 and the building programme began there and

Commemorative oars in LRC's entrance hall

then when Graham Hill, fresh from winning his second Formula One championship and wearing his helmet of appropriate livery, drove an old Morris Oxford which had been obtained for £5 head-on into the wall that separated the club from Spring Passage. The car was subsequently sold for £15! Hill made three runs to reduce the wall to rubble. Crosse's scheme comprised a new main entrance, staircase and office at the east end of the building, with new changing

The long room in the 1960s, showing the bar at the upstream end

and washing facilities behind on the ground floor, and a large club room – the Fairbairn room – and bar above. Unsurprisingly, costs soared above the best-laid estimates. By July 1970, when construction work caused rowing to be based at the Rutland boathouse in Hammersmith for all except for novices and irregulars, who could use boats kept on racks at Putney, the appeal rose from £32,000 to £64,000. In November that year, the best estimate was put at £62,142 and the appeal was £18,000 short.

Coni, with the support of the president, Farn Carpmael, maintained faith with his chum Crosse and adroitly expanded the appeal to meet its moving target. 'The spiralling effects of inflation made all this a gamble of hair-raising intensity,' the architect said later. 'Although I was frequently hauled over the coals, there was always the over-riding common aim to push the project through. I had to face a battery of barristers – LRC committees are always barrister-domi-nated. But the spirit and the will to win was strong on all sides. I am shattered and speechless when I think back to the courage of the committee which took the plunge and went ahead; it needed iron nerves.' There were hard decisions along the way, and casualties of the development were the all-glazed balcony, the fireplace for the Fairbairn room, the enclosed grandstand and many of the residential refinements. There were also unforeseen circumstances, such as the requirement for far more piling than planned under the new entrance because the spring under Spring Passage was springier than was first thought. Two local

The clubhouse in 2006

The tank

villains walked in one day and carried away the heavy copper boiler that was about to be installed for the heating system, never to be seen again. A high tide washed away the contractor's hut on the forecourt. When the newsletter declared in September 1971 that 'we now have the best rowing clubhouse in the country', the final cost had reached £71,000, with £14,000 yet to be raised. In January next year the Thirties Club pledged £1,000 as soon as £9,000 was raised from elsewhere. The appeal reached its final hurdle between re-opening of the building in June 1972 and the dedication of the new Fairbairn room by Graham Hill in November.

Crosse, who began rowing at London in 1950 as a student at the Architectural Association and left for Colin Porter's privateer programme at Barn Cottage eight years later, said in 2005 that Coni was the best client he ever had. 'He knew my heart was in the right place, but nothing else was. The result was that we got the building we really wanted.' In the 1971 newsletter, he told the members what he had done and what they must do to get the best out of it. 'Being architect to LRC is more exacting than rowing ten Boston Marathons in succession, or entering all seven events at the Olympics,' he wrote. 'Working at LRC, I have become appalled to see how what ten or fifteen years ago was a simple mess had degenerated into a sporting slum.' He explained that the aim of the exercise was to provide an efficient low-maintenance shell. It was then up to the members to furnish it, clean it, maintain it, improve and finish it, and enjoy it. His development confined rowing to the ground floor, with changing and shower facilities and a re-built boathouse for a hundred shells, with a workshop and the tank. The boathouse floor was sloped to enable flood water to exit; the old wooden racks were replaced by galvanised metal ones; the oar racks were now mobile, making

space for more boat racks; water was laid on to wash the floor, 'which warrants regular painting to keep the dust down'. Meanwhile, the first floor had a new lease of life. 'No other club that I know in the country will have such facilities or so much space. My prediction is that the cash turnover at the bar will soar. Beyond this, the club could do greatly increased business in letting out its clubroom and catering facilities.' The new captain's room above the entrance created space for

The members' room

enhanced kitchens on the first floor. Crosse gave a last piece of advice. 'If you want carpets and polished floors you must look after them yourselves and see to it that an impossible burden is not put on the steward and his wife.'

After the house re-opened, the social programme at this time took some surprising turns. Giles Chichester, son of Sir Francis, the pioneering solo round-the-world yachtsman, arranged a Christmas concert with St James's Piccadilly Music Society, St James's Choir and Miss Susan Drake on harp, where mulled wine was served. A ceilidhe with Hammersmith Folk Club was so successful that it became a regular fixture. A drag ball was organised by Stephen Rimmer. In July 1977 the club staged a ball to mark the Queen's jubilee, and in 1978 regular suppers on Wednesdays were re-introduced after a break of five years.

There was some evidence, too, that Crosse's pleas for respecting the building were heeded. As Coni said, London is now the premier club in the country where you can go to row, and you can be proud to take your friends there for the other activities.[2] There was an appeal for maintenance working parties in 1975, and in 1981 the long room was restored by friends of John Pepys (1930–80), 'recalling his services to LRC and oarsmen of many nations'. Coni announced a 125th anniversary appeal in that year to clear outstanding loans, buy furniture and

Top to bottom:
The Fairbairn room,
the long room,
and the gym

fittings – chosen by Joyce Conwy-Evans – and establish a reserve fund for the maintenance of the building. He estimated that inflation had increased the cost of running the club from £8,600 in 1969–70 to £39,000 a decade later, which had made the club's loan replacement scheme untenable. Without a new appeal to pay off the debts, the free loans could only be paid off by borrowing from the bank at the bank's rate of interest.

Attention had to be given to the roof in 1986, and in 1990 another extension was opened in the form of a shed for sculling boats erected between the boathouse and Barclays (now King's College School, Wimbledon), known as bays six and seven after the 'Sixes and Sevens' club who paid for it. In 1991 London's own thespian, Rodney Bewes, rescued the weathervane in the form of a sculpture of an oarsman which had fallen off the flagpole, and Peter Coni arranged for a new one to be welded on. The original, dating from around 1970, is thought to have been modelled on Chris Harris, but the subject for the replacement, made by George William Hammond, is not known.

Approaching its 135th birthday, the clubhouse is again in need of attention. A spanking new kitchen was installed in 2004 at a cost of £80,000, and the rooms were redecorated and the pictures and honours boards re-hung in 2005 in time for the sesquicentenary of the club. The problem now is not a simple mess degenerating into a sporting slum, but rather changed expectations of lifestyle and the proper accommodation of women, whose presence the club restricted to social invitation for its first 140 years. Carpmael's proud boast in 1971 that 'we now have the best rowing clubhouse in the country' is no longer true since several others, some of them aided by National Lottery grants, have undergone major refits, and in the case of Putney Town, a new building at Kew. In Putney alone, Thames have undertaken a huge

development of rowing facilities, Imperial College have enhanced their house with more boat bays, residential accommodation and a state-of-the-art gymnasium, and Westminster School's boathouse has been rebuilt. In the same period Barclays Bank, National Westminster Bank and Shell's club, Lensbury, have changed hands, and the new owners – King's College School, Dulwich College and Crabtree Boat Club have made changes, some of them extensive. Leander Club now has five-star facilities in Henley, the Royal Albert Dock has the superb London Regatta Centre, and Auriol Kensington at Hammersmith has transformed its facilities.

Alison and Mick Choy's wedding, 2004

So the London Rowing Club celebrates its sesquicentennial year by embarking upon a scheme at a projected cost of £1.4 million. The first two phases will add first-floor changing facilities for women, a large new crew room, a storage area, three or four extra bedrooms and access and toilet facilities for the disabled. The third phase will replace the unsightly boat shed between London and King's College School boathouse by more accommodation and social rooms above boat bays on the ground floor. The fourth phase will redevelop the present changing and shower area into a new gymnasium, ergo room and physiotherapy room, with men's changing and washing facilities above. A separate scheme will add a canopy to the balcony at the front of the club, enabling members to survey Putney reach in the open air on a wet day as they were able to do when the balcony was erected in 1920.

LEAN, MEAN AND KEEN 1971–1990

LEAN, MEAN AND KEEN

1971–1990

I F THE 1960S WAS A DECADE WHEN UNDERCURRENTS challenged poor management in British rowing, the 1970s saw poor performance turned on its head. London Rowing Club was at the epicentre. A snapshot of the 1977 season reveals a totally different picture than a living memory of the time could recall. In that year London's lightweight eight won the world title in Amsterdam, having qualified to wear GB hoops by winning the Vernon Trophy at the Head of the River Race,[1] the Thames Cup at Henley, and a gold medal at the national championships. London's coxless four were handed the Stewards' Cup at Henley on a plate by rowing over as the only entry and, like London's coxed pair, represented Britain at the world championships. The club entered seventeen eights in the Head, raised more than £1,800 for new boats and the Multiple Sclerosis Society by a sponsored row to Eel Pie Island and back, and won the victor ludorum trophies at the national championships and the Jubilee Serpentine Regatta. It headed *Rowing* magazine's table of wins for the season with 471 points, comfortably ahead of Nottingham and Union who scored 173. Mike Williams was captain; Peter Coni became chairman of the Amateur Rowing Association's executive committee and vice-chairman of Henley's management committee shortly after being elected a Steward; Chris Blackwall, London's Wyfold winner of 1969, followed Bob Janousek as national coach; and David Tanner, coach of London's coxless four, was made a junior selector.

The sponsored row was one of several organised in those years to supply sufficient good boats to sustain both the high volume and high level of rowing activity. When Mike Williams took over as captain, there were only two boats less than ten years old because the club had been devoting its limited financial resources to paying off the loans raised to pay for the 1970 redevelopment of the boathouse. A large fleet renewal programme was started, which initially involved borrowing a lot of boats from the Amateur Rowing Association followed by major fund raising to buy the club's own. These included three of the first six

Overleaf: *London Rowing Club, world champions in lightweight eights, Amsterdam, 1977*

Graeme Hall strokes the London lightweights at the world championships on Lake Ossiac at Villach, Austria, 1976

boats from Carbocraft's commercial production line (a four and two pairs), and a number of Karlisch and Empacher eights and fours. The lack of boats caused a lot of sharing and consequent re-rigging between heavy and lightweight outings, particularly of small boats during the winter, with the captain having to exercise the wisdom of Solomon in resolving competing claims of coaches. Boatman Frank Sims used to refer to the place as 'London Wrecking Club' because of the amount of wear and tear that resulted.

The seeds of the London lightweights were planted in 1974 when an invitation event for lightweight coxless fours was offered at the world championships in Lucerne. Britain's crew – Daniel Topolski, Chris Drury, Nick Tee and Graeme Hall – finished seventh there. Under Leander colours, they gained selection after winning the national championships, having lost to Porcellian of the USA in a semifinal of the Wyfold at Henley. Two of the crew, Drury and Topolski, had been around London for years. Drury first wore London's dark blue and white as a cox while at Emanuel School in 1967; Topolski, a former captain of rowing at Westminster School who was now coaching Oxford and using the club as the dark blues' tideway base, first appeared for London in the Wyfold in 1964. With the world championships due to take place on the new course at Holme Pierrepont, Nottingham, in 1975, these men, who were physically slight for rowing, seized the opportunity presented by the new lightweight category.[2] With

Blades commemorating world titles in lightweight eights, 1977 and 1980

Hall, who had stroked Cambridge to two Boat Race victories and Tee who rowed his third Boat Race for Oxford in 1974, they asked Ron Needs to coach them. Needs introduced them to the delights of the Grand Union canal at Brentford, convenient for his day job as administration director of Beecham Pharmaceuticals but, more to the point, a long straight stretch of flat, still water with no other traffic. It was there that Topolski, 'bossy in the

London leading Bedford RC in the final of the Britannia at Henley, 1970 (left to right): cox R Sherman, Daniel Topolski, Nick Cooper, David Sturge and John Dart

bow' by his own admission, learned to steer through narrow bridges. Drury had migrated to Thames Tradesmen in 1971 and spent three seasons with this burgeoning club at Kew. Hall was berthed at Tideway Scullers, where Topolski was also to be seen. In the winter of 1974 Drury was sculling at Leander, where Needs was a member of the coaching team, and it was Drury who recruited the others to have a shot at the lightweight fours. Once they had a world ranking of seventh under their belt, they sought and found a home at London, with the help of Peter Coni who had been assisting with coaching at Tradesmen. The club purchased a suitable boat from Crowland Rowing Club, and the London lightweights were in business.

The four decided to stay together. In 1975 they went to a regatta in Munich where they were eliminated, and earned the 'Tombstone Four' soubriquet from the *Times*. But they came home from Germany elated because, with the permission of coach Needs, they had a twenty-minute outing with Mike Spracklen who was coaching a lightweight eight under the Nautilus flag. 'He made us totally re-think the way we rowed,' Topolski said. They

The LRC and University of London combination beating Leander in the final of the Prince Philip at Henley, 1971

dropped their customary rating by three pips and went back on the Grand Union with Needs. Hall was unwell during the world championships. They led their opening race until going to pieces at the end, running out of puff and steering wildly. The *Guardian*'s headline on its account of the subsequent repêchage was 'The four muster in a bluster'. The crew mastered their opposition and a cross-headwind. Tee moved into the stroke seat for the semifinal, and their moment of truth arrived at the halfway point in the final, when they were in last place. 'The British were still last at 1,200 metres [1,312 yards], and the French, who had fallen to fifth, started to burn for the finish. Tee piled on the pressure and the British boat went with the French right through the field, with the rating up to 44 strokes to the minute when they crossed the line. Topolski's blade hit two buoys on the way but the crew corrected their steering without losing rhythm.'[3] They had cut through West Germany, Netherlands, the United States and then Australia to take the silver medal behind the French in the first-ever world championships for lightweights. The four's performance was, said Mike Spracklen, the ARA's lightweight co-ordinator, 'a breathtaking triumph... a truly great performance.'[4] Spracklen's composite lightweight eight won the bronze medal.

Winning medals made a huge difference to the attitude of lightweight oarsmen in other clubs, and London consolidated its position by funding and providing the equipment for a lightweight eight for the following season. Funding was sparse at the best of times and, for lightweights, almost non-existent, partly because there were no events for them in the Olympic games. A club willing to invest could therefore call the tune, and London required everyone who wanted to row in its eight to join, and to row under the blue and white colours at domestic regattas. As Chris Drury set about drawing together a 'positive galaxy of rowing talent', Peter Coni coaxed some financial support from Nottinghamshire County Council for a training camp at the National Water Sports Centre, but in the event the crew returned from Holme Pierrepont to the tideway because of strong wind which was slowing the boat and dragging down the morale of the crew. Two of the 1975 four were in the eight, Hall at stroke and Drury at six. They won the Metropolitan Regatta, Ratzeburg Regatta on both days, the West German open championships and the national championships of Great Britain. At Henley they lost their heat of the Grand by a third of a length to the eventual winners, Thames Tradesmen, who were two stone per man heavier. This was frustrating because they were as certain as certain could be that they could have won the Thames Cup. At the world championships in Villach, Austria, they appeared to have peaked too early, the gold medal outside their grasp by a half-a-length to the West Germans. Hall's career ended without a gold medal, but the rest were game for more.

At Thames I was a guest, but London was prepared to host us and to back us, which is not always the same thing.
— David Tanner, coach of Ealing High School's coxless four after they moved to London as a unit, 1975

Lightweights take the Thames Cup: beating Leander in the final, 1977, and on the medal podium

After Villach, the lightweight eight became the most desirable boat, and the new season began with a queue of men for the squad, enabling Needs to form a very strong boat. Only Drury, Colin Cusack and Nigel Read from the 1976 crew secured seats. Topolski returned after a season with Tideway Scullers in which he had won the Britannia Cup at Henley with three heavyweights in record time. Steve Simpole from Thames Tradesmen, Chris George and Paul Stuart-Bennett from London University, and Duncan Innes from Wallingford Rowing Club completed the crew, with Ray Penney, a veteran from Thames, in the cox's seat. Chris George summarised their feelings when he said: 'only a gold medal is acceptable.'[5] They went to Henley and waltzed through Hereford, Ghent and Vesta in the Thames Cup. A hard but successful semifinal against the University of London brought them up against Leander in the final, whom they beat in style by almost three lengths. Their time was ten seconds quicker than the supposedly faster Ladies' Plate. This was a poignant moment for Penney, who had been coxing for twenty years with no Henley medal to show for it. It would turn out to be his finest hour. But in Copenhagen, three weeks before the world championships, they lost to the Spanish lightweights by one second. 'I saw the gold medal disappearing down the plughole,' Topolski said. 'We trained like savages

for the world championships.' At the world championships in Amsterdam, the British lightweights had a problem all of their own. Ray Penney, the cox, was overweight. Reducing weight was causing him to lose his mental sharpness, and he knew it. He wanted to stand down, and was relieved when Pat Sweeney, cox of Britain's 1976 Olympic eight and present as a coach, was persuaded, reluctantly, to take his place for the races. Sweeney was on the minimum weight. 'He lifted us the minute he got into the boat,' Topolski said.

The eight, who had weighed in naked, won their heat and qualified directly for the final – and the Spanish did the same thing, only faster. Tensions were sky high, for with no repêchages or semi-finals to contest, the gap between heat and final for both crews seemed endless. There were several distractions of the wrong kind surging around Amsterdam's Bosbaan course, including rumours of illegal coaching via two-way radios (false), rumours of phoney illness to cover up defection of Soviet competitors (false, but it turned out later that an East German defected), and disputes over the fairness of lanes. The press's investigation of currents and wind shadows on the Bosbaan was at odds with the organisers', and questions met with a stonewall.[6] The lanes with the best results were one and two, and fortunately in the pulverising, punishing and stunning final, Spain drew lane one and GB lane two. The British led for 1,640 yards at which point the Spanish mounted a sustained attack which brought them level. A desperate charge for the line brought a photo finish and victory to London and their cox from Tradesmen by seven-hundredths of a second. The margin left the oarsmen relieved more than elated after this prime example of the closeness of lightweight races. Penney was first to welcome the crew ashore. His extra weight would have denied them their triumph, and when he died a few years later, it was clear that his most valued rowing treasure was the

GB winning the light-weight eight world title on the Bosbaan, Amsterdam, 1977.

Ray Penney coxed London's lightweight eight to victory in the Thames Cup in 1977 and then stood down at the world champi-onships because he was overweight.

Portrait by John Stephenson from a photo by Tony Owen

John Vigurs' boat is so good it's almost unsporting.

Henley medal that the champions whom he steered pulled for him.

This achievement was the first gold medal by a British eight for twenty-five years, since the European championships of 1952. Happily, it was not the end of London or Britain's lightweight story. It was the preamble to what Drury regards as the truly great year of 1978. Although the endgame was less dramatic than 1977, the achievements of the fours and eights supported by the club at several levels had, he felt, established a firm base under the lightweight springboard. Around forty appeared at London for lightweight selection. Needs had been nurturing younger men on the way up and found some new stars among the juniors, notably Clive Roberts, Bob Downie and Anthony French. Doug Melvin's son John and the GB single sculler, Peter Zeun, were also newcomers to the group. These five and former Oxford cox Colin Moynihan joined Drury, Simpole and Read in the line-up for the world championships. There was some animosity, Needs says, inevitably when someone who may not be up to scratch sets tension running high. But unquestionably, he had strength in depth. After winning the Head of the River Race, the Thames Cup at Henley and all their races in Europe except Lucerne Regatta where illness interposed, they won the world title in Copenhagen by a length, this time with Simpole in the stroke seat. Read described the excursion to Denmark as the best holiday of his life: 'With constant sunshine, temperatures in the eighties, a marvellous hotel in the woods by the lakes, topless bathing, entertainment from our cox, Colin Moynihan, and a gold medal! It would be difficult to better it.'[7]

Advertisement featuring the carbon fibre boat built by John Vigurs for the lightweight eight, 1977

Ron Needs, coach of lightweights

By the start of the 1979 season, some members of the group were receiving grants from the Sports Aid Foundation, an industry-backed charity that supported athletes with medal potential. Nottinghamshire County Council continued to give support, and London continued to supply equipment. A squad developed to produce an eight and a four. Although once again the available talent was terrific, the early results were not, and there were resentments in some quarters over London's requirement of membership. An eight emerged as the top boat and lost the final of the Thames Cup to a much heavier Leander crew. The Wyfold was won by a lightweight four from Wallingford who knocked out London's lightweights in the semifinal. There were several men who thought that there were four better men in the group than the one eventually selected. When the crews arrived at Bled, the enchanting venue for the world championships in what was then Yugoslavia, gold was no longer engraved upon the London eight. Performances were unsettled, Read was sick and had not recovered properly when he thought he had, and the final position was a disappointing fifth in a blanket finish. But the British light four, the also-rans of the squad, won gold.[8] They were the same London crew that lost to Wallingford at Henley. They were coached by Father Mark Jabale of Belmont Abbey, a recent convert to rowing from rugby.

Rudder commemorating London lightweights' 1977 season

As another Olympic games approached, Ron Needs left London to become a national coach, and Terry O'Neill who had had success with City Orient, a club on the River Lea, replaced him. A cheerful east ender with a sharp sense of humour, he was bent on extending his international experience. O'Neill's persona was different from Needs's quiet backroom voice, but the aim remained the same. Once more, lightweight talent gathered at London to be 'flogged up to Richmond and back' according to one who didn't succeed in getting a seat in the eight. What emerged was a crew of immense physical strength, but no money. The ARA left the lightweights to fight their own corner while it threw everything it had at the Olympic games in Moscow. The oarsmen ran discos and raffles to get to Belgium for their championships. They were unable to afford a foreign training camp, but obtained some financial support from Guinness and organised what turned out to be an excellent camp in Hereford. And in Hazewinkel they won another gold medal, this time by clear water. This was London's third world gold in lightweight eights. The crew was Colin Barratt, Dave Hosking, Bob Downie, Nick Howe, Peter Zeun, Clive Roberts, Nigel Read, Steve Simpole and cox Simon Jefferies.

Terry O'Neill, coach of lightweights

In 1981 the lightweight wheels came off the track at London. The national squad lost some coherence when its members and coach O'Neill moved to the

Hammersmith boathouse of the Amateur Rowing Association. Four London gold medallists from the 1980 crew plus cox Jefferies and Drury, who had been dropped that year, represented Britain in the lightweight eight in the world championships in Munich, where they finished tenth. This marked the end of London's run of success in big lightweight boats, although British lightweight rowing would continue to notch up successes for another ten years. Drury, who was there throughout, thinks that London was ahead of its time. 'There was support from the club throughout,' he said. 'There was commitment. Nobody ever failed to turn up. We had accuracy, good control, good coaching and the ability to change.' The combination of excellent coaching, enthusiasm from the club for its elite squads and the provision of resources was at the base of the achievements. 'All that went out of the window pretty soon after the squad moved. They never put anything in place of the London lightweights scheme which thrived for ten years,' Drury said. The centre of lightweight gravity moved to Nottingham, where Mark Lees became the first professional coach of the Nottinghamshire County Rowing Association, but that is another story.

The rise and rise of the lightweights was not the only story of London during the 1970s. A chance meeting between Mike Baldwin, London's captain, and David Tanner, coach of a very successful junior crew from Ealing High School and Cardinal Vaughan School, resulted in the arrival of a ready-made four who would make a significant mark in heavyweight rowing. In the autumn of 1975 Tanner's crew – John Beattie, Ian McNuff, Robin Roberts and Martin Cross – had put in their last appearance at the junior world championships in Montreal. They had silver medals round their necks, a mighty achievement at a championships where all the golds were shared between East Germany and the Soviet Union except for the coxless pairs, won by West Germany. To Tanner's surprise, the crew's meteoric record as juniors resulted in their desire to continue together to see where they could get to as seniors, and they asked him to coach them. Their base as juniors was at Eel Pie Island in Twickenham, and for two years they had used the Thames gym on their frequent visits to the tideway through the good offices of Dave Gramolt. Naturally, Tanner's first move to find a new home took him to the captain of Thames, to whom he explained that they wished to compete as a four and try for the national senior team. The response was that they were welcome to try out for the first eight for a couple of years, and then see how things go. Which was the wrong answer for the history master from Ealing and his students. On the day of the Pairs Head, they were in limbo, having no home and no money. They were also on the water in pairs, but not taking part in the time trial. London's Baldwin spotted them and asked Tanner who they were and why weren't they racing. The conversation went like this:

'It's not what we're trying to do.'

'What are you trying to do?'

'We're looking for a club to row at.'

Within two days Tanner, who knew nobody at London before this incident, received a phone call saying that the club was interested, and that they could use a Karlisch boat. Which was the right answer for the history master from Ealing and his students.

'We went down and really got quite involved. They had a sponsored row partly to help us, and we managed to run the Karlisch aground during it, so it wasn't the best starting point. But they were just totally helpful to us.' Tanner got to know Baldwin quite well, classifying him as a forward-looking captain who was looking to expand and get some success. He also found Ron Needs with his lightweight group in residence – another high performance thinker. He felt that the club was engaged in thought about international rowing. It was into creating new things and appealing to committed chancers and aspirants rather than buying in successful oarsmen from elsewhere.

Thus London secured an ambitious coach and four new, high calibre members very quickly in Beattie, McNuff, Cross and Derek Bond in place of Roberts, who did not want to continue. 'In that first year, we went and won the Wyfold for them, which was not such a bad thing to do, especially as it could have been Thames's. We were adopted by Farn Carpmael, and older members raised money so we could compete. They were great,' Tanner says.

David Tanner, coach of the Ealing four who joined LRC

For the 1976 season they were a complete club crew, winning all their races at home except for the national championships where they came second to Thames Tradesmen. The only foreign trip they took was to Ratzeburg, Germany. But when it came to training, they were going out twice a day. Only one British crew had trained as hard as the London four in the past, and that was the Thames Tradesmen junior four under Jim Railton, three of whom won silver medals in Bob Janousek's Olympic eight as London were doing their domestic circuit. Tanner's style is to seek the best. He had learned about junior rowing from the national coach Penny Chuter and the Wallingford Schools coach Bruce Grainger, and for seniors he sought out Janousek when the Czech moved from coaching Britain to making Carbocraft boats after the 1976 Olympics. 'He was very helpful with advice,' Tanner said. 'The big step we had made was to go out twice a day training. His eight had not done that. Only the double scullers Baillieu and Hart and ourselves were doing it. We were getting up there.'

Back at the club, Mike Williams succeeded Mike Baldwin as captain. 'I think by that time I had become an extremely demanding coach,' Tanner said. 'I remember Mike Baldwin shortly after Mike Williams took over saying, "I think you'll find that Mike will probably respond better to your requests if you don't shout at him," so I took that on board.' Tanner was challenged by Peter Coni who wrote to him to ask, in the spirit of being helpful, whether his guys should be quite as separate as they are; shouldn't they be joining in a bit more? 'I convinced him we did need to be doing our own thing; that was the way I wanted to drive it because we were doing something a bit new.' He interpreted the enquiry as aimed to help the crew to progress, not as a bleat about club ethos. He saw Coni as very supportive. 'I think the whole attitude of the club was excellent. We weren't standoffish at all. We were a unit, but anybody inside would see us as part of the club, properly a part, and that was important.'

The proof of the crew's stepping up was selection for the national team in 1977, where they finished tenth at the world championships in Amsterdam. They were not the only London men in the heavyweight team, for Henry Clay was with the eight, and Jamie MacLeod and Neil Christie represented their country in a coxed pair, steered by David Webb, as they had done at the Olympics in 1976. Clay was also at the Olympics with David Sturge in a coxless pair.

In 1978 Derek Bond dropped out, and David Townsend, an outstanding London University oarsman and a member of Britain's Olympic coxless four in Montreal, replaced him. At Henley they withdrew from a straight final in the Stewards' because of illness, allowing Trakia of Bulgaria to row over. The world championships were on Lake Karapiro in New Zealand, incurring heavy expenditure on behalf of the club and some very generous support from London's overseas members in Australia and New Zealand, all of whom had been contacted by secretary John Pepys before departure. Coni arranged the loan of a car for four weeks in Sydney to give them freedom of movement at the pre-championships training camp. The backing and the support were worth it, however: Messrs Beattie, McNuff, Townsend and Cross returned home with bronze medals. 'They earned their passage the hard way and maintained a good-humoured yet clenched-fist attitude to competition,' according to the *Almanack*.[9] The favourites were the East Germans who had held the title since 1974, but the Soviet Union put paid to their run. The Soviet oarsmen stole a four-second lead in the first 550 yards and held the front to the line. The British were second at halfway, and the East Germans left their last fling

Derek Bond, Ian McNuff, John Beattie and Martin Cross winning the Wyfold at Henley against Potomac Boat Club, 1976

Bobbie Prentice and Martin Spencer beating J H van Drooge and R Nolet of Nereus in the final of the Double Sculls at Henley, 1976

too late to take gold. This made the London crew unquestionably the best in the west. And it drew interest from the Sports Aid Foundation, so their funds were much healthier in the autumn of that year. Third place was maintained for the next two years, at the world championships in Bled and the Olympic games in Moscow. The season to Bled gave them first places at Manheim, Saltzgitter and Essen. The East Germans commanded the championship final, while the British crew pushed the Czechs hard for the silver medal. Their time of 6 minutes 6.65 seconds was a British best. The hat trick of bronzes was completed in Moscow in the strongest field yet. A hard heat forced Britain into a repêchage which they and the new power in rowing, Romania, were determined to win. The Londoners triumphed and fought a tough final which had East Germany and the Soviet Union battling for the gold and the rest battling for bronze. The Czechs, Romanians and Swiss lost it by half way, and it was 'a tribute to the crew and to their coach, David Tanner, that their mettle was tested in such demanding circumstances and not found wanting'.[10]

London's Christie and MacLeod also featured in the British team in 1979 (coxless) and 1980 (with Webb). Mark Bathurst was in the heavy eight in 1979, and Henry Clay in 1978 and 1980. Colin Moynihan steered the 1980 Olympic eight to a silver medal with his arms grasping the rudder yoke behind him after its strings broke. The four's Olympic bronze marked the end of them as a unit. Townsend retired, and the veteran Olympian Jim Clark of Thames Tradesmen replaced him for 1981, but the combination was not a success. The club newsletter contains a poignant Freudian slip when it described the crew as 'currently undergoing attitude training in South Africa' Moscow turned out to be the last medals won by Beattie and McNuff, and by the time Martin Cross won Olympic gold in Los Angeles in 1984, he had taken his oar to Thames Tradesmen. World and Olympic medals for London members were sparse during the rest of the 1980s, which was partly a reflection of the increasing ability of the governing body of British rowing to fund and organise a composite national squad, and partly the hard fact that there were only a handful of men capable of reaching the gold standard. In 1981 Moynihan again coxed the heavy eight to a silver medal at the world championships in Munich. In 1983 John Melvin won silver in the lightweight single sculls in Duisburg. In 1988 in Milan, Robin Williams and Nick Howe won silver medals in the light four, and next year the all-London four of Williams, Howe, Nick Strange and Stuart Forbes won bronze in Bled. Before we look at the international record of the 1980s, however, let us glimpse what else had been going on at the club since 1970.

The decade began with a doubling of the membership. On 1 March 1970 the new national coach, Bob Janousek, made one of his first visits since taking up his post, and was shown around by the chief club coach, David Kealey. There was a thirty-strong novice and junior squad under Bill Thompson, and a strong veteran squad which took Paris by storm, or at least took Montmartre, if not the Basin de Courcy, where Ted Porcher reported in the newsletter that the eight 'never fought, so was never defeated'. In Amsterdam, it was the storm that took the veterans' regatta, playing havoc with the races but not denying Doug Melvin and Graham Beech single and double sculling success. Ten scullers achieved places in the top forty of the Scullers' Head, among them the Irishman Sean Drea in seventeenth place, who had just arrived at London for coaching from Doug Melvin. London crews reached the final of the Thames and Stewards' cups at Henley and won the Britannia event for coxed fours. The Thames Cup eight and the sculler Drea represented England and Ireland respectively in the Home Countries International match. The club bought two pairs, a second-hand eight and a new tub pair, the latter from the Bath Boating Company. Andrew Paterson organised rowing for 'irregulars' – members who could only show up occasionally. There were sessions on the tank as well as in boats, land training and discussion at the bar.

In 1971 the Boustead Cup was revived, with London winning all four races. The club was represented at Ghent's centenary regatta. Scullers were active, Topolski winning junior-senior at Vesta Dashes and senior at the Metropolitan. Nick Cooper, Rob van Mesdag and Doug Melvin took the team prize in Norfolk; Cooper and Topolski were first and second at Eton, David Sturge and Cooper were first and second at Weybridge; Sturge won at Marlow, and at Henley he beat two Danes in the Diamond Sculls before going out to the eventual winner, Alberto Demiddi of Argentina. Chris Blackwall and Peter Harrison

London's lightweight eight in the Head of the River Race, 1980

were half of a composite coxed four that won the Prince Philip. Topolski, Sturge and Cooper finished third overall in the Fours Head of the River Race, with the veteran international sculler Nick Birkmyre in the stroke seat.[11] In 1972, fourteen eights were entered for the Head, one manned by Trinity College Dublin. Ghent was now a regular fixture, and the National Championships of Great Britain was a new event on the new six-lane international course in Nottingham. London's crews were absent save for one sculler, but the championships soon became a prime destination. The irregulars had become so popular that a place in a good boat was hard to find. Among those reporting to Paterson were former Olympic and trial cap oarsmen, and the national team's doctor. There was a new light-weight tub pair which could be carried to the water by three people and convert-ed to a double scull. A new programme was developed for those unable to train with the senior squad during the week but who could commit to regular outings at weekends. Veterans had clocked up thirty-five wins by November. In 1973 the final of the Diamonds was an all-London affair, except that the loser, Sturge, was sculling for Lady Margaret Boat Club of Cambridge, and the winner, Drea, for Neptune Rowing Club of Dublin.

In 1974 the veteran C eight won in Ghent with the assistance of 'our Turin members', an example of connections made from time to time with friends across the world. The irregulars now filled six eights for weekend outings. In 1975 the rules and regulations of the club were revised thoroughly under the guidance of Archie Nisbet. Paul Johnson revived London's rugby football club, and the team – decked out in shirts lent by London Welsh – lost to Mayfair Nomads by six points to twenty-six, and to Rosslyn Park by four points to eight-een. Chris Drury won Doggett's Coat and Badge in a dramatic race through the bridges from London Bridge to Chelsea, beating Poplar's John Dwan by less than a length. He and Topolski won the double sculls in the Pairs Head. Crews from the Swiss club Thalwil and the Dutch club Oceana were entertained as they passed by on their tour of the Thames. On 7 December a sponsored row to HMS *Belfast* and back raised £1,700 towards a new eight. Nine eights, eight fours, four pairs, five doubles, one quad, and fifty singles took part.

In July 1976 a London crew made up of Giles Chichester, Rob van Mesdag, David Addison, Simon Rippon and cox Graham Butler finished fifth in the Vogalonga, a race along the Grand Canal and round the lagoon in aid of the Venice in Peril Fund. The club was represented at the centenary of Mannheimer Ruderverein. This chapter started with 1977, the year of the first of London's three world titles in lightweight eights. In 1978 the *International Herald Tribune* was sponsoring the club, and Coni was elected chairman of Henley's manage-ment committee. The club's tally of 113 wins – including thirty-one in which a member of the Melvin family took part – spanned events on the Amstel, in

Amsterdam, Lea Spring, Mannheim, Poplar, Worcester, Monmouth, Hereford, Saltzgitter, Peterborough and Ratzeburg. A narrow victory was achieved by four men at Tooting lido in a swimming match against Putney Town, Thames and National Westminster Bank rowing clubs. The first four finishers in the Pairs Head were London's. In 1979 two London crews sank in the Head, in common with thirteen from other clubs, in conditions that blew into a rage at Putney when it was a spring-like calm four miles away at the start. Another sponsored row to Eel Pie Island raised about £3,000 that helped pay for a Karlisch eight purchased from Orange Coast College at Henley, and a new Land Rover, the previous one being written off. Mark Bathurst and Neil Christie won the Grand at Henley and the national title in the national eight. But while the lightweight squad won the eights and fours at the national championships, some of the club's own events were in trouble. The Green Fours and the club single sculls were deferred until the Christmas regatta because they were not receiving enough entries. The Curry Cup, the annual race between Calcutta, Singapore and Hong Kong, was held as it had been since the mid-1960s, and a party travelled to Singapore for the centenary of the Republic of Singapore Yacht Club.[12] London claimed members or associates in thirty-one countries, and was awash with Czechs when the FISA Masters Regatta was held in Nottingham. The club veteran D eight won a gold medal there. Keith Ticehurst followed Mike Williams as captain and was in office for four years.

In 1980 London had five eights in the top twenty-five of the Head of the River Race, counting composites in which they were represented. London III was Trinity College Dublin, and London VII was the Spanish national squad, coxed by 'Raymondo' Penney, who were given the slot as a thank-you for hospitality at Banyoles. The Amateur Rowing Association enacted new status categories.[13] A vigorous darts team, whose regulars were Keith Ticehurst, Mike Williams, Laurie Shindler, Ray Penney, Eddie Halpin, Tony Owen and Mrs Lillian Eagle, played a series of matches with mixed results. Sam Mainds organised a 102-mile row from Oxford to the clubhouse for a group of irregulars, taken in three stages with breaks at Pangbourne and Maidenhead.

In April 1981 London Rowing Club conducted a groundbreaking experiment by sending its coxless four to Johannesburg for two-and-a-half weeks' training at altitude.[14] Coach David Tanner, with his eye on the 1984 Olympics, observed that the Mexico Olympics of 1968 had been disastrous when crews were sent unprepared to compete at altitude, and while the British altitude camp before the 1972 games had indifferent results, some east Europeans were clearly gaining benefit from such training. He considered that most athletes would respond well to two altitude camps before competition, one in April and the second to end between ten and eighteen days before the event for which they were to peak. South Africa offered good water at a height of between 5,750 and 7,200 feet and an amenable temperature for the time of year. The complication was that both the International Olympic Committee and the Commonwealth banned sporting contact with South Africa because of the policy of apartheid.[15] Because the national squad was partly funded by the Sports Council, any such expedition must be entirely unconnected. Tanner sought advice from John Rodda, the *Guardian*'s athletics correspondent and expert on sports politics, who advised that any such visit should be private, with no official contact. Unsurprisingly, Peter Coni paved the way in his capacity as chairman of the International Rowing Committee by sounding out the Sports Council and informing the ARA of what was afoot. Both agreed that if there was no financial help, GB branding, or competition, there would be no objection. Coni and Tanner took pains to inform the press of the nature of the altitude training. The experiment was inconclusive because one athlete did not respond as the others did.

Neil Christie and Jamie Macleod, finalists in the Silver Goblets at Henley, 1981

John Melvin, silver medallist in lightweight single sculls, Duisburg, 1983

The 125th anniversary of the club was celebrated in 1981 by a dinner at the Mansion House and a win at Henley when the London-Thames Tradesmen coxless four won the Stewards', Christie and MacLeod in the Goblets and the eight in the Thames Cup were finalists, and the Wyfold and Britannia fours reached semifinals. The club won the victor ludorum at the national championships, and set a record of ten minutes for jumping the start in the Vogalonga in Venice.

In 1981 also, Keith Mason's marriage broke up and Robin Williams was searching for a place to continue rowing after he graduated from London University. They were to help shape London Rowing Club's progress from the 1980s towards the twenty-first century, the first as a captain, the second as a competitor, and both as coaches. Mason had grown up in Fulham and spent three weeks at Vesta when he was aged eighteen, but forsook rowing for family life and a career at Hoare and Co, the merchant bank in Fleet Street. When he moved back to west London aged thirty-eight, he was looking for a way to rebuild his life, and was introduced to London's irregulars under their coach, Andrew Paterson. Mason took to rowing like a duck to water, and became the fittest man at the club in his age bracket. He moved into the club and became captain in 1986. He introduced discipline and structure, sought out coaches and organised gym sessions and a senior 3 squad, and attracted lapsed members back to the club. Drury was one returnee who put together a good eight

for the Head, in which it finished second, and carried on to Henley. It lost the semifinal of the Thames Cup to the eventual winners, Ridley College of Canada.

The 1982 season had a bad start on 12 February, when two London lightweight crews collided in the dark near Chiswick Eyot. An eight which was completing a turn hit a four. Its bow ball severed, and the bows of the boat entered Simon Barker, 3-man in the four, at the back of his left hip and emerged below his rib cage. Miraculously, none of Barker's vital organs were in the way, but he spent five weeks in intensive care before his next outing, which was in the Pairs Head nine months later. The incident also caused the Amateur Rowing Association to reprimand the club and tighten up its night rowing rules.

During this time London continued to have representatives in the national squad. Clive Roberts and cox Simon Jefferies won the 1982 Head with the ARA crew, and there were two lightweight eights in the top ten – twenty-two of the forty-two members of the lightweight squad were from London, and four of the squad coaches.[16] London III, who finished twenty-fifth in the Head, had hoped to employ the services of Oxford's Sue Brown as cox, but that idea was vetoed because the club rules could not be altered. They then tried for Cambridge's Ian 'Gonzo' Bernstein, who was a member, but that did not find favour with CUBC. Brown was eventually smuggled on board.

At Henley in 1982, Beattie and Roberts won the Grand in the national composite, and with Moynihan coxing, finished sixth in the world championships in Lucerne. John Melvin was Britain's lightweight sculler. The GB light four and eight were all Londoners, with the eight finishing sixth and stroked by Robin Williams, with Drury behind him in the seven seat. The Pairs Head was won by John and Simon Melvin and the Fours Head coxless division by McNuff and Beattie of London, with Richard Stanhope and Andy Holmes.

In 1983 London combined with the University of London to win the Grand,[7] and the club eight reached the semifinal of the Thames Cup. Williams's lightweight four lost the final of the Wyfold to a heavy Lea crew. In the national championships, London won the victor ludorum for the third consecutive year, and John Melvin won the silver medal for lightweight sculls at the world championships in Duisburg. John Beattie, Simon Melvin and Steve Simpole also represented their country. Sam Mainds's irregulars, having completed an Oxford to Cookham voyage in 1982, went to Dunkirk where they 'maintained a hundred per cent record,' though at what is not clear from the newsletter.

London's name was engraved on the Grand for the third consecutive time in 1984, with Roberts and Moynihan labelled as members of the Olympic eight that was coached by Graeme Hall in Los Angeles. Beattie was also in the Olympic team, but the only significant result was the coxed four's gold medal. That crew included Martin Cross who was now rowing for Thames Tradesmen, plus Leander's Andy Holmes, University of London's Richard Budgett and Marlow's Steve Redgrave – the first of Redgrave's five Olympic golds. Adrian Ellison of London University was the cox. The lightweight championships were in Montreal, where the team was hit by influenza. Williams stroked Britain's eight on bow side, and it finished sixth.

By now there were several clubs supplying men to the lightweight squad, and true composites were being formed. Ron Needs was back as coach in charge of the London area squad, with Mark Lees his counterpart in Nottingham, and Brian Armstrong, an influential coach from Wallingford, newly appointed as national coordinator for the ARA. But the ARA was still forced to lean heavily on its member clubs to support the programme, and London continued to play a prominent role, in sharp rivalry with Nottinghamshire County Rowing Association which was founded by the former London lightweight Ian Wilson and first appeared at Henley in 1983. One of the ingredients London supplied was fun, both on and off the water. The contrast between the two, according to Williams, was that while London continued to be a club with activities on many levels, NCRA were much more clued up over what was required to achieve gold medals. 'On the tideway everything is a race,' he says. 'We thrashed ourselves all the time.' County had good equipment, still water at Holme Pierrepont, and a professional coach who set performance standards for training through the year, which rowers had to reach to stay in the scheme. Williams took 1985 off and tried for the single scull in 1986, without success. He also rowed in a double scull with Steve Chilmaid, but they were beaten by County's Carl Smith and Alan Whitwell who eventually won the world title on their home course. London's Nick Howe, Lynton Richmond, Simon and John Melvin and Charles Nelson were in the fifth-placed lightweight eight, plus County's Peter Haining who began his rowing on Loch Lomond and his international aspirations at London where he occupied the room next to Keith Mason.[18] The best that London's small entry at Henley in 1987 could achieve was the quarterfinals of the Thames Cup. Williams pursued his single sculling career in the Diamonds, but lost his first race and did not get into the national team. At the world championships in Copenhagen there were four Londoners – Bill Downing, Marcus Williams, Nelson and Howe – in the British lightweight eight.

Robin Williams then embarked on the best three years of his rowing life. He left his employment at the *Financial Times* to set up his own advertising business, which he could manage alongside his rowing activities. He and London's Nick Howe secured seats in Britain's light four and won the 1988 world silver medal in Milan. Next year an all-London crew – Nick Strange, Howe, Williams and Stuart Forbes – took the bronze medal in Bled, and the same line-up won the Wyfold in 1990 rowing as London A. The Wyfold was a tremendous achievement; four of the five selected crews, including London's B crew, were from the national lightweight squad.[19] Both London crews reached semifinals, A beating Thames Tradesmen, Thames and Bedford, and B beating Worcester, Club Laval (Canada) and Palm Beach (USA). The race against Laval was the seventy-fourth Henley race for Chris Drury, making him the oarsman with the largest number of races at the regatta.[†] In the semis B came to the end of their run against Notts County, also selected and quarterfinal victors against another selected lightweight crew, Lea. London A met the heavyweight selected four from Nottingham and Union in their semifinal, and in a well-paced race gradually built a lead of two lengths by halfway, and held it to earn their place in the final. The final was a fine race in difficult conditions. County lead by a canvas at the Barrier and London by the same margin at Fawley, where they set a rate of 37.5 strokes to the minute for the rest of the course and came home a length and a third in front. This was a particularly sweet medal for Nick Howe. It was his fourteenth appearance at Henley since he represented his school, Hampton, in 1975, when he lost the final of the Visitors'. Three years later he won the Wyfold with Molesey Boat Club, and between then and 1990 took part in five semi-finals and six finals without success.[20] He and Williams finished their partnership of four years in Tasmania later in the autumn, where they were once more in the light four which finished fifth at the world championships, deep in the forest wilderness of Lake Barrington.

In 1988 Richard 'Gonzo' Philips had taken over as captain from Keith Mason, and the benefits of Mason's business-like organisation were lining London up for another burst of success. The lightweight pair of Steve Chilmaid and Andy Butt lost the final of the Goblets to the American Olympians Ted Swinford and

---

† LRC 'B': Andy Butt, Lynton Richmond, Simon Melvin, Chris Drury. Drury, who was also rowing in Upper Thames RC's Stewards' four, was called up by LRC as reserve after two rounds of the Wyfold. This forced UTRC to withdraw, amid acrimony, because Henley rules forbid an individual to compete in more than one four-oared event. London's Daniel Topolski held the Henley appearances record previously.

John Riley. A pure club crew coached by Marcus Williams reached the semifinals of the Thames Cup, where Thames Rowing Club beat them. Simon Jefferies coxed the British eight at the Olympic games in Seoul, and Andrew Ostling and Sean Collins were in Britain's under-23 team. The novice squad notched up six wins at senior 3 and senior 2 levels. Two veterans, Simon Barker and Robert Rakison, each won ten times during the season, and club crews of veterans won four events at the FISA Masters Regatta. Peter Coni was elected president after Farn Carpmael died. For the 1989 season former captain Mason was coaching a novice squad that had more recruits to add to the twenty who started in 1988. The club entered twelve crews for Henley's sesquicentenary birthday regatta, and revived the twelve-oar for the occasion.[21] Of the twelve crews, four failed to qualify, one withdrew with sickness, one scratched because an oarsman was called to the national squad after close of entries, and the Wyfold four was disqualified over its status. The first eight beat Thames in the Ladies' Plate before losing to the University of Pennsylvania.[22] The second eight lost to Lea in the Thames cup; the coxed four in the Britannia beat Aberdeen Boat Club and lost to Isis; Howe and Robin Williams lost to the national squad heavyweights in the Goblets; Steve Chilmaid and Sean Collins lasted one round in the Double Sculls.

Theft of much of the club's best silverware blighted 1990, but on the water the early season was lively. The national lightweight squad was based at the club again, and nine trained eights entered the Head, seven of whom rowed in the Veterans' Head next morning – including the lightweight eight who had attended Robin Williams's stag night between the two. Several upriver clubs were accommodated when floods curtailed activity on their home waters. The Scullers' Head took place in difficult conditions in which only thirty-three completed the course, including all of London's entries. Sean Collins won Doggett's Coat and Badge, and Rorie Henderson ended Steve Redgrave's five-year reign in the Wingfield Sculls.[23]

Robin Williams intended to stop pulling for London and Britain when he crossed the line at Lake Barrington, Tasmania. But in 1991 he became London's first professional coach, and was to lead the club through the glorious nineties.

Leander and LRC lead the University of Washington in the final of the Grand at Henley, 1984. The cox is Colin Moynihan

14

MOVERS, SHAKERS AND CONI

The London Rowing Club's capacity to attract movers and shakers both inside and outside the sport has continued since the second world war, and one who stands out among a galaxy of candidates is Peter Richard Carstairs Coni, OBE, QC. He joined the club on graduation from Cambridge in 1959 and set about setting records: 'The only man who rowed seven consecutive times for the same club [in the Grand] and never getting through a single heat,' he told Frank Keating in the *Guardian*. He fell in love with Henley on his first visit: 'I remember like yesterday morning the smells and sensibilities and the early sunlight on the water, the first time I ever set eyes on Henley. Midsummer 1957, and my St Catharine's Cambridge crew being beaten by Eton in the first round of the Ladies' Plate.'[1] Coni's love affair with London took him from the captaincy to the presidency; his love affair with Henley took him to the chairmanship of the committee of management; his love affair with rowing made him chairman of the Amateur Rowing Association and treasurer of the international rowing federation (FISA); his love of and skill at administration led him to seats on the British Olympic Association, the Central Council for Physical Recreation and the Thames Water Authority. In 1986 he combined all of these faculties with his knowledge, his lightning intelligence and his sense of humour to deliver the biggest and best world championships in Nottingham since international championships began in 1893.[2]

Peter Coni, OBE

Coni was a multi-tasker with a fast analytical mind. It is said that he kept a law book on the foot-stretcher of his boat on the Cam to fill in the recovery time. He could certainly sit through complicated meetings while reading a brief or doing a crossword and then come up with a precise solution to arguments that raged around him. His favourite footwear was trainers, often combined with full Henley or London regalia. He smoked Balkan Sobranies in a tortoiseshell holder; he drank gallons of tea from a particular cup at his house in Victoria, which served as lodgings for several London members and a drop-in centre for rowers with projects or problems; he got around in an exceptionally battered Mini but also possessed his late aunt's 1938 Bentley and a Ferrari which he reluctantly sold near the end of his life on the grounds that 'alas, in my present state of health I'm just not fit to drive it, even though I keep telling them that at 159 mph there will always be a better chance of me missing the oncoming traffic'.

Coni's rowing career at London was distinguished by his lack of success at Henley, but was not totally devoid of achievements elsewhere. He won events at the Chiswick, Kingston, Thames Ditton, Maidenhead, Hereford and the Metropolitan regattas. As an office holder, however, he made an enormous contribution towards ensuring that his club thrived in changing times from the 1960s to the 1990s – changes often influenced by himself.[3] He was vice-captain from 1961 to 1965 except for 1963 when he was captain, and he ran with the reformers inside and outside the club. He was house steward in 1961 and 1962, and treasurer from 1967 to 1977, seeing London through financial pitfalls during the period of renovation.[4] He was vice-president from 1978 and president from 1988 until

Chairman of Henley Royal Regatta

his death in 1993. Whatever the office, his clarity of thought made for lively committee meetings, as the following account shows. 'Avoiding clashes with his many other committees and Coronation Street, he would arrive at high speed along the embankment; usually in a Mini... though sometimes, to the alarm of both rowers and wildlife, in his Ferrari. Sweeping into the club with the appropriate drawer from his filing cabinet for that meeting, he would collect a drink in his 1861 LRC tankard whilst at the same time demanding to know why the rest of the committee was not seated and ready to start. Removing his LRC blazer in the members' room to reveal the latest outrageous t-shirt, Peter would open the *Times* at the almost-completed crossword together with assorted other papers (legal or rowing) on which he proposed to work during the meeting. Whilst completing the crossword intermittently, the meeting could rely on Peter not only to sum up clearly a lengthy debate but also to offer a "wholly sensible" suggestion to close the discussion.'[5]

Coni spent twenty-nine years representing London on the Amateur Rowing Association council. When elected, he was the only member under forty, and the only member still rowing. But he was soon joined by others who were intent on wholesale reform of the selection board and the council itself. He joined the executive in 1968 and was chairman from 1970 to 1977. When he retired in 1991, he recalled his first, somewhat embarrassing, meeting: 'Two weeks earlier the ARA had been sent a letter which was virtually a vote of no confidence signed by myself as captain of London, and by the captains of Leander, Thames, Kingston, Molesey, National Provincial Bank and the University of London – effectively all the clubs which mattered on the current rowing scene.' Their demands included a full-time coach, an independent selection board and a regular newsletter.[6] 'It speaks highly for that body of elder statesmen that, far from closing their ranks and telling us to mind our own business, within two years all those demands had been put into effect.' They did not stop there. During the next five years the average age of the council took a significant plunge as young activists presented themselves for election.[7]

Coni's abilities were soon spotted by Henley Royal Regatta. He was made a steward in 1974 and progressed rapidly to the chair of the management committee in 1977, where for fifteen years he presided over a fist of change to fit out the regatta for the approaching century. London had its own man at the head of the regatta where its founders aimed to achieve glory. When the chair passed to Mike Sweeney in 1992, a new headquarters had been built, new umpires' launches cruised the course, Temple island had been secured for the stewards and its pavilion restored, a new charitable trust was pouring money into rowing at the grassroots, and, above all in Coni's gratification, women were competing at the regatta.[8]

'It has been a most enjoyable as well as demanding task,' he said when he relinquished the chair. 'I can't think of anything in my life that I could have to look back on which I would enjoy more than those fifteen years running this regatta.' Henley had experimented with events for women early in the 1980s, but it was the inclusion of world cup events for male and female scullers in 1993 that heralded a permanent presence of women on the water at Henley. Coni always recognised that international cooperation and participation were key to Henley's and Britain's rowing prosperity. He negotiated recognition of his traditional regatta by FISA, became FISA's treasurer from 1990 to 1993, and he encouraged Britons to help shape world affairs, so that during the 1990s the number of British office holders and commissioners serving FISA reached double figures. One of his early acts on becoming chairman was to propose Thomas Keller, the president of FISA, for election as a steward.

One among many of Coni's skills – one which goes some way to explaining his success – was to find round pegs for round holes. He had a knack of seeing hidden talents in others and persuasively releasing them. An example is the way in which he recruited the author to act as press chief for the 1986 world championships. He telephoned at midnight and put the question out of the blue. The conversation, interspersed with some persuasive suggestions as to backup and how little time such a task will take up, went:

'Thank you for thinking of me, Peter, but regrettably the answer is no.'

'Well, will you think about it?'

'Yes Peter, I've thought about it, and the answer's no.'

'Well, will you sleep on it?'

'All right, Peter, I'll sleep on it.'

Next morning's post brought a bulletin containing the announcement of my appointment. The experience was one of the best things that ever happened to me. I'm pretty sure, too, that this wasn't the only adventure of mine which Peter was behind, nor that I was the only victim of such tactics.

Coni was also a brilliant lawyer. Called to the bar in 1960, the young barrister would arrive at his chambers in Gray's Inn in traditional pin stripes, slamming the door of his battered Mini, cigarette holder with Sobranie clenched between teeth, a pile of books and briefs under his arm, leading with his eyebrows like a walking Spy cartoon.[9] When he became a Queen's Counsel in 1980 solicitors with crime and matrimonial cases were queueing for his services. He was a deputy judge in the family division and a bencher of the Inner Temple. But his devotion to rowing deprived the legal world of an outstanding judge while dealing a great favour to rowing and sport in general – ably abetted by his chief clerk, London's Chris Drury, who kept his summer case load quiet. Coni chaired the committee of enquiry into drug abuse in British sport in 1988, concluding that one in ten of those preparing for the Seoul Olympics may be guilty. He had already played a role in keeping rowing clean by advocating both FISA's and the ARA's introduction of random dope testing from 1981.

His reports and recommendations on any subject are models of sense and clarity, dubbed 'Conigrams' and covering such problems as the navigation rules for the tideway, hands-in-the-till investigations at the club, or selection disputes at the ARA. He was an active participant on the committees of the Metropolitan Regatta, the Head of the River Race and the River & Rowing Museum, to name but a few. He also caught a member of Henley's stewards' enclosure selling tickets on the

Coni by Ticehurst,
Regatta, *July 1988*

Sir Richard Westmacott's statue of Achilles, paid for by subscriptions from the ladies of England as a memorial to the Duke of Wellington, was set up at Hyde Park Corner in 1822, complete with fig leaf to protect his nudity. In the 1960s his fig leaf was severed by members of LRC. The original was restored at the expense of the chief perpetrator in 1992.

Right: *The fig leaf*

black market by answering advertisements while subscribing to the *Tatler* in the guise of his alter ego, Samantha Carstairs.

Peter Coni also enjoyed eclectic enthusiasms which ranged from theatre ('a bravely appalling actor with the Cambridge University Theatre Group, a band of mostly gay senior members and amateur dramatic club rejects,' according to a contemporary); philately (complete collections of the stamps of Gambia and Bosnia-Herzegovina), art (particularly David Hockney), Mensa (in whose directory he described himself as 'in theory a keen radical, in practice a lazy pragmatist') and Coronation Street (during which you would get a sharp earful if you phoned him). One of his best escapades was carried out in the cause of finding a suitable door knocker for London Rowing Club's new entrance in 1970, as he later revealed in the course of a debate in the *Guardian*.[10] This addressed the vexed question of whether there is any truth in the suggestion that sculptures of male nudes in the British Museum had their sexual appendages diligently removed by the Victorians, and it drew this contribution:

'Mr G Jerman is not entirely correct about the demise of the original fig leaf on the Achilles statue at Hyde Park Corner. I can assure your readers that it was not apt to come loose, nor did it fall off in the frost. It required a great deal of hard work with a hacksaw; the blades of which snapped frequently, to get the fig leaf away. It was secured by three very solid brass bolts, and it was necessary to get a park chair in order to climb up onto the plinth of the statue and then to put a second chair between the feet of Achilles in order to reach up between his legs to get at the fig leaf. As I remember, it took us about six hours of sawing on different nights to get through the three bolts. We were fortified by pints of beer from The Nag's Head in Kinnerston Street.[11]

'We had in mind attaching the fig leaf to the door of London Rowing Club at Putney as a spectacular door knob, but it was so heavy it proved unsuitable. Last year I spoke to the minister of works in charge of the statues in Hyde Park and asked whether it would be acceptable if I were to return the fig leaf and pay for its reinstatement or whether she would take a serious view that we had been defacing a work of art. Happily, she thought the whole affair very amusing and I paid a substantial sum for its reinstatement. So, Achilles is now again wearing his original "underwear" – a much more impressive fig leaf than his temporary one in the 1960s.' – Peter R C Coni, OBE, QC, London SW1.

Peter Coni made things happen. In the words of his former clerk, 'Peter stepped into something [Henley] that needed life breathing into it. He got very lucky.' He put his money on lightweights at London, on women at Henley. He brought talents and skills of others together in the world arena, and he realised opportunities for generations of rowers. He summarised his love of rowing like this: 'The satisfaction, the mental and physical thrill, when a boat begins to go really fast because the crew is moving it properly is indescribable; but I am sure it beats the satisfaction of serving an ace in tennis, or getting the timing exactly right when driving off on a golf course, or of co-ordinating perfectly the run-up and take-off on a pole vault,

because rowing combines those technical skills and perfect timing with total physical commitment and exhaustion. And when you get it right, it is a satisfaction beyond any that I know.'[12]

Jenny Owen, first woman to win for London

In view of Peter Coni's fulfilled wish to have women competing at Henley, he would have surely encouraged and welcomed the opening of his club's doors to women. London had a long life without them. Giles Chichester made the first recorded claim at his wedding in 1977, when he said that this was the first marriage between two members. Certainly the rules for non-rowing member-ship allowed ladies and gentlemen over the age of eighteen to join. Anne Carpmael became a member when she was elected vice-president in 1999, an election accompanied by cheering and voting with both hands at the annual general meeting. This was in recognition of more than being married to two presidents – Jock Wise and Farn Carpmael – in succession. It was for being a marvellous hostess at her home by the river in Goring, where Henley crews were invited on the Sunday before the regatta. It is a moot point whether the hospitality enhanced or hindered their performance chances at the regatta. 'The garden party was eagerly looked forward to by the crews. Part of the joy of winning your seat in one of the crews was that you had won your invitation to Withy Mead,' said the club's newletter.

Female coxes slipped under the net soon after the recruitment of small males became difficult, although this had not happened in 1982 when the Oxford cox Sue Brown was lined up to help one crew in the Head out of a hole. The committee was dead against her inclusion, so she was smuggled aboard after the crew had boated, and she disappeared before it de-boated. This was not an isolated case. The club turned a blind eye to female coxes in events not governed by the international federation's rules. They were admitted as non-rowing members, barred from using the facilities or equipment (other than sitting in a boat, presumably) but were not required to pay full rates.

In 1997 the proposal to admit women as full rowing members came up at the AGM and was passed, but nobody asked to join for another five years. This may have been because of the ungracious but understandable wording that accompanied the new rule, to the effect that the men's facilities should not be reduced as a result of allowing women in. Or it may have been the lack of facilities for women, which was a real problem, and one of the reasons for considering buying the boathouse next door. In March 2002, however, Jenny Owen applied, and was approved as a member on 13 May. She came via Surrey University, Northwich Rowing Club, Tideway Scullers, Thames Rowing Club and former-London oarsman Peter Haining's sculling group. When at Thames, she enjoyed a lot of social life at London, which was seen from along the river as a successful club. In September 2001 Smith married Mike Owen, a London resident. Soon after her membership came through, she won the senior 3 single sculls at the Metropolitan Regatta. Jenny Owen is thus the first woman and the first winner – unless, that is, you count Nicola Tee, who won medals with London from 1975 when she was Mr Nicholas Tee. As a loner who wanted to scull in a single, Owen was made to feel important when she took the London colours. She was impressed by the unobtrusive attention which she received from Paul Reedy and the others on the coaching team.[13] 'The coaching meant something. They could explain things,' she said. London also suited her because she was not patronised, and there were no politics. She puts this down to the rowers being a single, big squad instead of in separate squads she encountered at Thames. She says that if you have good relations with the people round you, you enjoy being there. 'Women bitch, men don't.' Reedy's take on women at the club is that there are two issues: 'They should strive to do a good job and be successful, and not be detrimental to what we're already doing.' He's considering an eight for the Remenham Cup at Henley Royal in London's sesquicentennial year.

Meanwhile, no account of women at the club would be complete without mention of Mrs Lillian Eagle. She first wielded mops and brushes in April 1959 when she arrived at the club from Felixstowe, and she kept the premises in proper order, not to mention the members, until 1995. She also served in the bar and at table, and was often to be found clearing up after functions in the small hours before cycling home, 'suitably attired in reflective yellow, criss-crossing Wandsworth like a glittering angel'. When she first moved to the area, Mrs Eagle joined Hurlingham Yacht Club and raced dinghies. She joined Alpha women's rowing club in 1977 which later merged with Mortlake Anglian, and won her novice and novice sculls in 1978. She went on to become a veteran medal winner and travelled to many continental regattas to take part and to support London crews. Her bicycle bell on the Putney towpath was another manifestation of her enthusiasm for the club. She went afloat in her sculling boat three times a week. She also fed many feathered friends outside the club, nursing injured birds back to health. In 1995 she was a guest at the annual dinner, and in 1996 a dinner was held in the long room to honour her, attended by seventy members and twenty riverside friends – boatmen and their wives from other clubs. A boat was named *Lillian* in her honour. She continued to work shorter hours, but was diagnosed with leukaemia and spent increasingly long spells in hospital. On the last day of 1997 she learned that she had been awarded an MBE for services to the club, and the Central Chancery of Orders of Knighthood answered her son Eric's appeal for the award to be presented in hospital. On 3 February 1998 Field Marshal Lord Bramall, lord lieutenant of London, presented the medal, and Lillian died, aged sixty-eight, two days later.

A remarkable number of London members have put back what they took out

A letter from Lillian Eagle

of the club as competitors, enriching the lives of future members. Here we will meet some of those who by their actions at the oar, in the committee room, and often in remarkable careers outside rowing, have given the club life and character. We met Archie Nisbet in the 1920s when he arrived at London from Pembroke College, Cambridge and, after a brief sojourn at Thames, brought the coach who had inspired his college and the upstream rivals with him. There are several versions of how Steve Fairbairn arrived at London in 1926, but whatever the details, it was Nisbet who held him to a promise. The version printed in the club's death notice says that when Nisbet heard that Steve had been replaced as captain of Thames, he cut short an outing and took a taxi to Steve's hotel, the Hyde Park, and reminded him that he had accepted an invitation to come to London should he ever be available.[14] Nisbet became captain in 1924 at a low ebb in the club's fortunes and breathed energy and enthusiasm into it, following his convictions and introducing new methods. He resigned the captaincy after the 1927 season and became house steward, while winning a silver Olympic medal in Amsterdam in 1928. After that he coached continuously (in tandem with Pembroke College until 1935), together with his brother-in-law Charles Rew and Jock Wise, both disciples of Steve. The Fairbairn years produced thirteen wins at Henley in the decade after the coach's arrival, success built on Nisbet's foundation. Nisbet continued coaching after the Second World War, retired from the London seat on the Amateur Rowing Association council in 1975 and became chairman of the Head of the River Race two years later. Goodness knows when he found the time to practise as a solicitor. He was a gentle, kind man, who expired in 1986.

Rew joined Thames in 1919 and followed his master, Fairbairn, to London

Left to right: *Farn Carpmael, Jock Wise and Archie Nisbet*

after honourably seeing out his 'contract' with Thames for the 1926 season. He suffered for his faith, dead-heating with Thames in the first place in the Head in 1927, losing the final of the Grand to his old club in the same year, and losing again to Thames in the Stewards' in 1928. On this occasion he had stroked the London crew for only a week after being drafted in as a substitute, and leading by a length all the way up the course until the very end. But as coach the luck ran with his skill in 1930 when his crews won the Grand, the Stewards', the Wyfold and gold medals for an eight and four at the Empire games. Three Henley medals followed in 1931 and another empire gold in 1934. He was a vice-president from 1951 until his death in 1972.[15]

Claude 'Jock' Wise joined London in the autumn of 1905. He was a light-weight, winning the Wingfield Sculls in 1913 when he weighed 10 stone 1 pound, 'an extraordinarily fine waterman and uses his head well. Wise's performance was a brilliant one,' said a contemporary report. He made twelve appearances in the Thames Cup. He rowed in the Grand and Wyfold in 1908 and again in 1920 and 1921. He contested the Diamonds in 1912 and 1913, but never won a Henley medal. He became the assistant secretary in 1912 and held continuous office until his death in 1971, being captain in 1920, vice-president in 1946 and president from 1951. A gentle and kindly man, Wise was a father figure of the sport. 'His respect from all came from his quiet and sensible counsel combined with an active interest in the activities of not only those in his club but also of anyone connected with the sport,' said the *Times*.[16]

Philip Nevil 'Farn' Carpmael was another who slid down the conduit from Cambridge to London, a Fairbairn disciple from Jesus College, Cambridge. He was educated at Oundle before going up to Jesus in 1928, and he won the Boat Race in 1930 and 1931, changing sides in the process. In the latter year he won the Grand and the Stewards' with London, his four being the object of Drinkwater's praise as the finest coxless four he had seen in thirty years.[17] Farn spent twenty-five years competing at Henley until 1952, and at the age of forty he won the Wingfields in 1948, and defended them successfully next year. In 1959 he began a three-year stint as captain in similar circumstances to Nisbet in the twenties, a fallow period in which Farn laid the foundations for a return to the forefront of the rowing scene. He had a particular fondness for the Phelps fami-ly of watermen, and championed watermen in general, being instrumental in opening London's doors to down-river men keen to scale the heights of amateur rowing in the post-war era — men no longer tarred with the guilt of profession-alism by association. In 1976 Carpmael became president when Edgar Howitt died. He broke down the barriers of age and seniority. He exuded the spirit and teaching of Fairbairn. At dinners and functions, the room would be enveloped in a crescendo of 'Faaaaaarrrrrrn'. He was a president who rowed because of the pleasure it gave him, who acted with simplicity and honesty in all he did, and a president who recognised that friendship and fun were part of going from strength to strength.[18] His expertise at 'cockfighting' was also legendary.[†]

For many years, Oliver Philpot was a familiar figure on Head day and at the Metropolitan Regatta, decked out in a top hat as chief boat marshal. He stroked eights at Radley and Worcester College, Oxford, and was a Thames Cup finalist for London in 1937. During the Second World War he was shot down off the Norwegian coast while attacking a convoy as pilot of a Beaufort torpedo bomber, and he finished up in the high security prisoner-of-war camp called Stalag Luft III in Sagan, Silesia. His riveting account of his successful escape, with two others, via a tunnel under the wire dug with the aid of a wooden horse to conceal the goings-on has some references to rowing. Waking up on the day of the escape, Philpot says: 'I felt in a trance as before my one appearance at Henley.' Buying a ticket at Sagan station after getting out of the tunnel: 'I had that screwed-up feeling that I got a fraction of a second before the gun at the bumping races on the river at Radley.'[19] Disguised as a Norwegian margarine sales-man, he travelled to Danzig (now Gdansk) and jumped a collier to neutral Sweden. In civilian life, Philpot's career included managing Wall's Ice Cream, Fropax Eskimo Food, and Remploy. He spent three years as overseas administra-tor of Help the Aged, and worked on behalf of the disabled. He was a Christian philanthropist who was a supporter of the European Union and enjoyed political canvassing. He also sculled the Boat Race course every Saturday until he was in his seventies.

Many members of London who served and survived in the Second World War distinguished themselves even if they did not all earn distinctions. Colonel Dell Rothschild was in the Royal Electrical and Mechanical Engineers carrying out anti-aircraft work with Bill Atkinson, John Pinches and Thames's Tim Wilson. After the war Rothschild joined the Newmark company and set up watch-making from scratch until manufacture reached a million timepieces a year. His management style was humane. 'No-one loses their jobs over this,' he would say during a crisis. 'You don't get off that easily.' He ran radio systems for the Head of the River Race, coached clubs including King's College London, the Royal Navy and the Royal Marines, worked with St John's Ambulance, and part-nered Peter Coni for years on health and safety matters concerning rowing and the tideway.[20] Edward Sturges spent some of the war operating alone as a Special Operations Executive officer behind the Japanese lines organising the Karens in

†Two men would lie next to each other head to toe. Each would raise the leg closest to his rival to an upright position, and battle would commence to force the opponent's leg to the ground.

guerrilla activities. Before that he fought in Africa, Burma and the Far East with 44 Commando, and afterwards taught gymnastics near Sloane Square, tutoring various members of the royal household.[21] Colonel Sankey was a Royal Engineer who served in both world wars, and was notable for designing the first eight-man rowing tank. He rowed in the Thames Cup five times and the Wyfold three times between 1907 and 1914, but never won. Small, wiry, virile and vigorous, Sankey was a main stay of the London old men's eight for a very long time, and lived in the club for many years until he had to be moved to a nursing home.[22] Of the post-war generation, Peter Jackson became commanding officer of the 10th Hussars, where David Edwards, son of 'Jumbo', was an officer. He presented his 1962 Commonwealth games oar to the sergeants' mess, who have cursed it ever since because it is such an awkward object to move around. When Jackson asked his CO permission for time off for the games, the senior rank was reluctant because leave had already been granted for Henley. 'So Peter picked him up and held him over the banister of the stairwell until he agreed,' Edwards says.

John David Forbes Pepys started rowing in the Far East in the 1950s and joined the club in 1959. Thus 'Pepys Promotions' was born, a series of innovations by an energetic secretary (1973–75) and then treasurer. He encouraged oarsmen from foreign clubs affiliated to London to use the premises when visiting or moving back to their roots. He founded the 'irregulars', outings for people who could not train regularly, followed by dinner on Wednesdays. He edited the newsletter for twelve years, organised cleaning parties for parts of the building, and founded the annual Curry Cup race in 1965, an encounter between Singapore, Hong Kong and Calcutta oarsmen on the Tuesday before Henley for a trophy which was originally for a yacht race in Calcutta. Pepys's philosophy of winning races was 'you have to row until you see black' which aptly illustrates his determination in all he did. How amazed, therefore, were his companions when he suddenly asked for an 'easy' during a casual outing. Only months later when cancer was detected were his crew mates reminded of this. True to his nature, he suffered his illness courageously.

London Rowing Club's first waterman was Fred Phelps, succeeded by his son Edwin 'Shaky Ted' Phelps (father of the boat builder Edwin Phelps), succeeded by Charles Phelps's son Jack, succeeded by Jack's brother Tom. Thus from the beginning until Tom's retirement in 1967, London was in the capable hands of a dynasty of Fulham and Putney Phelpses, almost all of whom worked in and around boats at Putney for generations. Tom, like his father before him and two of his four brothers, won Doggett's Coat and Badge in 1922. His uncle 'Bossy' Phelps taught him to scull and sent him out with his amateur pupils, and Tom became mentor and

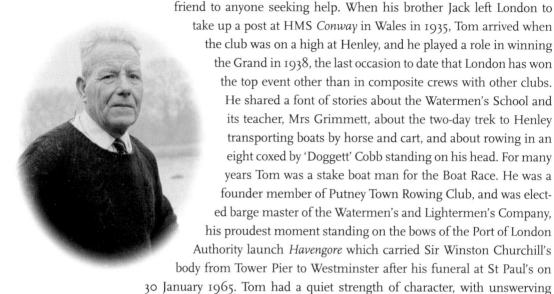

friend to anyone seeking help. When his brother Jack left London to take up a post at HMS *Conway* in Wales in 1935, Tom arrived when the club was on a high at Henley, and he played a role in winning the Grand in 1938, the last occasion to date that London has won the top event other than in composite crews with other clubs. He shared a font of stories about the Watermen's School and its teacher, Mrs Grimmett, about the two-day trek to Henley transporting boats by horse and cart, and about rowing in an eight coxed by 'Doggett' Cobb standing on his head. For many years Tom was a stake boat man for the Boat Race. He was a founder member of Putney Town Rowing Club, and was elected barge master of the Watermen's and Lightermen's Company, his proudest moment standing on the bows of the Port of London Authority launch *Havengore* which carried Sir Winston Churchill's body from Tower Pier to Westminster after his funeral at St Paul's on 30 January 1965. Tom had a quiet strength of character, with unswerving loyalty and immense knowledge of water, boats and crews. His obituary said that as a true Englishman he would have heard the trumpets on the other bank when extracts from Pilgrim's Progress were read at his funeral.[23]

Tom Phelps, the fourth member of the Phelps family to act as London's waterman, who retired in 1967

In the early 1960s Tom Phelps acquired a helpmate in Fred Jones, who was introduced to the club by Farn Carpmael of the North Thames Gas Board. Jones worked at the board's research station upstream of Wandsworth bridge, and he assisted Phelps with the launching of boats and their maintenance, and continued to do so with his successors Eddy Halpin, Frank Sims and Bill Colley. He was also Father Christmas, drains-fixer and barman to the club, although his battle with the new fancy cash till sometimes resulted in a four-figure bill for a pint of beer. After an overland trip to Prague with the boat trailer during the cold war, Fred was shocked by the condition of the people under the Communist government, and made a point of telling his union leader so when he returned. He outlived two wives and a girlfriend before departing to the boathouse in the sky in 2003, where he is no doubt pulling pints.[24]

Hugh Robert Arthur Edwards was universally known as 'Jumbo'. He led life on the edge of a blade, on the edge of a joystick and at the narrow end of a megaphone, all permeated by a cultivated slowness of speech and a hesitant, gap-toothed sentence structure that made him at times a baffling coach but also a hilarious raconteur. He began his rowing at Westminster School and then outstretched himself in the Boat Race when he collapsed in 1926. With London he reached the final of the Grand in 1927. 'Steve Fairbairn was then coaching London, who were rapidly recovering from the doldrums they had been in for forty years,' he wrote in his autobiography. 'Under Steve's tuition I gradually became a proficient oarsman.'[25] In 1930 he rowed for Oxford a second time and won the Grand and the Stewards' with London, capping his year with a gold medal at the Empire games. Next year he won three Henley finals on the same day, and in 1932 two Olympic golds on the same day, the first in a Christ Church pair with Lewis Clive and the second as a substitute in the Thames RC coxless four.

'Jumbo' joined the RAF in 1931 and attained the rank of squadron leader in 1938. He was awarded the AFC in 1943 after flying a damaged Hampden bomber safely back home from an air raid over Cologne, and a DFC in 1944 after bringing his crippled Liberator down off the coast of Cornwall while on convoy patrol, and being rescued by sculling his rubber dinghy into a shipping lane. He took command of 53 squadron when his brother Cecil was killed in action, and he retired with the rank of group captain in 1956. After the war 'Jumbo' became a prominent, experimental coach, with mixed results. Although clearly influenced by the Fairbairnism at London when at the height of his powers in a halcyon period for the club, he looked more to the orthodox methods to be found at Eton and Oxford for his own coaching ideas. He introduced longer oars, bigger blades, more severe gearing, interval training, and the use of strain gauges, ergometers and accelerators to calculate the work output through the stroke cycle. But in nineteen years with Oxford, his crews were successful in only five Boat Races. According to Richard Burnell, his coaching was marred because he did not spot the need to hold fast to a fixed datum point.[26] His insistence on uniform and uniformity from the practice outing to the dinner table caused him a lot of trouble, and his lack of skills as a motivator, linked with an excess of booze, sometimes let him down.[27] 'Jumbo', though, despite the impression his speech gave, was by no means aloof. He coached the British eight in 1960 and launched the Nautilus scheme in 1964 at the behest of the ARA. This had mixed results, but was the beginning of the revolution which eventually tore selection for Great Britain away from the pre-cast club unit towards mixing the best wherever they were found. 'Jumbo' coached many clubs, including London, from time to time, and when based at Putney he always made his headquarters on the premises. He was also a racing pilot, coming second in the King's Cup in 1933, and a keen sailor, taking part in the first round-Britain race in 1966 (and often crossing the Channel for duty frees). He collapsed on his yacht in the Hamble and died later in December 1972, a true legend in his lifetime.[28]

Petty Officer Graham Hill, RN, walked into London Rowing Club in 1952 and asked to join. John Pinches, the captain, thought quizzically about 'gentlemen' but liked the cut of his jaw, and when Hill said he was willing to ride his motorcycle from Chatham barracks each day for training, Pinches took him on. Hill previously rowed at Auriol Rowing Club in Hammersmith and Southsea Rowing Club while stationed at Portsmouth, and he was also coaching at Stuart Ladies' on the River Lea, where he was courting his future wife Bette whom he had met at a Boxing Day party at Auriol. From joining London until 1954 he rowed in twenty

Graham Hill at Monaco Grand Prix, 1964

finals, usually as stroke, eight of which resulted in wins. He also stroked the Grand eight at Henley in 1953, losing a semi-final to Union Sportif Metropolitaine des Transports, France, by a length. During that year Hill answered a magazine advertisement placed by the Universal Motor Racing Club which offered four laps of Brands Hatch for six guineas. He was hooked. After the Head in 1954, in which he rowed in the crew which followed RAF Benson in the pecking order and won the first Vernon Trophy, he resigned his job at S Smith and Sons, component manufacturers, and signed on the dole to take an unpaid job as mechanic to the new racing drivers' school at Brands Hatch. He was soon employed by Lotus as a mechanic before switching to the BRM team as a Formula 1 driver. There followed a glittering career at the wheel. Hill was world champion in 1962 with BRM and again in 1968 with Lotus. He was runner-up three times between them. He won the Indianapolis 500 in 1966 and Le Mans in 1972, and raced in 176 grand prix before retiring in 1975 to concentrate on management. Through his racing career he continued to support rowing and London, turning out to make accomplished speeches, beginning the demolition to make way for the extension to the boathouse by driving an old Morris into the wall, and opening the new Fairbairn room when the work was done. He famously adopted London's blue-and-white colours on his racing helmet, attributing his driving successes to what he learned from rowing:

'I really enjoyed my rowing. It really taught me a lot about myself, and I also think it is a great character-building sport,' he wrote. 'You have to have a lot of self-discipline and a great deal of determination. You not only get to know about

London's twelve-oar on parade at Henley, 1989

yourself, but you get to know about other people – who you would like to have in a boat with you over the last quarter-mile of a race when you are all feeling absolutely finished. With seven other fellows relying on you, you just can't give in. The self-discipline required for rowing and the "never say die" attitude it bred obviously helped me through the difficult years that lay ahead before I began to achieve my real ambition: the Le Mans 24-hour, the world title and the Indianapolis 500 – in other words, the hat-trick so far unique in motor racing history.'[29] In his youth a wild man at the wheel of old bangers, Hill became a campaigner for road safety and a leading abolitionist of the three-wheel invalid carriages and their replacement by a safe vehicle. He was also an active president of Springfield Boys Club in Upper Clapton, east London. Tragically he was killed in 1975 at the controls of his own Piper Aztec when it crashed in a copse at Arkley golf course, Elstree, while trying to land in mist. He was returning from testing the latest Embassy-Hill Formula One car at the Paul Ricard circuit in the south of France, and five members of his team died with him. He was forty-six. His son Damon also became a world champion Formula one driver, and he, too, drove in London colours.

John Marsden was known as the 'Quiet One'. The tall, strong, good looking soldier by instinct, housemaster at Eton by profession, drove to Putney every evening to cover 3,000 miles in his sculling boat by the time he won the Wingfield Sculls at the age of forty-one. He was one of the group of scullers based at London during the 1950s which included Tony Fox with whom he reached the final of the Double Sculls in 1954 and Doug Melvin with whom he did the same in 1956.[30] He won the first Scullers' Head in 1954. After rowing in the Eton eight in 1934, Marsden did not go out in a boat again for fifteen years. He studied languages in Bonn and at the Sorbonne and was awarded the American Bronze Star and the Croix de Guerre and a mention in dispatches for his war work in intelligence. He was parachuted into Africa, took part in the

Lofoten Islands raid in Norway, and was attached to General Eisenhower's headquarters. He was an inspiring teacher and housemaster with a steely smile and quick wit, organising expeditions such as a row from Lechlade to Greenwich in two quads in the depth of winter. One sank below Tower Bridge, and the rescued boys took a taxi back to London Rowing Club – where else? Marsden later became a stockbroker and farmer, and set up Marsden tutors in London to teach not necessarily bright kids to speak German. This had evolved into Collingham College, a large independent sixth form college, by the time of his death in 2004.[31]

Among the colourful figures of the club, particularly on the booms near the progress board at Henley, is the actor Rodney Bewes. He rowed for London and the gig club at Cadgwith Cove in Cornwall, and when on the booms he always wears his club cap. Best known now for his one-man show of Three Men in a Boat (performed at the club on 23 November 1993), he has led a distinguished career on stage and screen, playing opposite Tom Courtney in Billy Liar, opposite James Bolam in the long running Likely Lads television series, and Flute to Sir Ralph Richardson's Bottom in a production of A Midsummer Night's Dream which toured Europe and Latin America. His skiff *Frank* and his dinghy *Maurice* have won the Chaplin Prize for best restoration and maintenance at Thames Traditional Boat Club rallies.

The lesson of attempting to untangle the history of London Rowing Club and the people who make it tick is that behind every coach and captain is a team, a situation which runs the risk of unsung heroes and mis-targeted praise. Nick Cooper, for example, attributes his winning of the Wingfield Sculls in 1967 to the stern tutoring of Doug Melvin and Graham Beech. He praises Peter Hilditch, captain in 1969, for his determination to end a long period without Henley success which resulted in tremendous support for himself and his crew mates Daniel Topolski, Chris Blackwall and Peter Harrison for their capture of the Wyfold, followed by the Britannia a year later with David Sturge, John Dart, Alan Sherman and Topolski. Cooper was propelled into the treasurer's office when John Pepys died in 1980, 'in blissful ignorance of the enormous size of the

overdraft which had been caused by the modernisation work.' Backs were to the wall, and while the house steward, David King, worked wonders with the bar, Cooper's wife Lotte organised the catering, and customers and money began to roll in. Cooper resigned in 1983 when he secured a job as an Outward Bound mountaineering instructor, leading climbs of Kilimanjaro each month. This heralded a career in mining and precious metals followed by thirteen years as bursar of a school when he and his family tired of travelling. 'The willingness of many to help so effectively when the chips are down showed the club spirit at its best, and will always be greatly appreciated,' is his epitaph to LRC.

Doug Melvin (left), sculler, coach, mentor and president 2001 to 2004, with Ian Watson, captain 2001 to 2002

Captains have run the spectrum of first-class athletes, organisation men and even cartoonists, for during Keith Ticehurst's four-year reign and beyond, the summons to Christmas parties and Guy Fawkes nights were enlivened by his sharp eye and keen jokes. Paid coaches have been engaged by London for only fifteen years. Before that, the time-honoured practice since the founding members guided form and fitness from the back seat of twelve-oars has been to pass expertise down through generations of oarsmen. This continues, usually accompanied by ARA qualifications, alongside the club professional. Doug Melvin is one example, a sculler from Lancaster whose rowing life and gentle voice weaves through competition, coaching, committee work and the presidency at London, and extends through his sons John and Simon. Alongside Melvins, there is also a succession of people who have carried the club's influence abroad in both senses, either by holding office in national and international rowing bodies, such as Peter Coni and the current president, Mike Williams, or by striking accord with clubs in many countries, such as Rob van Mesdag who brings Dutch, Belgian, Irish and Venetian connections in his baggage. In 1990, when the author visited Leningrad (now St Petersburg), he was amazed to see an LRC sticker on his airport taxi. The driver turned out to be an Olympic medallist who had also raced against London as a veteran. But then again, it's not as surprising as it first appeared, given London's outlook on rowing life.

Richard 'Gonzo' Philips, captain 1988 to 1990

A Blueprint in Our Minds 1991–2005

A BLUEPRINT IN OUR MINDS
1991–2005

A NEW ERA BEGAN IN DECEMBER 1991 when Robin Williams was appointed rowing manager, becoming the first club outside the universities and Leander to employ a professional coach. The reverse of this coin was that Bill Colley became the last boatman, a hard decision to make, but a reflection of the times. As plastic composites increasingly replaced wood for boat and oar construction, so there was less call for equipment maintenance, while as composite crews were now the norm in the national team, there was more call for continuous high-level coaching to produce club crews which could hold their own in the world of domestic regattas. Williams was contracted for twenty hours a week and become rowing master for City of London school at the same time. The contract, he says, was a joke, but he had three enjoyable and successful years producing strong open weight crews as well as knocking novice, intermediate and lightweight crews into shape. In 1991 Williams and Nick Strange raced in the national lightweight squad eight in the Ladies' Plate, while the club's eight, coached by Doug Melvin, reached the semifinal of the Thames Cup. In 1992 Williams reported that more people were rowing out of the club than had been seen in ten years, and there were occasions when every boat was out on the river. Plans were being made for winter weekends off the tideway, and there would be more lectures on rowing. This followed a season at Henley during which Williams survived two days of the Diamond Sculls before being beaten by an international from Melbourne University, Paul Reedy. Reedy went on to lose a close final against the former London sculler Rorie Henderson, who was wearing Leander colours and had a point to prove, having been rejected by the British team for the Olympic regatta coming up later in the year. Reedy hit the booms after clearing Temple Island, and at Fawley the scullers were level. Reedy was a length ahead at the mile, where Henderson began a relentless burn

Overleaf: Winners of the Thames Cup at Henley received their medals from LRC's patron, HRH Prince Philip, 1998

at a cool rating of 33 strokes to the minute. Reedy took his rate up desperately at the grandstand, but his bubble burst, and Henderson came through to win by three lengths, a verdict which did not really reflect the race. The twenty-four hours leading to this moment were doubly difficult for both men because Reedy was sharing his friend Henderson's flat and car. The evening of the Diamonds final was, understandably, 'a bit quiet'.[1] London's coxed four won against Nereus in the first round of the Britannia easily, and against Neptune in the second with difficulty, bursting through at the enclosures. Tough races followed against University of Bristol and Nottingham and Union, both selected crews. But Goldie, who had two men who won the Goblets earlier in the day, contained London and commanded the final.[2]

Andy Butt and Nick Strange won silver medals in the British lightweight eight at the world championships in Montreal, signifying the continuing presence of London oarsmen in the lightweight squad. From henceforth, the dynamics of lightweight rowing changed because of the momentous decision by the International Olympic Committee to include lightweight events in their programme. From now on, the ambitious would seek seats and the funding that came with them in fours and doubles, the boat classes admitted to the Olympic regatta, at the expense of eights, which were not. Club successes after Henley at Henley Town and Visitors', Oxford, Peterborough, and Ghent contributed to an increase in the squad from fifty to ninety in the autumn, excluding a strong squad

London's women at Henley: Anne Theophilus, Bryony Britten, Anna Crawford and Helen Mangan in the Princess Grace at Henley Royal, and with Kate Hoey, MP, as winners of the lightweight quadruple sculls at Henley Women's, 2004

London winning the Wyfold against Leander at Henley, 1993. From the bow: Marcus Williams, Sean Sinclair, Robin Williams and Bill Baker

of veterans. There was plenty of winter activity, such as video shows by 'Gonzo' Philips, fat tests by the Olympic doctor, Richard Budgett, lectures by 'Gonzo' Bernstein and training alongside Molesey and the Searle brothers, one of two British crews who won gold medals at the Olympics in Barcelona.[3] The Henley campaign led to a stunning win in the Wyfold, made all the more poignant because the prizes were given away by the president of the club, Peter Coni, who would pass to the great enclosure in the sky ten days later. London entered two crews, both lightweights. The A crew were selected and progressed to a meeting with the B crew, containing coach Williams, after dismissing Gloucester and then Stourport. London B arrived in the all-London quarterfinal by way of successful outcomes against Molesey, who led the early stage, and then Wallingford. London A had steering problems against their club mates after being only half a length down at the Barrier. Quintin were easy meat for the B crew in the semifinal. In the final Leander had a length lead at the Barrier, but London took the lead at Fawley, and rowed right away along the enclosures.[4] Another lightweight, Ned Kittoe, won a Henley medal in double sculls with Reg Redpath of Tyrian. Four more London lightweights lost the final of the Ladies' Plate to Brown University of the USA in a composite crew with Nottinghamshire County Rowing Association.

Coni had stepped down as chairman of Henley's management committee at the beginning of the year when his doctors gave him a death sentence. He said farewell to London in a 7 minute 31 second speech before the annual dinner at Simpson's, and delivered a typically robust farewell speech at Henley as he drew tears to the eyes on a sunny Sunday evening on 4 July 1993, having witnessed his own club have a part in two trophies and having witnessed Maria Brandin win the first event for female single scullers at his regatta. His departing signature tune was the theme from Coronation Street which he chose to accompany the prizegiver's procession from the secretary's tent to the grandstand, played by the band of the Royal Military School of Music. It set a challenge for Major Stuart Watts, the conductor, because it is a very short piece, and attempts to find its composer to lengthen it failed.

Peter Coni (seated, centre) with the winners of the Wyfold and the Double Sculls, and presenting Robin Williams with his medal, 1993

In 1993 there were seven London athletes and three coaches in the GB team. Mike Williams succeeded Coni as treasurer of the International Rowing Federation (FISA), and was also elected a steward. Robin Williams made a plea for commitment and reliability in his annual report: 'One of the lessons we have learned over recent seasons is that to win at top events, like Henley, requires a standard approaching that of international crews. This means a lot of training, having the necessary physiology, acquiring the technique, and leaving as few gaps in each individual's performance as possible.' It concerned him that Henley was widely seen as the crowning glory of the season, when it is actually only midway. 'We should explore other goals and racing at the sometimes scorned national championships and the home countries, for example. Many schools manage to arrange overseas tours, so why not LRC?' he asked, citing Australian Henley, the head of the Charles in Boston, Hawaii and Cannes. This was prescient: many of his ideas have been taken up and developed by himself and his successors.

Ned Kittoe and Tyrian's Reg Redpath winning the Double Sculls at Henley, 1993

Robin Williams's last year as coach, 1994, saw twenty-five members reach semifinals or finals at Henley, twenty-two London athletes and coaches involved in the English team for the Commonwealth regatta[5] or the British team for the world championships, and a frustratingly bold and brilliant year for Andy Butt, Ian Watson, Nick Strange and Ben Helm, the lightweight

four. They set a world's best time for a coxless four – light or heavy – of 5 minutes 18 seconds in the world cup in Paris, lost two Henley finals and came away from the world championships with nothing. While the Paris race put down a marker, the Henley adventure of attempting two events was an insurance policy against coming up against very big guns in the Stewards'. Henley turned into their charge of the light brigade, where bravery was not enough. Most of their races were hard, beginning with a dead-heat in the opening round of the Queen Mother for quadruple sculls. This was against Sykes Rowing Club, Australia's national light-weights, and was just what London did not need. The Australians led by a length at the first signal. London began to inch back after the Barrier. Sykes had a canvas at the bottom of the enclosure, and London forced a dead heat. The re-row followed the same pattern for the first mile, but then London moved ahead and Sykes could not answer. After an easy race against Tideway Scullers B, they next had a tough semifinal against Leander, who had weight advantage of nearly three-and-a-half stone per man. The heavier crew led by half-a-length at the Barrier, London took the lead at Fawley and led by a length from the mile to the finish.

Meanwhile, in the Stewards', the same London crew began by beating College Boat Club, the US lightweight squad, by half a length after the Americans led by

London's eight winning the Commonwealth championship for England, 1994

a length at halfway. Next came Charles River and San Diego, the US heavy squad, who were three-and-a-half stone per man heavier. London changed a half-length deficit to a lead of four feet at Fawley. They drew this out to two-and-a-half lengths at the finish. They thus reached the final in both events. Now, Goliath appeared in two guises. Boulogne and Lyon, in the Stewards', were the reigning world champions in coxless fours, and had beaten the GB squad four, rowing as Molesey, in the semifinal. With a weight deficit of almost three stone and having covered the course four more times than their opponents, London's name was never on this trophy. The French won by one-and-a-half lengths, but were harried all the way, only securing clear water at the enclosures. The Queen Mother was a worse fate for London. Treviris and Böllberg of Germany had made one change since winning the world title in 1993, and they were four stone per man heavier and, again, had expended far less effort to get where they were. The Germans led by two lengths at quarter-mile and five at the finish. The London crew came away with respect and honour.[6] After Henley they donned GB shirts and went to Eagle Creek, Indianapolis, where they won the lightweight fours B final for a world ranking of seventh. The glory there came to the lightweight eight, coached by Sean Bowden of Nottinghamshire County and Cambridge, two clubs on the ascendant and linked by their coaches.[7] In September, Williams became chief coach at Cambridge.[8]

The lightweight composite crew of Nottinghamshire County and London won the Stewards' in 1996. Bill Baker substituted for Andy Butt on the last two days because Butt's wife was having a baby. The others were Chris Bates (NCRA), Ian Watson and Jonty Williamson

The 1995 season was under the coaching of Antony Patterson, who arrived at London from Australia and departed for King's School, Parramatta, after a year, a move caused by a visa problem. The year began with a good showing on the tideway against Oxford but a mauling by Cambridge, sixth place in the Head for the top crew, four pennants in the Scullers' Head, a win in the Boustead Cup, and a win for the lightweight eight at the Metropolitan Regatta for the new Coni Cup. At Henley, the fallen heroes of 1994, Helm, Butt, and Strange, plus Jonty Williamson and cox Lisa Ross-Magenty, were members of the Ladies' Plate crew who lowered two records but lost to Princeton by three feet in a semifinal. Roger Everington paired up with Mark Partridge of Nottinghamshire County to contest the final of the Goblets against the all-conquering Steve Redgrave and Matt Pinsent. The club's lightweight eight and coxless four won the national championships, and the four won their event for England in the Home Countries International in Cork. There was also a crop of good results in post-Henley regattas, including Peterborough Summer, Oxford City, Maidenhead, Bristol,

Ross-on-Wye and Greenwich. At the world championships in soggy Tampere, Finland, Butt, Williamson, Strange, and Helm won silver medals in the lightweight eight. The newsletter thanked Wandsworth Council for floodlighting Putney bridge, which it described as a great view from the balcony. It also lamented the passing of Brian Longfellow who used to take an old wooden pair out with Alastair Duncan and amble along against the tide before subtly increasing pressure as other crews tried to overtake on the inside.

To provide rowing at high level for men and women who are not able to be full-time athletes but who want to win at Henley, the national championships and other leading regattas; and to be a centre of excellence for lightweight men.
– Mike Williams, president of The London Rowing Club, on the club's aims in 2006

London's lightweights were to the fore at Henley in 1996, Olympic year, teaming up in squad crews with Nottinghamshire County in the Ladies' Plate and the Stewards'. The eight in the Ladies' eventually lost to Leander who in turn lost the final to Goldie (Cambridge University). The Stewards' four first beat Commercial of Ireland after hitting the booms soon after the island, secondly a Nottinghamshire County and Auckland combination, and then Goldie in an action-packed final in which the boats clashed and had to re-start.[9] There were also London lightweights in the Queen Mother, where both the London entry and a combination with London University survived for one round. The Thames Cup A crew, mostly lightweights, did better, reaching the semifinal to be defeated by the Dublin club Neptune, the eventual winners. Two Londoners made the Olympic team in Atlanta, Ben Helm as stroke of the light coxless four and Nick Strange in the light double with Andrew Sinton. Seven Londoners rowed in British lightweight crews at the world championships for non-Olympic events in Strathclyde.

London's best Henley performances in 1997 were the final of the Wyfold and the quarterfinal of the Thames Cup. The Wyfold four had a good opening race against Worcester. They beat the Americans from Stanford Rowing Club in the second round, and in the quarterfinal found the gods on their side against the selected crew from Nottingham Boat Club. A clash at the end of the island stopped the race and the umpire ordered an immediate re-row. London led by two lengths at the mile with erratic steering which resulted in warnings, and came under pressure from their opponents. Nottingham closed along the enclosures when they hit the boom by the progress board, and the race was over.

The semi-final was London's by two-thirds of a length after University of London Tyrian pressed them all the way. In the final, Molesey, considerably heavier, reduced London's lead of a length at the Barrier to a foot at Fawley, and came through to win the cup by two-and-a-quarter lengths.

The Thames Cup was a tough event in which London defeated Garda Siochana in a notable race before bowing out to Thames Tradesmen. An oddity at this Henley was a selected boat in the Double Sculls manned by Melbourne University's Reedy and Olympic champion Peter Antonie who were also sculling with two Italians in the Queen Mother. They were beaten in the first round of both. Meanwhile, the old firm of Butt, Watson, Strange and Williamson represented Britain as the light four at the world championships in Aiguebelette, France, while James Brown had a seat in the lightweight eight. Since Patterson left the coaching chair, Mike Ivey had taken the rowing manager role, supported by a large number of part-time coaches. But on 1 December John MacArthur began work as London's coach, having arrived via a post as Hong Kong's rowing director and stints as the ARA's development coach in the west midlands and lower Thames areas.

Early next season, on 29 March, there was a memorial outing for Mrs Lillian Eagle, London's faithful cleaning lady and Mortlake, Anglian and Alpha's faithful sculler. The four *Lillian*, rowed by men and women from both clubs, was accompanied to Barnes bridge and back by the launch *Casamajor* and several crews. They returned at the top of a very high tide, causing Mrs Eagle's son Eric, her sister Pat and family members to be shouldered from *Casamajor* to tea at the clubhouse by oarsmen up to their knees in the Thames. The MacArthur era began with second place overall in the Head, and continued with the first win in the Thames Cup at Henley for twenty years. In the first round, this home-grown crew nurtured by coach Chris Jones beat the Americans of Penn Athletic Club, and in the second removed London's B crew, the verdicts being three lengths and two-and-three-quarters respectively. Nottingham Boat Club was the third victim, and then Molesey in a stroke for stroke encounter in which London had a half-length lead at the Barrier and held off repeated attacks to win by that distance. The final against Bowbridge (Oxford Brookes University's old boys and friends), who had also won their semifinal against Sydney Rowing Club by half-a-length but in a much slower time, followed a similar pattern to the race against Molesey. London had half-a-length at the Barrier and two-thirds at Fawley, consistently under-rating Bowbridge and increasing their advantage to a length at the three-quarter-mile signal. Bowbridge closed up, but not enough.[10] Who should pop up to present them with the Thames Cup but their patron, Prince Philip, wearing his Casamajor tie.

At Putney the premises were busy because Imperial College joined London as a temporary home while their clubhouse was being rebuilt. It was good year for Ian Watson, winning the London Cup for single scullers at the Metropolitan Regatta and the Fours Head in a composite lightweight quadruple scull. James Brown and John Warnock rowed in the British light four at the world championships in Köln, finishing fourth.

The fireworks were in the Thames Cup in 1999 as the club tried to hang on to the trophy. The A crew beat Queen's Tower (Imperial College's old boys and friends) in the first round, an emotional race because the two shared the club-house and had trained alongside each other. Tower took the lead to the first signal but were caught before the Barrier and were behind by three-quarters of a length at Fawley. Tower closed before London found a bit of clear water after the mile. The London B crew beat Mitsubishi in the first round and then went out to the A crew, who continued to the semifinal after removing Hamburg Germania. They met their match in Molesey, who built a three-quarter-length lead when they reached the Barrier. London attacked continually and lost a great race by quarter of a length. The London crew in the Britannia lost a re-row against Worcester after a dead heat in the second round. London's lightweights combined with Mainzer Ruderverein for the Ladies' Plate but lost the first round to the University of California Berkeley.

Appalling weather disrupted the season and caused the cancellation of the Metropolitan and Docklands regattas on the Royal Albert Dock. The coaching team lost their professional, MacArthur. Brown and Warnock again represented their country in the lightweight coxless four at the world championships in St Catharine's, Ontario, but their result was a disappointing eleventh.[11] Anne Carpmael, the widow of both Jock Wise and Farn Carpmael and a long-time generous financial supporter of the club, was elected an honorary vice-president.

None of the club's seven crews at Henley in 2000 progressed farther than a second round. Both entries in the Britannia were beaten by the Yorkshire club Blacksheep, and both Wyfold crews lost to the eventual winners, Worcester Rowing Club. The club's only representation in the Olympic team in Sydney was Lotte Miller who coxed the British women's eight. The Sydney games were notable for the fifth and last gold medal won by Steve Redgrave in a coxless four with James Cracknell, Tim Foster and Matt Pinsent; the first Olympic gold by a British eight since 1912; and the first Olympic medal for a British women's crew, silver for the quadruple scullers. On 20 October Paul Reedy, the Diamonds finalist of 1992, arrived from Melbourne to take up residence as coach, charged with 'providing opportunities for members to be successful domestically,

*Celebrating victory
in the Thames Cup,
1998. London beat
Bowbridge in the final*

internationally and at Henley'. Reedy won medals at the 1984 Olympics, the 1986 Commonwealth games and the 1990 world championships, and he won the Queen Mother in 1988, representing Melbourne University.

Reedy quickly got the measure of his job. 'The typical member comes from a provincial university or moves to London, many from overseas, to work,' he said. The first test is land training on Thursday nights, after which he says that eight out of ten won't return. The cornerstone is that everyone trains together, with flexibility worked in to accommodate working hours and to deal with the winter by using rowing machines and going elsewhere for cycling and other activities. There are compulsory sessions at the weekends for testing, mentoring and monitoring. The typical programme is two sessions a day at weekends and, during the week, two morning and four evenings, all round the year. The season begins on 1 September, and the squad usually starts with eighty people and settles at around fifty. Reedy and his team of volunteer coaches aim to cover the bases and expect to win, with special attention paid to developing the next generation. They want everyone to be able to row with anyone. 'We would like to be the best club. We should be able to win an event at Henley every year, but you have to be opportunistic in choosing the event.'

He began by introducing some 'Aussie sporting environment', insisting that everybody starts on the same footing, everyone trains together, and every tenth word is 'that's good'. The observation skills that he learned as a physiotherapist transferred well into rowing. His approach to selection is to enable anybody to slot into any crew. 'Then it comes down to physiology, who gets in.' Social events are important in his plan also, to ensure that the club maintains a network of support, to avoid crews or groups forming cliques, and to make it plain to the guys at the top that they have support.

The members responded. A sequence of events at Henley has led to two wins and several near misses since Reedy's first season. In 2001 the lightweight Wyfold four lost to Leander's lightweights, who were victors over London's heavy crew in the previous round and the eventual winners, in a semifinal. Handling two oars each in the Queen Mother, the same London crew in a different seating order[12] beat a London and Queen's Tower combination before going down to a heavy Leander crew. The Leander crew consisted of three national sculling squad men and a late call-up of Sir Steve Redgrave who won his twentieth and last Henley medal. In the Thames Cup London lost to the old enemy, Thames, in a semifinal. The crew in the Visitors' for coxless fours was selected but lost to an Imperial College and Queen's Tower combination in the second round.[13]

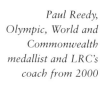

Next year there were fifty blues-and-whites in fourteen boats at Henley. The Wyfold four reached the final and the Britannia coxed four reached a semifinal. The selected lightweights in the Wyfold beat Molesey, London B, Crabtree (Cambridge old boys) and Leander before losing to Aberdeen Boat Club, and the Britannia crew beat Union of Boston, Nereus of Amsterdam and Galway of Ireland before meeting their match in Harvard. Three club crews started in the Thames Cup, the A boat having the most success by beating the Army in a good race in the opening round, and then Curlew on the next day. Then they met the crew from Homberger Ruderklub who beat them by a length and three-quarters in the fastest quarterfinal. The Henley Regatta recorder was of the opinion that with hindsight, Homberger and the eventual winners, Leander, should have been kicked upstairs into the Ladies' Plate on the grounds that the first were selected for the German under-23 team as soon as Henley finished, and the second had been doing rather too well before the regatta. Leander beat Homberger in a semifinal while earning a false start for themselves in the final for 'unsporting behaviour'. This was for shouting abuse at the Germans, and their written apology was insufficient to abate the ire of the Henley stewards. Leander beat Nottinghamshire County in the final.

Paul Reedy, Olympic, World and Commonwealth medallist and LRC's coach from 2000

Drama continued around Homberger in 2003, when a completely different line-up arrived in the final of the Thames Cup against London's A crew, some of whom rowed in the 2002 crew. There was considerable bad feeling created by the rumour that this time the crew contained athletes in the under-23 team, but status checks carried out by the stewards and relayed to the press refuted this. This time London had four entries in the Thames Cup. The D crew lost to Thames Tradesmen in the first round. The A crew disposed of the B crew in the first round and the lightweight C crew in the second, although the latter was stroke for stroke from the Barrier with A being warned several times for bad steering. Thames Tradesmen were their victims in the quarterfinal and Lady Elizabeth (Trinity College Dublin's old boys) in the semifinal. In this race London were trailing by a canvas at the Barrier and led by two feet at Fawley. They reached the line half-a-length in front. Then came the final, 'a splendid race, only marred by the behaviour of London Rowing Club's cox in defeat,' said the regatta report.[14] Homberger led by half-a-length at the quarter mile, three-quarters at Fawley and a length at the three-quarter mile signal. The regatta report takes up the story: 'London attacked very strongly from here to the finish but were warned several times for their erratic steering. While they continued to close it appeared that their cox was concentrating more on her opponents than on her course and there has to be a suspicion that, had this not been the case, the result might possibly have been different – Homberg holding on to win by half a length.' The view from the press box was that, coming along the enclosures on the Berks station, London had Homberger in their grasp while tight on the booms, exactly where they had been advised they should have been, and making ground fast. 'Then at around the progress board, cox Jasmine Khan steered out towards Bucks and Homberger. The London boat's wake left a huge arc, while the verdict to the Germans was half-a-length. London could have settled the argument in the best possible way, but their cox robbed them of the chance to do so by shouting insults about the Germans to the press box. She was lucky that the only riposte she had from the stewards was to be told to calm down.'[15] She did, however, get a roasting in the press.

Mike Williams, Henley Steward and LRC's president from 2004, in London blazer and Trinity Hall BC tie

Reedy's era brought about changes in training. In February 2001 trial eights were held between crews named 'Brumby' and 'Dingo' – wild horses and wild dogs – from Mortlake to Putney. Training camps in Europe were now the norm in such venues as Aiguebelette, Ghent and Banyoles, and this year's was at Lac Saint-Cassien, north of Cannes. London finished a respectable fifth in the Head, occupied the first two places in the Brugge Head in Belgium, and was overall winner of the Veterans' Head. Back at base, a new laundry room was created by reorganisation in the men's changing rooms, a necessity when the launderette in Lower Richmond Road closed for business. Two new Empacher eights, plus a four and three pairs were added to the fleet. Goodenough College, a graduate college for Commonwealth and American students, trained at London with their coach, the 1976 Olympic medallist Lenny Robertson.

Reedy kick-started the next season on 1 August. Nick Wakefield and Ian Watson were the fastest pair in the Pairs Head, and Mark Watkin won the club single scullers' division of the Head of the Charles in Boston, Massachusetts, in the autumn.[16] A series of committee headraces for a series prize was introduced for singles and pairs from the club flagpole to Barnes bridge and back in November, January and February. An inaugural visit to the Australian sporting environment took place for the first Rowing Ashes, staged in Melbourne as part of the 150th Australia Day celebrations. The Ashes stayed at home on this occasion. During that winter there was a dinner for former captains, and nineteen showed up from a possible twenty-nine. Wednesday dinners took the form of three courses with a speaker once a month and one course during the weeks in between. March's Head was heralded by a 'fly-past' of eight eights at Putney. Only six were allowed in the head itself, and five finished in the top fifty – four of them ahead of the neighbours, Thames I. London went to the head at Kingston and got three boats into the top five in Brugge. The club became an Amateur Rowing Association high performance centre for lightweights, and Chris Drury joined the coaching team as a result. An expedition to Paris led to winning the Trophée Européen à l'Aviron against mainly university crews. Jenny Owen, the first woman to become a rowing member, won the senior 3 single sculls at the Metropolitan Jubilee Regatta. There were numerous club representatives in teams for the Commonwealth championships in Nottingham, where the London lightweight eight took a gold medal for England. Helen Mangan, representing Northern Ireland, became the first London woman to win an international medal when she took the silver medal for lightweight single sculling. The lightweight pair of James Brown and Jonty Williamson won silver for England, and three London coxes also won medals. Reedy was in charge of lightweights for the national team for the third round of the world cup in Lucerne and the world championships in Seville. John Warnock rowed in the British lightweight four in Seville, and he and Martin Harris became the fastest pair in the Pairs Head. Thirty-four scullers completed the Scullers' Head, held after a twenty-month hiatus after shifting its date in the calendar from April to November. Kate Hoey, the former minister for sport, spoke at the annual dinner that, for the second time, was aboard the Thames cruise ship *Silver Sturgeon*.

The year 2003 began with a second visit to Melbourne. A fifteen-day camp – together with Thames's women's squad! – culminated in the Ashes race on Australia Day, 26 January. London, on the north station of the River Yarra, beat Melbourne on the south station by two-and-a-half lengths. The Thames women also won. The April camp was at Lake Legutiano in the Basque region of Spain. The early season saw London oarsmen involved in the Remenham Challenge, fixtures against Oxford, Cambridge and City of Bristol, the ARA's trials and the committee headraces. Lea were beaten on the line at the Brugge Head, and London were the victors in a side-by-side race against KRB Ghent. Either side of Henley, the season chalked up wins by eight crews at Docklands Regatta, two at Marlow, eleven medals at the national championships and five pennants at the Wallingford Long Distance Sculls. Several scullers accompanied Ian Watson and his Westminster School squad to Berne for the Armada Cup. Warnock, Harris and Danny Harte raced in the British lightweight eight at the world championships in Milan, where they finished sixth.

At the annual dinner in February 2004 the new captain, Mark Watkin,

Theodore Ramos in his Chelsea studio with his copy of Alfred de Prades's 1860 club portrait commissioned to mark LRC's 150th anniversary. The original was lost as a result of enemy action whilst in storage in Chiswick during the Second World War

directed attention to the season ahead: 'We should not follow a path,' he said. 'We should leave a trail.' Watkin began competing at Henley in 1990 and had been with London since 1995. He was one of a strong group who had experienced highs and lows at the regatta since Reedy began coaching four seasons before. He was approaching his twelfth Henley as one of five men still available who had been narrowly beaten by Homberg, and the club had really felt that defeat. 'I wanted to win as much as I wanted LRC to win,' he said. Watkin believed, like Reedy, that there was no replacement for hard work and routine, and he followed the current London maxim of 'looking after one per cents'. Physical and mental attributes were strong. So at the beginning of his year as captain he sat down with the chief coach, and said that the club could win two events at Henley this year. 'Paul remarked "We should be happy with one", which was right, in a way.' Winter training had been strong, beginning with a January cycling camp at Club La Santa, Lanzarote, when five hundred miles were completed in volcanic scenery. There was also a better indoor environment because in the previous October, the gym had been renovated with new flooring, mirrors and weights, and was decked out in blue and white. This was an extension of emphasis placed on recognisable club kit for Wednesday and weekend outings, and encouragement of supporters to sport the colours at regattas.

The racing season began gingerly when the Head was hit by atrocious weather and cancelled just before it was due to start, but thirty crews took part in a hastily-arranged time trial two hours later on a calmer tideway. London finished third and had three boats ahead of Thames. At Easter, good light and heavy fours emerged from a camp in Seville. The only setback there was Rob McKenzie's tenosynovitis that put him out of the boat for a month. At Wallingford Regatta on Dorney Lake, the open eight bucked its ideas up after strong words followed a bad heat. London beat a strong Henley crew in the final that ignited a healthy rivalry between the two clubs for the rest of the season. Four members of this eight also won the open fours. The one per cents were adding up. Tents were erected at regattas so that crews could rest and receive massage from Claire Buckley, the captain's fiancée. Watkin, McKenzie, Mark Evans and Colin O'Malley got into the final at the Metropolitan, relieved to be up and running again. By now a Thames Cup eight was emerging as a strong unit. And at Henley Women's Regatta came another first when Anna Theophilus, Bryony Britten, Anna Crawford and Helen Mangan set up the club's first title for a London women's crew in the lightweight quadruple sculls.

Watkin's hopes and the coaching team's preparation were on target when Henley arrived. After a windy week, two London crews were in finals. The Thames

Cup eight[17] beat Staines and Quintin comfortably in the first two rounds before a hard race
against Combined Services, which went stroke-
for-stroke for three-quarters of a mile. Here
London pulled away to win by a length and
three-quarters. Meanwhile, the London B eight
beat Auriol Kensington before losing to
Mitsubishi in the second round. This was unfortunate because the Japanese club was afterwards
disqualified for including a world champion in its crew. This breach of the status
rules for the Thames went undetected by the stewards until the damage had been
done, and consequently Reuss Luzern had a row-over in the quarterfinal.
Meanwhile, London A met Lady Elizabeth, for the second time in two years, in the
semifinal, and were down by three-quarters of a length at halfway. A sustained
effort approaching Remenham reduced the deficit to half a length at the three-
quarter-mile signal. At the mile signal they were in the lead by a canvas, and they
went away to win by a length-and-a-half in a well-judged race and a disciplined
performance. On the last day came the Swiss, who had beaten London's rivals,
Henley, in the other semifinal. The crews were level at the first signal and Reuss
led by a foot at the Barrier, where they settled at 40 strokes to the minute with
London set on two strokes lower. At Fawley, approximately halfway, London had
taken the lead by a canvas, and they increased this to three-quarters-of-a-length at
the mile. In a terrific, thundering race for the finish, Reuss closed the gap, but
London won by half-a-length in 6 minutes 50 seconds, fastest time of the week.

The four in the Wyfold had been listening to the end of this at the back of the
boat tent while they prepared to go down the track for the last time.[18] Over the

*Winning the
Commonwealth
championships
for England,
Nottingham 2002,
and the crew with
coach Tam
Richmond*

London's eight in Melbourne, winners of the Rowing Ashes on Australia Day, 2003, with the trophy, an inscribed cocktail shaker. Back row (left to right): Tam Richmond (coach), Colin O'Malley, Mark Watkin, Danny Harte, Jonathan Smith, Jonathan Curran, Pete Robertson, Paul Reedy (chief coach). In front: Brian Ulliott, Phelan Hill, David Finn

previous four windy days, with Watkin steering, they had beaten crews from Henley, Reading, Cambridge 99, and Nottinghamshire County. In the first race, Watkin's main concern had been to avoid being blustered onto the booms when coming off the island. On the start, there was a diversion. London noticed that Henley had taped the lettering 'LRC A' to their boat as a wind-up. Its effect was to make the Londoners laugh, helping them to relax in the inevitable first-night nerves. When the race started the Henley crew also shouted and screamed in an attempt to put them off. At the end of the island an enormous gust of wind met them, putting the blades within a foot of the booms. But they did not touch, and London were able to take their rating down to below 30 strokes to the minute for the second half of the course. 'If they had transferred their vocal chords onto the ends of their blades they may have gone faster,' said Watkin of Henley. Thursday's race against Reading went the same way, but without the shouting. Friday's against Cambridge 99 produced another repeat of race pattern and verdict. For the third time they took a bag of re-hydrating drinks on board at the boat tent pontoon before paddling through the bridge for a wind-down and landing for a de-brief from Reedy. After exchanges with friends and family, they washed out the remaining lactate on rowing machines, received a massage from Claire, and ate a snack. Saturday's semifinal was against Notts County B whose previous close race had ended in their opponents, County A, being disqualified for steering infringements. Nobody at Henley takes a County crew lightly, but London again went ahead early in the race and, in head-wind gusts that almost stopped them dead, won by four-and-a-half lengths.

Saturday night, before the final, was quiet night at their house in Bix, at the top of the Fairmile outside Henley. Coach Reedy turned up for his last briefing, a routine of analysing the race just performed to identify what they must concentrate on next day. 'We had broken the course down stroke by stroke on paper. We knew how many strokes between markers, how many strokes gone from the start and how many strokes to the finish. We had analysed all the markers commonly known down the course, together with markers not so well known. The course was a blueprint in our minds,' Watkin said. Their last opponents were the Army, losing finalists from the year before and two stone a man heavier. They felt ready. Early next morning they were out for their last practice, with Reedy beside them on a bike on a towpath which would be impossible to penetrate when they returned to race at 2.40 pm. But at this hour there were few people about. They picked up the Cambridge University four in the Visitors' for a 'brush' and moved away from them while under-rating them. This felt good. They returned to Bix for breakfast.

For the final they would be on the Berks station for the first time, closest to the enclosures, giving Watkin booms to watch for on stroke side, and now, as the commentary and the roars and the shouts from the water told them that London had won the Thames Cup, they tried to stay calm in bay L of the boat tent. The message was double-edged: they were pleased for the eight, but now there was extra pressure on themselves to perform. A warm-up on land, a final discussion with Reedy and a delay for a heavy shower preceded going afloat to cheers from the victorious eight and the London supporters. They began the lonely haul to the start.

London's final warm-up was performed downstream of Temple island, and as the red Army came into view, the blue-and-whites remained 'all-eyes forward in our own bubble, concerned only with ourselves'. Attached to the start platform, Watkin's heart pumped, relieved by deep breathing. The chatter and hubbub faded to silence before a solitary, distinctive voice of London treasurer John Rew boomed: 'Have the race of your lives, London!' Watkin takes up the story:

'The umpire stood up at the front of the launch. We all knew the procedure. We just wanted to start now. Before we knew it the words came. "Attention, Go!"

Our first stroke felt so strong, I knew by the time we came forward for the second stroke that this would be our race. By five strokes we had gained half a length. The start sequence was awesome. By the end of the island we had opened to three-quarters of a length. Completely in tune with our race plan, we executed everything. By the Barrier we had generated over a length lead. The support and shouts from the bank got louder as we went up the course and

as we approached Remenham Club, a deafening but huge lift for us could be heard. We had reached a two length lead which we held through Remenham and we felt well in control of the race.

'We consolidated our lead as we came through the enclosures and we held off the pushes from the Army crew. I kept calling "One at a time" meaning keep it simple and just take one stroke at a time. The enclosures were alive with noise and support. Then we crossed the finish line. All I could feel was numbness from racing hard, and jubilation. My arms went up in the air. Twelve Henleys with numerous semifinals and a final. I grabbed Rob in front of me with whom I'd tried five times previously to win at HRR. It felt extra special having achieved our goal together in the same crew.'[19]

The Wyfold four beat the Army by a length and a quarter in 7 minutes 1 second, again the event's fastest time of the week. Medals and trophies were received from Prince Albert of Monaco. Winning two

Henley success in 2004: London beating Reuss Luzern in the Thames Cup, and leading Army Rowing Club in the Wyfold

trophies was a massive and significant day for London, and it took a long time to sink in after the hugs and cheers, the shouts and tears subsided. London really had left a trail behind in 2004. The Thames Cup crew laid a ghost, acknowledged by the regatta's recorder who wrote: 'The crew were greatly in debt to their coxswain [Martin Haycock] who performed outstandingly well throughout the regatta and particularly in the final.'[20] And Dougie Melvin, president of the club, touched the Wyfold crew when, a few days later, he handed Watkin an envelope containing a note which said 'a small memento of your special Henley.' With it

*Thames and Wyfold
winners at Henley,
2004*

were five Henley programmes, one for each day of the regatta, with every single
entry on each race completed. Watkin remembered the wisdom of his coach.
'Look up to the ideals but do not run away from reality. Make an endless wish,
and if you concentrate and perfect yourself, you will break down the barriers.'
In 2002, Reedy wrote in the club newsletter: 'I believe we have a training
programme to accommodate hard training and success on the water together
with the challenges of full-time employment. I am in awe of the commitment
demonstrated by squad members. The standard of rowing and the physical
preparation of squad members is impressive and has improved significantly this
year. It will continue to improve.'[21] He can say that again.

In 2005 the Boustead Cup against Thames was won, bringing the total since
1947 to London twenty-six, Thames twenty-two, with eleven missed years. At Henley
the best result was in the Thames Cup where the A crew, one of three London
entries, went out to the eventual winners, Henley RC, in a semifinal. Except, that is,
for the lightweight James Lindsay-Fynn who, together with his partner Mark Hunter
of Leander, won the Double Sculls against the Dutch heavyweight internationals
Ivo and Alvin Snijders. All their victims were much heavier than them. Lindsay-
Fynn, who won a Henley medal as an Eton cox in 1991, put London's name on this
trophy for only the third time since the Double Sculls began after the Second World
War.[22] He and Hunter went on to win the world championship B final for a ranking
of seventh in Gifu, Japan.

*Mark Hunter
(Leander) and James
Lindsay-Fynn
winning the Double
Sculls, 2005*

And so we must leave off more or less where we came in. As The London Rowing Club enters its next 150 years, coach Reedy sits in his office filing the emails which log his squad's training progress, and trawling the internet to find out who is coming to Henley from other parts of the world. As the day passes, ergos whirr and weights pump in the gym below, water swirls in the tank and boats come and go from the bays in the boathouse. Back in the office, Julian Ebsworth addresses the same tasks as Herbert Playford performed from 5

*Keith Ticehurst,
cartoonist*

Hotham Villas in 1856 – issuing notices about payment of subs amidst a host of other chores that befall the secretary and his assistant, Nigel Smith. Dominic Saunders, the house manager, is clearing up from the night before and setting up for today's event, which if it's a Wednesday is members' dining night – much the same as has happened since the imposing original boat-house opened in 1871. Mike Williams, the president, spreads tentacles to the rowing world as an executive member of both the national and international rowing federations, a member of Henley Regatta's management committee and treasurer to the Boat Race foundation – much as the founders made their presence felt in tideway, upper Thames and even international rowing. Mike Baldwin, vice-president, is chairing the 2006 world champi-

onship organising committee – just as Peter Coni did for 1986. Through the week, scullers and crews, oarsmen and oarswomen, youngsters and veterans, captain Dan Pring and his cohorts, members and committee come and go, some legging it along the high street from the Waterloo trains, just as their predecessors did in answer to the first invitation 150 years ago. From the walls of the members' room, the long room and the Fairbairn room, founders and legends look on, and much of what they see they would recognise. Coaches and captains may no longer run affairs on the water from the back of a twelve-oar or a horse on the towpath, as Nottidge, Casamajor and the Playford brothers used to do, but the dedication, the forward-thinking, the resolution and the thoroughness which permeates upstairs, downstairs and in boats – all would resonate with them. As long as the world offers regattas, and as long as the Thames ebbs and flows along the tideway, the blue-and-white will boil the water aft.

APPENDICES

Acknowledgements

The author is grateful to many who have contributed to Water Boiling Aft and made its creation an adventure. Principal among them are Julian Ebsworth, LRC's honorary secretary, who was assiduous at digging detail, and Tony Owen, the club's librarian and archivist, whose encyclopaedic knowledge of rowing and the world of watermen brought added value. Mike Williams, Nigel Smith and Rob van Mesdag read the manuscript as it evolved and improved it immeasurably by spotting howlers and offering good suggestions. Jaap Oepkes's photography of the club's collection of historic images and John Shore's photography has enriched the book immensely, and I am also grateful to Michael Dover of Weidenfeld and Nicolson who has looked after production, and to the skills of both designer Justin Hunt and editor Jennie Condell. Chris Sprague and the anniversary committee which he chairs have given encouragement and support throughout.

While the skeleton for this book was supplied by LRC's annual records published during its first hundred years and the club's newsletters since, flesh and colour has been added by memoirs, documents, reminiscences, cuttings and pictures contributed by the following: Philip Barker, Graham Boyes, Owen Bryant, Goran Buckhorn, Simon Crosse, Chris Drury, David Edwards, Alan Foster, Lionel Judd, Rupert Hare, Guy Harris, Jeremy Hudson, Colin Kester, Daniel Kirmatzis, Paul Littleton, Paul Mainds, Keith Mason, Tony Mason, Doug Melvin, Bill Miller, Ron Needs, Jenny Owen, John Pinches, Robin Poke, Dan Pring, Robert Rakison, Nigel Read, Simon Rippon, Bill Robertson, Michael Rowe, David Tanner, Daniel Topolski, David Townsend, Mark Watkin, Robin Williams and Chris Woodall.

London Rowing Club Officers

*HRH Prince Philip,
Duke of Edinburgh,
patron of LRC 1952–*

Presidents

1860-75	J. Layton, JP
1879-93	The Rt. Hon. The Earl of Londesborough
1894-1935	The Rt. Hon. The Lord Ampthill, GCSI, GCIE
1936-46	R. S. Bradshaw
1947-50	G. Fraser
1951-71	C. W. Wise
1973-75	E.G.L. Howitt
1976-88	P. N. Carpmael
1989-93	P.R.C. Coni, OBE, QC
1994-2000	J. Ormiston
2001-04	D. V. Melvin
2005-	M. D. Williams

Vice-Presidents

1859-63	E. Belfour
1864	C. Boydell
1865-70	J. S. Virtue
1872-82	H. H. Playford
1883-94	F. Playford
1892-98	E. Monteuuis
1897-1907	B. Horton
1905-35	R. S. Bradshaw
1936-45	J. Baker
1947-50	C. W. Wise
1951-86	R. A. Nisbet, OBE
1951-73	C. H. Rew
1967-76	Sir Charles Wheeler, KBE
1978-88	P. R. C. Coni, OBE, QC
1987-93	J. Ormiston
1989-2000	D. V. Melvin
1994-2004	M. D. Williams
2000-03	Mrs Anne Carpmael
2001-	J. Ormiston
2004-	M. B. Baldwin
2005-	D. V. Melvin

Captains

1856	F. Playford
1857-58	J. Paine
1859-62	Frank Playford
1863	C. Boydell
1864	H. N. Custance
1865-66	H. H. Playford
1867	F. Fenner
1868	J. C. F. May
1869-78	F. S. Gulston
1879-80	S. Le Blanc Smith
1881-85	B. Horton
1886-87	J. F. Stilwell
1888	P. Adcock
1889-93	G. B. James
1894-95	R. S. Bradshaw
1896	B. B. Cubitt
1897	W. J. Thompson
1898-1904	F. S. Lowe
1905-06	E. D. Hay Currie
1907-08	R. B. Freeman
1908	P. Adcock
1909	L. Balfour
1910-14	H. Lumb
1919	P. Adcock
1919	W. T. Raikes
1920-21	C. W. Wise
1922-23	W. P. Trotter, MC and Bar
1923	F. A. G. Medd
1924-27	R. A. Nisbet
1928	A. J. Peppercorn
1929-30	T. N. O'Brien
1931-32	F. M. L. Fitzwilliams
1933-35	E. G. L. Howitt
1936	P. H. Jackson
1937-38	A. B. Fraser
1939	M. P. Lee
1946	T. B. Langton, MC
1947	D. A. Bristol
1948	R. P. M. Bell
1949	N. K. G. Rosser
1950	R. P. M. Bell
1951	M. H. N. Plaisted
1952	J. H. Pinches, MC
1953	J. M. G. Andrews
1954-55	W. H. Atkinson
1956	M. J. Langton
1957	J. R. Mayhew-Sanders
1958-59	D. Ashton
1960-62	P. N. Carpmael
1963	P. R. C. Coni
1964	G. Plumtree
1965	P. A. Littleton
1966	G. R. Marks
1967-68	S. E. Rippon
1969	J. Kitto
1970-71	P. R. Hilditch
1972	P. N. Carpmael
1973	P. E. Harrison
1974	R. C. R. Twallin
1975	F. C. Carr
1976	M. B. Baldwin
1977-78	M. D. Williams
1979-82	K. A. Ticehurst
1983	S. M. Jefferies
1984-85	P. A. H. Fitzwilliam
1986-87	K. E. Mason
1988-90	R. A. Philips
1991-92	S. A. Harris
1993	J. D. Kinsella
1994	P. P. Halford
1995	C. L. Richmond
1996-97	R. W. A. Hare
1998	S. A. B. Simms
1999	M. B. D. Helm
2000-01	I. D. J. Watson
2002-03	J. E. Williamson
2004	M. R. Watkin
2005	C. M. O'Malley
2006	D. R. Pring

Secretaries

1856-57	H. H. Playford
1857-58	F. Playford
1858-60	A. A. Casamajor
1862-63	J. Owen
1864-67	J. C. F. May
1868-70	C. E. Innes
1871	T. Rouse Ebbetts
1872-74	C. H. Warren
1875-79	E. Monteuuis
1880	C. G. Ells
1881-82	T. Rouse Ebbetts
1883-84	G. R. B. Earnshaw
1885-86	P. D. Ullmann
1887-91	J. Donaldson
1892-94	P. A. N. Thorn
1895-97	F. E. Thorn
1898-1901	C. Harden
1902-11	I. N. Cameron
1912-14	H. S. Hackman
1915-18	P. Adcock
1919-20	G. K. Rose
1920-21	H. S. Hackman
1922-24	G. H. Fairbairn
1925	J. A. Giuseppi
1926-36	Col C. E. P. Sankey, DSO
1937-39	Capt. C. S. Dodwell
1940-46	H. S. Hackman
1947-56	T. D. M. Boyland
1953-60	R. P. M. Bell
1957-73	A. J. Tressidder
1977	J. D. F. Pepys
1978	K. A. Ticehurst
1978	C. M. R. von Patzelt
1979-82	M. Rayner
1983-2003	N. A. Smith
2004-	J. R. R. Ebsworth

Treasurers

1856-64	J. S. Virtue
1856-64	J. Ireland
1865-68	C. Boydell
1865-69	J. Owen
1869-70	J. C. F. May
1871	T. Burrowes
1872-74	J. C. F. May
1875-76	C. E. Innes
1877-85	W. H. Lowe
1886	R. Mould
1887-88	W. H. Lowe
1889-90	R. Mould
1891-92	W. H. Lowe
1893-95	B. Horton
1896-1909	L. Maclean
1910-11	H. Roberts
1912-14	H. E. W. Lutt
1915-17	J. J. Craggs
1919	H. E. W. Lutt
1920-24	G. S. Craggs
1925-32	H. S. Hackman
1933-34	F. M. L. Fitzwilliams
1935	A. E. C. Drake
1936-37	T. D. M. Boyland
1938-39	E. R. Nicholas
1940-45	W. G. A. Burgess
1946-54	P. S. Beale
1955-56	W. P. Trotter, MC and Bar
1957	W. B. Hiscocks
1958	N. K. G. Rosser
1959-66	P. S. Beale
1967-77	P. R. C. Coni
1978-80	J. D. F. Pepys
1980-83	N. P. Cooper
1984-93	M. D. Williams
1994	R. A. White
1995-2001	M. Rayner
2002-	J. H. B. Rew

The Club had paid secretaries in 1861 (Mr Richardson), 1974-5 (C. J. Oberst) and 1976 (K. C. W. King).

WINS AT HENLEY ROYAL REGATTA

THE GRAND CHALLENGE CUP
1857, 1859, 1862, 1868, 1872, 1873, 1874, 1877, 1881, 1883, 1884, 1890,
1930, 1931, 1933, 1938, 1979†, 1982†, 1983†, 1984†

THE THAMES CHALLENGE CUP
1875, 1877, 1878, 1880, 1883, 1885, 1886, 1931, 1932, 1935, 1977, 1978, 1998, 2004

THE STEWARDS' CHALLENGE CUP
1856*, 1857, 1858, 1864, 1868, 1869, 1871, 1872, 1873, 1874, 1875, 1876, 1877, 1878, 1895, 1896,
1930, 1931, 1977, 1979, 1981†, 1996†

PRESENTATION CUP FOR FOUR OARS WITHOUT COXSWAINS
1872

THE WYFOLD CHALLENGE CUP
1856*, 1860, 1862, 1879, 1880, 1889, 1895,
1905, 1906, 1914, 1926, 1930, 1932, 1933, 1936, 1937, 1938, 1969, 1976, 1990, 1993, 2004

THE PRINCE PHILIP CHALLENGE CUP
1971†

THE BRITANNIA CHALLENGE CUP
1970

THE SILVER GOBLETS & NICKALLS' CHALLENGE CUP
1856*, 1858, 1860, 1865, 1869, 1871, 1872, 1874, 1876, 1879, 1895, 1896, 1927, 1947

THE DOUBLE SCULLS CHALLENGE CUP
1976, 1993†, 2005†

THE DIAMOND CHALLENGE SCULLS
1856*, 1857, 1858, 1860, 1861, 1862, 1868, 1876, 1923, 1951, 1953

*†composite crew *rowing as Argonaut Club*

WINNING CREWS AT HENLEY ROYAL REGATTA
THE GRAND CHALLENGE CUP

	1857			1859			1862	
Bow	J Ireland		Bow	G A Dunnage		Bow	H Hood	
2	F Potter		2	W Foster		2	W Stout	
3	C A Schlotel		3	F Potter		3	G P R Grubb	
4	J Nottidge		4	W Dunnage		4	G Ryan	
5	J Paine		5	W Farrar		5	C Boydell	
6	W Farrar		6	J Paine		6	A Hodgson	
7	A A Casamajor		7	A A Casamajor		7	F Fenner	
Str.	H H Playford		Str.	H H Playford		Str.	G R Cox	
Cox	H Edie		Cox	H H Weston		Cox	E T Weston	

Beat Oxford University B C by 1¼ lengths in 7m. 55 secs. | *Beat Cambridge University B C by ¾ length in 7m. 45 secs.* | *Beat Trinity College, Oxford, by 3 lengths in 8m. 5secs.*

	1868			1872			1873	
Bow	C H Warren		Bow	S Le B Smith		Bow	C E Routh	
2	B P Seare		2	C E Routh		2	C S Routh	
3	J G Walker		3	C S Routh		3	James B Close	
4	W C Cross		4	B P Seare		4	W F Pitchford	
5	A de L Long		5	R M Barton		5	R M Barton	
6	G Ryan		6	John B Close		6	John B Close	
7	S Le B Smith		7	A de L Long		7	A de L Long	
Str.	F S Gulston		Str.	F S Gulston		Str.	F S Gulston	
Cox	V Weston		Cox	V Weston		Cox	V Weston	

Beat Eton College by 1¼ lengths in 7m. 20 secs. | *Beat Kingston R C by 6 lengths in 8m. 27 secs.* | *Beat Eton College by 3 lengths in 7m. 52 secs.*

	1874			1877			1881	
Bow	B Horton		Bow	B Horton		Bow	P Adcock	
2	C S Routh		2	C H Warren		2	W A D Evanson	
3	C E Routh		3	E Slade		3	C G Ousey	
4	E B Parlour		4	A Trower		4	W W Hewitt	
5	A de L Long		5	A de L Long		5	H Butler	
6	F L Playford		6	F S Gulston		6	W R Grove	
7	S Le B Smith		7	S Le B Smith		7	H H Playford	
Str.	F S Gulston		Str.	F L Playford		Str.	F L Playford	
Cox	V Weston		Cox	W F Sheard		Cox	W F Sheard	

Beat Eton College and Thames R C by ⅔ length in 7m. 41 secs. | *Beat Thames R C by 1¼ lengths in 8m. 2½ secs.* | *Beat Leander Club by 1 length in 7m. 23 secs.*

	1883			1884			1890	
Bow	G R B Earnshaw		Bow	G R B Earnshaw		Bow	M W Mossop	
2	C E Earnshaw		2	C E Earnshaw		2	H W Reeves	
3	W Bergh		3	W Bergh		3	F E Coulson	
4	A S J Hurrell		4	J F Stilwell		4	J Baker	
5	C G Ousey		5	H J Hill		5	A G Aldous	
6	W R Grove		6	A S J Hurrell		6	R S Farran	
7	J T Crier		7	J T Crier		7	R S Bradshaw	
Str.	W W Hewitt		Str.	W W Hewitt		Str.	G B James	
Cox	W F Sheard		Cox	W F Sheard		Cox	W F Sheard	

Beat Twickenham R C by 1 length in 7m. 51 secs. | *Beat Twickenham R C – not rowed out – in 7m. 27 secs.* | *Beat Brasenose College, Oxford, by 1¼ lengths in 7m. 4½ secs.*

	1930		1931		1933
Bow	R Close-Brooks	Bow	R Close-Brooks	Bow	R J D Forbes
2	E G L Howitt	2	T D M Boyland	2	T D M Boyland
3	G H Crawford	3	D St J Gogarty	3	P N Carpmael
4	H C Boardman	4	P N Carpmael	4	G B Wood
5	H R A Edwards	5	H R A Edwards	5	P H Jackson
6	A J Harby	6	A J Harby	6	E G L Howitt
7	F M L Fitzwilliams	7	F M L Fitzwilliams	7	D H Mays-Smith
Str.	T N O'Brien	Str.	E G L Howitt	Str.	T Turner
Cox	J A Brown	Cox	P B Geoghegan	Cox	W H W Cane

Beat Leander Club by 1¹/₂ lengths in 6m. 59 secs. · *Beat Thames R C by ¹/₂ length in 7m. 33 secs.* · *Beat Berliner Ruder Club by ¹/₄ length in 7m. 36 secs.*

	1938		1979		1982
			Composite crew with Thames Tradesmen's R C		Composite crew with Leander Club
Bow	M P Lee	Bow	L D Robertson	Bow	D McDougall
2	H C Fraser	2	E R Sims	2	J G Suenson-Taylor
3	J H Pinches	3	M D Bathurst	3	J Clark
4	R Parker	4	A N Christie (LRC)	4	J M Beattie (LRC)
5	P H Jackson	5	J MacLeod (LRC)	5	A J Holmes
6	W F McMichael	6	G A Rankine	6	J M Pritchard
7	T R M Bristow	7	C G Seymour	7	M R McGowan
Str.	P L M Hartley	Str.	J A Roberts	Str.	R C Stanhope
Cox	D R Rose	Cox	A F Inns	Cox	S M Jefferies (LRC)

Beat Trinity Hall, Cambridge, by 1¹/₂ lengths in 6m. 58 secs. · *Beat Yale University, USA, by 2¹/₂ lengths in 6m. 35 secs.* · *Beat University of London and Tyrian by ¹/₂ length, no time taken*

	1983		1984
	Composite crew with University of London B C		Composite crew with Leander Club
Bow	I T McNuff (LRC)	Bow	D McDougall
2	J M Beattie (LRC)	2	C J Mahoney
3	D A Clift	3	S F Hassan
4	M P Cross (LRC)	4	J M Pritchard
5	R G McB Budgett	5	D A Clift
6	T A D Cadoux-Hudson	6	C G Roberts (LRC)
7	R C Stanhope (LRC)	7	M R McGowan
Str.	J L Bland	Str	A Whitwell
Cox	A Sherman	Cox	C B Moynihan (LRC)

Beat Cambridge University BC by 4 lengths in 6m. 26 secs. · *Beat University of Washington BC, USA, by 3 lengths in 6m. 22 secs.*

THE THAMES CHALLENGE CUP

	1875		1877		1878
Bow	W A Willmott	Bow	E S Prior	Bow	E S Prior
2	P Adcock	2	E F Stearns	2	E F Stearns
3	W B Webb	3	C J Ringrose	3	B E Holland
4	H Laming	4	G J Nesbitt	4	W A D Evanson
5	J H Dickson	5	W W Hewitt	5	H Butler
6	F E Parlour	6	H H Playford	6	G J Nesbitt
7	J Knight	7	C K Greenhill	7	C G Ells
Str.	G C White	Str.	P Adcock	Str.	P Adcock
Cox	V Weston	Cox	W F Sheard	Cox	W F Sheard

Beat West London R C by over 2 lengths in 7m. 33 secs. · *Beat Thames R C by 1¹/₂ lengths in 8m. 29 secs.* · *Beat Ino R C by over 2 lengths in 7 mins 55 secs.*

	1880		1883		1885
Bow	J Farrell	Bow	L Maclean	Bow	L Maclean
2	E S Prior	2	H W Page	2	W C Rivett
3	J I Ward	3	J Kerr	3	G Beeson
4	F P Ousey	4	C Wood	4	C Wood
5	G H C Tucker	5	W R Lyne	5	W R Lyne
6	J F Stilwell	6	F W Earnshaw	6	A S Bryden
7	A S J Hurrell	7	P D Ullmann	7	P D Ullmann
Str.	E J Beal	Str.	H C Roberts	Str.	G B James
Cox	W F Sheard	Cox	W F Sheard	Cox	W F Sheard

Beat Twickenham R C by 2 lengths in 7m. 24 secs. — *Beat West London R C by over 1 length in 8m. 5 secs.* — *Beat Thames R C by ½ length in 7m. 36 secs.*

	1886		1931		1932
Bow	A B Vaux	Bow	R J D Forbes	Bow	J Grumbar
2	H Shirreff	2	G B Wood	2	F R Derry
3	P D Ullmann	3	R W Burkitt	3	A E C Drake
4	C E Brown	4	B T Hill	4	B T Hill
5	W R Lyne	5	J M Fraser	5	P H Jackson
6	A S Bryden	6	F T Coulton	6	R W Burkitt
7	G Beeson	7	D H Mays-Smith	7	R J D Forbes
Str.	G C Vaux	Str.	T Turner	Str.	E D Wetton
Cox	W F Sheard	Cox	A B Wayte	Cox	J A Brown

Beat Thames R C by ½ length in 7m. 5½ secs. — *Beat Magdalene College B C by 2 lengths in 7m. 43 secs.* — *Beat Imperial College B C by 4 feet in 7m. 41 secs.*

	1935		1977		1978
Bow	O L R Hills	Bow	N S Read	Bow	A J P French
2	J F Gibson	2	C P Stuart-Bennett	2	J N Melvin
3	J H Pinches	3	C J D George	3	P Zeun
4	C C Bass	4	D G Innes	4	C G Roberts
5	R Carver	5	C M Cusack	5	R A Downie
6	G M Rushmore	6	S A Simpole	6	C M Drury
7	O St J Hamlin	7	D Topolski	7	N S Read
Str.	P V Ormiston	Str.	C M Drury	Str.	S A Simpole
Cox	G Harris	Cox	R L Penney	Cox	C B Moynihan

Beat Pembroke College B C, Cambridge, by ¼ length in 7m. 5 secs. — *Beat Leander Club by 2¼ lengths in 6m. 37 secs.* — *Beat Leander Club by 2½ lengths in 6m. 54 secs.*

	1998		2004
Bow	M H W Harris	Bow	P M Beard
2	G N Gillespie	2	J D Smith
3	S R J Woods	3	A B MacFarlane
4	A J Macpherson	4	J A McGrail
5	R W A Hare	5	S D Craig
6	B P Hopkins	6	S J Masterson
7	T D Atkinson	7	P J S Robertson
Str.	T P Hudson	Str.	D R Pring
Cox	C A Miller	Cox	M N Haycock

Beat Bowbridge B C by ⅔ length in 6m. 35 secs. — *Beat Ruder Club Reuss, Lucerne, Switzerland, by ½ length in 6m. 50 secs.*

THE STEWARDS' CHALLENGE CUP

1856		1857		1858	
(Rowed as Argonaut Club)					
Bow	J Nottidge	Bow	A A Casamajor	Bow	A A Casamajor
2	A A Casamajor	2	J Nottidge	2	W Farrar
3	J Paine	3	J Paine	3	J Paine
Str.	H H Playford	Str.	H H Playford	Str.	H H Playford
Cox	F Levien	Cox	H H Weston	Cox	H H Weston

Argonaut Club rowed over in final, after beating LMBC by 2 lengths in first heat.

Beat Lady Margaret B C by about 4 lengths in 8m. 25 secs.

L R C rowed over.

1864		1868		1869	
Bow	J C F May	Bow	S Le B Smith	Bow	G Ryan
2	H N Custance	2	F S Gulston	2	F S Gulston
3	G Ryan	3	A de L Long	3	A de L Long
Str.	F Fenner	Str.	W Stout	Str.	W Stout
Cox	E T Weston	Cox	V Weston	Cox	V Weston

Beat University College, Oxford, by 1¹/₄ lengths in 8m. 45 secs.

Beat Oscillators Club by 4 lengths in 8m. 22 secs.

Beat Oxford Radleian Club by 2 lengths in 8m. 36 secs.

1871		1872		1873	
Bow	C E Routh	Bow	S Le B Smith	Bow	James B Close
2	G Ryan	2	John B Close	2	F S Gulston
3	A de L Long	3	A de L Long	3	A de L Long
Str.	F S Gulston	Str.	F S Gulston	Str.	John B Close
Cox	V Weston	Cox	V Weston		

Beat Kingston R C by over 1 length in 9m. 9 secs.

Beat Kingston R C by several lengths in 9m. 21 secs.

Beat Kingston R C by 3 lengths in 8m. 23 secs.

1874		1875		1876	
Bow	S Le B Smith	Bow	S Le B Smith	Bow	C H Warren
2	F L Playford	2	F L Playford	2	F S Gulston
3	A de L Long	3	A de L Long	3	S Le B Smith
Str.	F S Gulston	Str.	F S Gulston	Str.	F L Playford

Beat Thames R C by 3 lengths in 9m. 0 secs.

Beat Leander Club by 2¹/₂ lengths in 7m. 56 secs.

Beat Thames R C on a foul in 8m. 27 secs.

1877		1878		1895	
Bow	S Le B Smith	Bow	S Le B Smith	Bow	A S Little
2	F S Gulston	2	F S Gulston	2	H W Stout
3	A de L Long	3	A Trower	3	V Nickalls
Str.	F L PLayford	Str.	F L Playford	Str.	G Nickalls

Beat Thames R C by 2 or 3 lengths in 9m. 7 secs.

Beat Shoe-wae-cae-mette BC, USA, easily in 8m. 37 secs.

Beat Thames R C by 1¹/₄ lengths in 7m. 43 secs.

1896		1930		1931	
Bow	W B Richards	Bow	F M L Fitzwilliams	Bow	F M L Fitzwilliams
2	H W Stout	2	A J Harby	2	P N Carpmael
3	V Nickalls	3	H R A Edwards	3	H R A Edwards
Str.	G Nickalls	Str.	H C Boardman	Str.	A J Harby

Beat Thames R C by 1 length in 8m. 42 secs.

Beat Leander Club by 1¹/₂ lengths in 7m. 34 secs.

Beat Piacenza R C, Italy, by 3 lengths in 8m. 45 secs.

1977		1979		1981
				Composite crew with
				Thames Tradesmen's R C
Bow	D Bond	Bow	J M Beattie	Bow	J M Beattie (LRC)
2	J M Beattie	2	I T McNuff	2	I T McNuff (LRC)
3	I T McNuff	3	D G H Townsend	3	J Clark
Str.	M P Cross	Str.	M P Cross	Str.	M P Cross (LRC)

L R C rowed over in accordance with Rule XIX in 7m. 24 secs.

Beat Oxford University easily in 7m. 19 secs.

Beat Vesper B C, U S A, easily in 7m. 48 secs.

1996	
Composite crew with	
Nottinghamshire County	
Rowing Association	
Bow	C Bates *(Fri.)*
	W J Baker (LRC) *(Sat. and Sun.)*
2	I D J Watson (LRC)
3	J E Williamson (LRC)
Str.	A D J Butt (LRC) *(Fri.)*
	C Bates *(Sat. and Sun.)*

Beat Goldie BC by 4 lengths in 6m. 44 secs.

THE WYFOLD CHALLENGE CUP

1856		1860		1862	
(Rowed as Argonaut Club)		Bow	F Potter	Bow	H Hood
Bow	J Nottidge	2	A Schlotel	2	G P R Grubb
2	A A Casamajor	3	C A Schlotel	3	F Fenner
3	J Paine	Str.	W Foster	Str.	W Stout
Str.	H H Playford	Cox	H H Weston	Cox	E T Weston
Cox	F Levien				

Beat Royal Chester RC by 1 length

Beat Kingston R C by over 1 length in 10m. 8 secs.

Beat West London R C easily in 9m. 20 secs.

1879		1880		1889	
Bow	C G White	Bow	E J Beal	Bow	G C Vaux
2	W A D Evanson	2	W R Grove	2	H W Reeves
3	C G Ells	3	W W Hewitt	3	B B Cubitt
Str.	P Adcock	Str.	P Adcock	Str.	P A N Thorn

Beat Thames R C by many lengths in 9m. 56 secs.

Beat Third Trinity, Cambridge, by several lengths in 8m. 4 secs.

Beat Thames R C by 4 lengths in 7m. 58 secs.

1895		1905		1906	
Bow	A F G Everitt	Bow	E D Hay Currie	Bow	J N Balme
2	F S Lowe	2	R B Freeman	2	J R K Fenning
3	F P Barton	3	W R Gaskell	3	R B Freeman
Str.	W J Thompson	Str.	G R Davis	Str.	P Dewar

Beat Third Trinity, Cambridge, by 2¹/₂ lengths in 8m. 16 secs.

Beat Reading R C by 1¹/₂ lengths in 7m. 59 secs.

Beat Thames R C by 2¹/₄ lengths in 7m. 58 secs.

1914		1926		1930	
Bow	T McK Hughes	Bow	C F K Mellor	Bow	R Close-Brooks
2	H Lumb	2	A J Peppercorn	2	E G L Howitt
3	F S Laskey	3	W E E Webb	3	G H Crawford
Str.	M S Ell	Str.	T N O'Brien	Str.	T N O'Brien

Beat Lady Margaret B C by 1¹/₄ lengths in 8m. 35 secs.

Beat Lady Margaret B C by 4 feet in 7m. 59 secs.

Beat Vesta R C easily in 7m. 52 secs.

1932		1933		1936	
Bow	R Close-Brooks	Bow	J G Webb	Bow	J H Pinches
2	G B Wood	2	R W Burkitt	2	R R Lack
3	D H Mays-Smith	3	A E C Drake	3	M P Lee
Str.	T D M Boyland	Str.	E D Wetton	Str.	O St J Hamlin

Beat Nottingham Union R C easily in 8m. 29 secs.   *Beat Westminster Bank R C by 2 lengths in 8m. 28 secs.*   *Beat Reading R C by 3 lengths in 8m. 26 secs.*

1937		1938		1969	
Bow	J Ormiston	Bow	A B Fraser	Bow	D Topolski
2	H Carter	2	W T Robertson	2	N P Cooper
3	J H Pinches	3	T E Hendrie	3	P E Harrison
Str.	C L Morris	Str.	I G Esplin	Str.	C I Blackwall

Beat Walton R C by ¹/₂ length in 8m. 20 secs.   *Beat Royal Chester R C by 4 lengths in 7m. 41 secs.*   *Beat Trident R C, South Africa, by 2¹/₂ lengths in 7m. 16 secs.*

1976		1990		1993	
Bow	D Bond	Bow	N J Strange	Bow	M C H Williams
2	I T McNuff	2	N J Howe	2	S J Sinclair
3	J M Beattie	3	R M W Williams	3	R M W Williams
Str.	M P Cross	Str.	S R W Forbes	Str.	W J Baker

Beat Potomac B C, U S A, by ¹/₂ length in 6m. 56 secs.   *Beat Nottingham County R A by 1¹/₂ lengths in 7m. 26 secs.*   *Beat Leander Club by 4¹/₂ lengths in 6m. 55 secs.*

2004	
Bow	M R Watkin
2	R J McKenzie
3	J A M Evans
Str.	C M O'Malley

Beat Army R C by 1¹/₄ lengths in 7m. 01 sec.

PRESENTATION CUP FOR FOUR OARS WITHOUT COXSWAINS

1872	
Bow	John B Close
2	F S Gulston
3	A de L Long
Str.	W Stout

LRC rowed over.

THE PRINCE PHILIP CHALLENGE CUP

1971	

Composite crew with
University of London B C

Bow	P E Harrison (LRC)
2	C I Blackwall (LRC)
3	A A Bayles
Str	D Warbrick-Smith
Cox	P J Sweeney

Beat Leander Club by 1²/₃ lengths in 7m. 39 secs.

THE BRITANNIA CHALLENGE CUP

1970	
Bow	D Topolski
2	N P Cooper
3	D P Sturge
Str.	J K G Dart
Cox	R Sherman

Beat Bedford R C by ²/₃ length in 7m. 48 secs.

THE SILVER GOBLETS & NICKALLS' CHALLENGE CUP

1856		1858		1860	
(Rowed as Argonaut Club)					
Bow	A A Casamajor	Bow	H H Playford	Bow	A A Casamajor
Str.	J Nottidge	Str.	A A Casamajor	Str.	W Woodbridge

Beat H H Playford and J Paine of Argonaut Club easily.

Beat E Warre and A P Lonsdale of Balliol College by 1¹/₂ lengths

Beat D Ingles and N Royds of First Trinity by 2 lengths in 11m. 50 secs.

1865		1869		1871	
Bow	J C F May	Bow	A de L Long	Bow	A de L Long
Str.	F Fenner	Str.	W Stout	Str.	F S Gulston

Beat H Snow and E Warre of Eton by 3 or 4 lengths in 9m. 7 secs.

Beat W C Calvert and T K McLintock-Bunbury by 3 lengths in 9m. 20 secs.

Beat James B Close and John B Close of First Trinity, Cambridge, by 1¹/₂ lengths in 10m. 17 secs.

1872		1874		1876	
Bow	A de L Long	Bow	A de L Long	Bow	S Le B Smith
Str.	F S Gulston	Str.	F S Gulston	Str.	F S Gulston

Beat J J Croskell and T G Thompson of Lancaster by 2 lengths

Beat J Mair and A Trower of Kingston R C easily in 10m. 3 secs.

Beat A E Campbell and R G Davey of Twickenham easily in 8m. 55 secs.

1879		1895		1896	
Bow	R H Labat	Bow	V Nickalls	Bow	V Nickalls
Str.	F S Gulston	Str.	G Nickalls	Str.	G Nickalls

Beat W H Eyre and J Hastie of Thames R C by several lengths in 11m. 6 secs.

Beat W Broughton and S D Muttlebury of Thames R C, not rowed out, in 9m. 11 secs.

Beat W E Crum and C M Pitman of New College, Oxford, easily in 9m. 10 secs.

1927		1947	
Bow	R A Nisbet	Bow	J H Pinches, MC
Str.	T N O'Brien	Str.	E M Sturges

Beat G O Nickalls and H O C Boret of Leander Club by 1¹/₄ lengths in 9m. 23 secs.

Beat J R W Gleave and D G Jamison of Magdalen College, Oxford, by 2¹/₂ lengths in 8m. 46 secs.

THE DOUBLE SCULLS CHALLENGE CUP

1976	1993	2005
	Composite crew with University of London Tyrian Club	Composite crew with Leander Club
Bow R Prentice Str. M S Spencer	Bow E W M Kittoe (LRC) Str. R F Redpath	Bow M J Hunter Str. J W Lindsay-Fynn (LRC)
Beat J H van Drooge and *R Nolet of ASR Nereus, Holland,* *by 2½ lengths in 7m. 22 secs.*	*Beat I W Hopkins and M Pollecutt* *of Molesey BC by 2 feet in* *7m. 32 secs.*	*Beat I M Snijders of ASR* *Nereus and A F Snijders of* *DSR Proteus-Eretes, Holland,* *easily in 7m. 26 secs.*

THE DIAMOND CHALLENGE SCULLS

1856	1857	1858
(Sculled as Argonaut Club) A A Casamajor	A A Casamajor	A A Casamajor
Beat C Stephens of Reading B C *easily.*	*Beat J Paine of LRC by* *4 lengths.*	*Sculled over.*

1860	1861	1862
H H Playford	A A Casamajor	E D Brickwood
Beat E D Brickwood of LRC *in 12m. 8 secs.*	*Beat E D Brickwood of LRC* *by 3 lengths in 10m. 4 secs.*	*Beat W B Woodgate of Brasenose* *College by several lengths* *in 10m. 40 secs. after a dead heat.*

1868	1876	1923
W Stout	F L Playford	M K Morris
Beat W C Crofts of Brasenose *College by 2 lengths in* *9m. 6 secs.*	*Beat R H Labat of LRC by* *4 lengths in 9m. 28 secs.*	*Beat D H L Gollan of Leander* *Club by 1 length in 8m. 23 secs.*

1951	1953	
(Sculled in Pembroke College, Cambridge, colours) T A Fox	T A Fox	
Beat E Lassen of Koge Roklubb, *Denmark, by 4½ lengths in* *8m. 59 secs.*	*Beat R George of Union Nautique* *de Liege, Belgium, by 4 lengths* *in 8m. 12 secs.*	

WINNING CREWS AT HENLEY WOMEN'S REGATTA
LIGHTWEIGHT QUADRUPLE SCULLS

2004
Composite crew with Auriol Kensington RC

Composite crew with Auriol Kensington RC
Bow   A-L Theophilus (LRC)
2   B J Britten
3   A C Crawford (LRC)
Str.   H Mangan (LRC)
Beat Mortlake Anglian B C by 2½ lengths
in 5m. 10 secs.

WINNING CREWS IN THE HEAD OF THE RIVER RACE

	1926	1927	1928
Bow	A J Peppercorn	R A Nisbet	E G L Howitt
2	C H Rew	T N O'Brien	K Fawssett
3	R A Nisbet	A O Hughes	H C Boardman
4	G A Block	J N Rofe	R E James
5	W E Webb	W E Webb	H R A Edwards
6	J N Rofe	W A Rowat	J N Rofe
7	A F Long	A F Long	A J Peppercorn
Str.	T N O'Brien	C H Rew	T N O'Brien
Cox	E A B Griffith	C K Stopp	J A Brown
Time	20 m. 1 sec.	18 m. 41 secs. (1st= with Thames RC)	18 m. 41½ secs.

	1929	1930	1931
Bow	F M L Fitzwilliams	R Close-Brooks	R Close-Brooks
2	E G L Howitt	E G L Howitt	T D M Boyland
3	A J Harby	A Graham	D H Mays-Smith
4	K Fawssett	H C Boardman	R V Dudley-Clarke
5	G H Crawford	G H Crawford	H R A Edwards
6	H C Boardman	A J Harby	A J Harby
7	H R A Edwards	F M L Fitzwilliams	F M L Fitzwilliams
Str.	R Close-Brooks	T N O'Brien	E G L Howitt
Cox	J A Brown	J A Brown	J A Brown
Time	19 m. 24 secs.	19 m. 12 secs.	19 m. 24 secs.

	1932	1933	1934
Bow	R Close-Brooks	R Close-Brooks	O L R Hills
2	T D M Boyland	T D M Boyland	T D M Boyland
3	B T Hill	P N Carpmael	P N Carpmael
4	G B Wood	E G L Howitt	R G Sankey
5	J M Fraser	P H Jackson	P H Jackson
6	P N Carpmael	G B Wood	G B Wood
7	D St J Gogarty	D H Mays-Smith	A E C Drake
Str.	T N O'Brien	T Turner	T Turner
Cox	C D Eberstein	W H W Cane	G Harris
Time	16 m. 11 secs. (shortened course)	19 m. 54 secs	20 m. 17 secs

	1935	1936	1939
Bow	B S Beazley	J H Pinches	M P Lee
2	E D Wetton	B S Beazley	H C Fraser
3	P N Carpmael	O St J Hamlin	P J Stone
4	R G Sankey	G M Rushmore	P N Carpmael
5	P H Jackson	P H Jackson	G A Morris
6	E G L Howitt	A B Fraser	P L Hartley
7	A J Barrett	T R M Bristow	P H Jackson
Str.	T D M Boyland	T D M Boyland	D A L Lawrence
Cox	G Harris	H D Winkworth	D Rose
Time	19 m. 41 secs.	20 m. 9 secs.	19 m. 21 secs.

	1949	1950	1978
Bow	P D Secretan	D P Trotter	A J P French
2	R P M Bell	F H M Rushmore	J N Melvin
3	F L Whalley	J F B Douglas	P Zeun
4	E M Sturges	R P M Bell	C G Roberts
5	J H Pinches MC	M H N Plaisted	R A Downie
6	P N Carpmael	T A Fox	S A Simpole
7	N K G Rosser	J H Pinches MC	N S Read
Str.	B Goult	P N Carpmael	C M Drury
Cox	J M Johnston-Noad	J M Johnston-Noad	C B Moynihan
Time	19 m. 35 secs.	18 m. 52 secs.	17m. 47.49 secs.

INTERNATIONAL REPRESENTATIVES FOR GREAT BRITAIN

1908 Olympic Games London

J R K Fenning	M2-	Bow	Gold
J R K Fenning	M4-	3	Silver

1928 Olympic Games Amsterdam

R A Nisbet	M2-	Bow	Silver
T N O'Brien		Stroke	
D Guye	M2x	Bow	
H C Boardman		Stroke	

1932 Olympic Games Los Angeles

H R A Edwards	M2-	Bow	Silver
L Clive		Stroke	
H R A Edwards	M4-	3	Silver

1936 Olympic Games Berlin

T R M Bristow	M4-	Bow	Silver
A J Barrett		2	
P H Jackson		3	
J D Sturrock		Stroke	

1951 European Championships Macon

T A Fox	M1x	Silver

1952 Olympic Games Helsinki

T A Fox	M1x	4th

1953 European Championships Copenhagen

T A Fox	M1x

1954 European Championships Amsterdam

A J Marsden	M2x	Bow	4th
T A Fox		Stroke	

1955 European Championships Ghent

W H Atkinson	M4+	Bow
P MacQuisten		2
J P C Vigurs		3
S C Crosse		Stroke
S G B Underwood		Cox
D V Melvin	M1x	

1956 European Championships Bled

R A Wheadon	M8+	Bow
T A Fox	M1x	

1956 Olympic Games Melbourne

R A Wheadon	M8+	Bow	
T A Fox	M1x		9th

1958 European Championships Poznan

S C Crosse	M4+	2
J P C Vigurs		3

1959 European Championships Macon

S C Crosse	M4+	2

1960 European Championships Rome

C M Davis	M8+	Stroke	
J P C Vigurs	M4-	3	5th
S C Crosse	M4+	2	

1961 European Championships Prague

J P C Vigurs	M8+	3	5th

1962 World Championships Lucerne

J P C Vigurs	M8+	3	9th
J M Howard-Johnston		Cox	

1964 European Championships Amsterdam

N P Cooper	M4-	2	9th
R N Carpmael		3	

1965 European Championships Duisburg

N P Cooper	M2x	Bow	8th

1966 World Championships Bled

R N Carpmael	M8+	5	4th
N P Cooper	M2x	Bow	9th

1967 European Championships Vichy

N P Cooper	M8+	2	7th
R N Carpmael		7	

1969 European Championships Klagenfurt

D Topolski	M4-	Bow
N P Cooper		2
P E Harrison		3
C I Blackwall		Stroke

1971 European Championships Copenhagen

P E Harrison	M2+	Bow
C I Blackwall		Stroke
R Sherman		Cox

1974 World Championships Lucerne

D Topolski	LM4-	Bow	7th
C M Drury		3	

1975 World Championships Nottingham

D Topolski	LM4-	Bow	Silver
C M Drury		2	
G F Hall		3	
N D C Tee		Stroke	
J H Clay	M2-	Bow	
D P Sturge		Stroke	

1976 FISA Lightweight Championships Villach

D Carpenter	LM8+	Bow	Silver
B S Fentiman		2	
M Harris		3	
S Fraser		4	
C M Cusack		5	
C M Drury		6	
N S Read		7	
G F Hall		Stroke	
H J H Wheare		Cox	

1976 Olympic Games Montreal

J H Clay	M2-	Bow	12th
D P Sturge		Stroke	
J MacLeod	M2+	Bow	7th
A N Christie		Stroke	
D Webb		Cox	

1977 World Championships Amsterdam

N S Read	LM8+	Bow	Gold
C P Stuart-Bennett		2	
C J D George		3	
D G Innes		4	
C M Cusack		5	
S A Simpole		6	
D Topolski		7	
C M Drury		Stroke	
J H Clay	M8+	3	5th
D Bond	M4-	Bow	10th
I T McNuff		2	
J M Beattie		3	
M P Cross		Stroke	
J MacLeod	M2+	Bow	10th
A N Christie		Stroke	
D Webb		Cox	

1978 FISA Lightweight Championships Copenhagen

A J P French	LM8+	Bow	Gold
J N Melvin		2	
R A Downie		3	
C G Roberts		4	
P Zeun		5	
C M Drury		6	
N S Read		7	
S A Simpole		Stroke	
C B Moynihan		Cox	
D Topolski	LM2x	Stroke	7th

1978 World Championships Karapiro

J M Beattie	M4-	Bow	Bronze
I T McNuff		2	
D G H Townsend		3	
M P Cross		Stroke	
J H Clay	M8+	2	7th

1979 World Championships Bled

J M Beattie	M4-	Bow	Bronze
I T McNuff		2	
D G H Townsend		3	
M P Cross		Stroke	
M D Bathurst	M8+	3	6th
A N Christie		4	
J MacLeod		5	
R J Stuart	LM8+	Bow	5th
D G Innes		2	
P Zeun		3	
J N Melvin		4	
N S Read		5	
C M Drury		6	
C M Cusack		7	
S A Simpole		Stroke	
P Jenkinson		Cox	

1980 FISA Lightweight Championships Hazewinkel

C N Barratt	LM8+	Bow	Gold
D B Hosking		2	
R A Downie		3	
N J Howe		4	
P Zeun		5	
C G Roberts		6	
N S Read		7	
S A Simpole		Stroke	
S M Jefferies		Cox	

1980 Olympic Games Moscow

J H Clay	M8+	3	Silver
C B Moynihan		Cox	
J M Beattie	M4-	Bow	Bronze
I T McNuff		2	
D G H Townsend		3	
M P Cross		Stroke	
J MacLeod	M2+	Bow	9th
A N Christie		Stroke	
D Webb		Cox	

1981 World Championships Munich

J M Beattie	M4-	Bow	10th
I T McNuff		2	
M P Cross		Stroke	
C B Moynihan	M8+	Cox	Silver
C M Drury	LM8+	2	
R A Downie		3	
N J Howe		4	
C G Roberts		6	
S A Simpole		Stroke	
S M Jefferies		Cox	

1982 World Championships Lucerne

J MacLeod	M2-	Bow	12th
A N Christie		Stroke	
C G Roberts	M8+	2	9th
J M Beattie		4	
C B Moynihan		Cox	
J N Melvin	LM1x		8th
R A Downie	LM4-	Bow	9th
S A Simpole		2	
P Zeun		3	
N J Howe		Stroke	
S J Chilmaid	LM8+	Bow	6th
P J Head		2	
P Connors		3	
D R Hampton		4	
R M Counihan		5	
J P Edwards		6	
C M Drury		7	
R M W Williams		Stroke	
C P Berners-Lee		Cox	

1983 World Championships Duisburg

J M Beattie	M4+	Bow	6th
R Stanhope	M4-	Bow	10th
J N Melvin	LM1x		Silver
S E Melvin	LM8+	Bow	7th

1984 Olympic Games Los Angeles

C G Roberts	M8+	4	5th
C B Moynihan		Cox	
J M Beattie	M2-	Bow	12th

1984 FISA Lightweight Championships Montreal

J N Melvin	LM1x		4th
S J Chilmaid	LM2x	Bow	11th
R M W Williams	LM8+	5	6th
N J Howe		Stroke	
S M Jefferies		Cox	

1985 World Championships Hazewinkel

C M Drury	LM4-	2	7th
S E Melvin	LM8+	2	9th
N J Howe		3	
C Nelson		7	

1986 World Championships Nottingham

C L Richmond	LM8+	2	8th
S E Melvin		3	
C Nelson		4	
J N Melvin		6	
N J Howe		Stroke	

1987 World Championships Copenhagen

W D Downing	LM8+	Bow	5th
M C H Williams		3	
C Nelson		4	
N J Howe		6	

1988 World Championships Milan

R M W Williams	LM4-	Bow	Silver
N J Howe		2	
W D Downing	LM8+	Bow	8th
C Nelson		6	

1989 World Championships Bled

R Henderson	M4x	2	
N J Strange	LM4-	Bow	Bronze
N J Howe		2	
R M W Williams		3	
S R W Forbes		Stroke	
A D J Butt	LM8+	Bow	6th
W D Downing		5	

1990 World Championships Barrington

N J Howe	LM4-	Bow	5th
R M W Williams		Stroke	
N J Strange	LM4x	2	12th

1991 World Championships Vienna

N J Strange	LM8+	3	5th
S E Melvin	LM4x	Stroke	8th

1992 World Lightweight Championships Montreal

A D J Butt	LM8+	3	Silver
N J Strange		5	

1993 World Championships Roudnice

M C H Williams	LM2-	Bow	9th
W J Baker		Stroke	
M B D Helm	LM8+	2	5th
A D J Butt		3	
N J Strange		5	

1994 World Championships Indianapolis

R D T Everington	LM2-	Bow	6th
A D J Butt	LM4-	Bow	7th
I D J Watson		2	
N J Strange		3	
M B D Helm		Stroke	

1995 World Championships Tampere

A D J Butt	LM8+	3	Silver
J E Williamson		4	
N J Strange		7	
M B D Helm		Stroke	
I D J Watson	LM4-	2	5th

1996 Olympic Games Atlanta

M B D Helm	LM4-	Stroke	10th
N J Strange	LM2x	Bow	12th

1996 World Championships Strathclyde

I D J Watson	LM8+	4	4th
J E Williamson		6	
A D J Butt		7	
J M A Brown	LM2-	Bow	10th
J M Keys		Stroke	
E W M Kittoe	LM4x	Bow	6th
S R W Forbes		Stroke	

1997 World Championships Aiguebelette

A D J Butt	LM4-	Bow	9th
I D J Watson		2	
N J Strange		3	
J E Williamson		Stroke	
J M A Brown	LM8+	5	Silver

1998 World Championships Cologne

J M A Brown	LM4-	Bow	4th
J S Warnock		Stroke	

1999 World Championships St Catharines

J M A Brown	LM4-	Bow	11th
J S Warnock		Stroke	

2000 Olympic Games Sydney

C A Miller	W8+	Cox	7th

2000 World Championships Vilnius

J M A Brown	LM8+	2	Silver

2001 World Championships Lucerne

J S Warnock	LM8+	6	5th

2002 World Championships Seville

J S Warnock	LM4-	Stroke	12th

2003 World Championships Milan

J S Warnock	LM8+	2	6th
M H W Harris		3	
D B Harte		6	

2004 World Championships Banyoles

J S Warnock	LM2-	Stroke	9th

2005 World Championships Gifu

J W Lindsay-Fynn	LM2x	Bow	7th
D B Harte	LM2-	Stroke	7th

Glossary

CHISWICK BRIDGE
Ibis and Quintin Boathouses
MORTLAKE
Ship Inn
Stone
FINISH 4 miles 374 yards
Practice Finish
Mortlake Brewery
Mortlake Church
CHISWICK
White Hart
3¾ miles
Barnes Terrace
Emanuel School Boathouse
Duke's
Bandstand
Meadows
Fuller's Brewery
M I D D L E S E X
BARNES BRIDGE
Corney Reach
Chiswick Church
Chiswick Eyot
Chiswick Steps 2 miles 1020 yards
Chiswick Mall
Chiswick Reach
BARNES
S U R R E Y
St Paul's School
The Doves
Pier

THE BOAT RACE COURSE
FROM PUTNEY TO MORTLAKE

HAMMERSMITH BRIDGE
1 mile 1180 yards
Harrods Depository (formerly Soap Works)
Barn Elms (Ranelagh)
Mile Post
Crab Tree Reach
HAMMERSMITH
Beverley Brook
RIVER THAMES
The Crab Tree
Boathouses
Fulham Football Ground
Craven Steps
PUTNEY
Fulham Reach
Hole in the Wall
FULHAM
Duke's Head
Star and Garter
Fulham Wall
University Stone
Pier
START
PUTNEY BRIDGE

→ N

feet 1500   1000   500   0   500 yards

PUTNEY TO MORTLAKE

Also known as the Boat Race course and the Championship course, the stretch of the tideway between Putney and Mortlake is 4 miles 374 yards long, marked by a stone on the embankment at each end. The course is a huge S-bend. The Boat Race normally runs from Putney to Mortlake on the incoming tide, and the Head of the River Race normally runs from Mortlake to Putney on the outgoing tide. The key markers are the mile post (one mile above the Putney stone), Hammersmith bridge, Chiswick steps and Barnes bridge.

STATUS RULES

Rowing has two disciplines, rowing and sculling. The international categories for each are senior and under-23 (open weight and lightweight) and junior (under 19). In Britain the categories for men and women are senior (including novice, and lightweight), junior. For a hundred years from the foundation of London Rowing Club, 'junior' meant the second crew and was not governed by age. There are also age-related categories for veterans (also known as masters).

ROWING INSTITUTIONS

ARA: the Amateur Rowing Association (1882) is the governing body of rowing for Great Britain and England. Scotland, Wales and Ireland have their own governing bodies. **FISA:** the Fédération Internationale des Sociétés d'Aviron (1892) is the governing body for international rowing, and the oldest international sports federation. FISA events, including world championships and world cup regattas and regattas run under FISA

rules such as the Olympic Games, use multi-lane courses of 2000 metres. **Olympic games:** rowing is a founding sport of the modern Olympic games, first held in 1896. **World rowing championships:** the world rowing championships began in 1893 as the European championships, and are run by FISA, the international rowing federation. **British Empire and Commonwealth games:** rowing was an official sport in the Empire and Commonwealth games until 1986. Since then Commonwealth championships have been held during the same years as the Commonwealth games.

CONVERSION TABLES

Imperial to metric

1 mile	1760 yards	1.6093 kilometres
1 nautical mile	6080 feet	1.852 kilometres
1 knot	1 nautical mile per hour	0.914 metres
1 yard	3 feet	0.914 metres
1 foot	12 inches	0.3046 metres
1 inch	2.54 centimetres	

Metric to imperial

1 kilometre	1000 metres	0.62137 mile	1093.6 yards
1 metre	100 centimetres	1.0936 yards	3.281 feet
1 centimetre	10 millimetres	0.3937 inch	

Weights

1 cwt		50.8 kilograms
1 stone	14 pounds (lb)	6.3504 kilograms
1 pound (lb)	16 ounces (oz)	0.4536 kilogrammes
1 kilogramme	2.20462 (lb)	

Old money

£1	20 shillings (s)	240 pence (d)
1 shilling (s)		12 pence (d)
1 guinea	£1: 1s	252 pence (d)
New £1	100 pence	

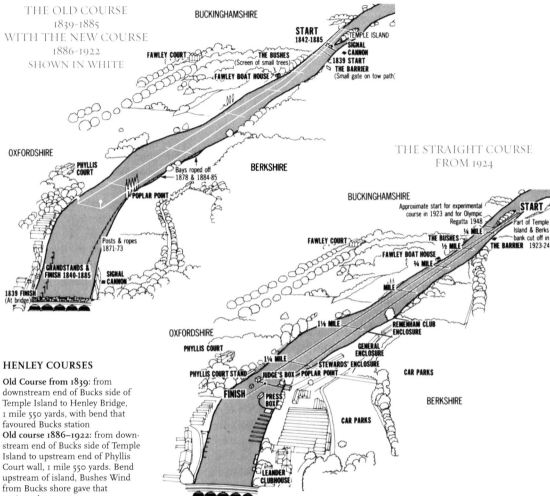

THE OLD COURSE
1839-1885
WITH THE NEW COURSE
1886-1922
SHOWN IN WHITE

THE STRAIGHT COURSE
FROM 1924

HENLEY COURSES

Old Course from 1839: from downstream end of Bucks side of Temple Island to Henley Bridge, 1 mile 550 yards, with bend that favoured Bucks station

Old course 1886–1922: from downstream end of Bucks side of Temple Island to upstream end of Phyllis Court wall, 1 mile 550 yards. Bend upstream of island, Bushes Wind from Bucks shore gave that station advantage.

1923: experimental straight course 1 mile 440 yards from upstream end on Berks side of island to Finish.

1924 to date: from downstream end on Berks side of Temple Island to Finish, 1 mile 550 yards straight course, 80 feet wide.

HENLEY ROYAL REGATTA

Henley Royal Regatta: founded in 1839, Henley regatta is run against the stream on a two-lane course of 1 mile 550 yards (2112 metres). It is operated under its own rules by Stewards who are elected for life. Until 1946 the events for which London RC was eligible were the Grand, Stewards', Thames and Wyfold challenge cups, plus the Silver Goblets and the Diamond Sculls. Since 1946 new trophies have been added, and qualification rules for many events have changed. Trophies open to club crews are described on the right:

Grand Challenge Cup (1839): top ranking eight-oared open event.

Ladies' Challenge Plate (1845): second ranking eight-oared event, opened to clubs in 1985.

Thames Challenge Cup (1868): eight-oared event for club crews.

Stewards' Challenge Cup (1841): top ranking four-oared open event.

Visitors' Challenge Cup (1847): four-oared event with same qualification rules as Ladies' Plate, opened to clubs in 2001.

Wyfold Challenge Cup (1847): four-oared event from 1855; same qualification rules as the Thames Cup from 1996.

Prince Philip Challenge Cup (1963): open coxed fours event with same qualification rules as the Grand, discontinued in 2004.

Britannia Challenge Cup (1969): coxed fours event for club crews since 2004 with same qualification rules as the Thames Cup.

Queen Mother Challenge Cup (1981): open event for quadruple sculls with same qualification rules as the Grand.

Men's Quadruple Sculls (2001) quadruple sculling event with same qualification rules as Ladies' Plate.

Silver Goblets and Nickalls' Challenge Cup (1845): open event for pair-oars.

Double Sculls Challenge Cup (1946): open event for double sculls.

Diamond Sculls (1844): open event for single sculls.

Remenham Challenge Cup (2001): open event for women's eights.

Princess Grace Challenge Cup (2001): open event for women's quadruple sculls.

Princess Royal Challenge Cup (1997): open event for women's single sculls.

Bibliography

London Rowing Club

Reports of the London Rowing Club, 1856 to 1953

Rob van Mesdag Ed, LRC 1856 to 1981, One Hundred and Twenty-five Years of Rowing, LRC, 1981

Memorandum and Articles of Association of the London Boat House Company Limited, incorporated 22 January 1870

Henley Royal Regatta records, 1839 to 2005

Rowing

Richard Burnell and Geoffrey Page, The Brilliants, A History of the Leander Club, Leander Club, 1977

Elizabeth Carter, Furnivall Sculling Club, in preparation

Hylton Cleaver, A History of Rowing, Herbert Jenkins, London, 1957

Christopher Dodd, The Oxford and Cambridge Boat Race, Stanley Paul, London, 1983

Christopher Dodd and John Marks (Eds), Battle of the Blues, P to M, London, 2004

Christopher Dodd, The Story of World Rowing, Stanley Paul, London, 1992

H R A Edwards, The Way of a Man with a Blade, Routledge & Kegan Paul, 1963

Ian Fairbairn Ed, The Complete Steve Fairbairn, Nicholas Kaye, London. 1951 (reprint with additional material, The Kingswood Press, London, 1990)

Niall Ferguson, Empire, How Britain made the Modern World, Allen Lane, London, 2003

Eric Halladay, Rowing in England: A Social History, Manchester University Press, 1990

R C Lehmann, The Complete Oarsman, Methuen, London 1924

Thomas C Mendenhall, The Harvard-Yale Boat Race 1852-1924, Mystic Seaport Museum, Mystic, 1993

John Munro and others, Frederick James Furnivall, A Volume of Personal Record, Henry Frowde, OUP, 1911

G O Nickalls, A Rainbow in the Sky, Chatto and Windus, London, 1974

Guy Nickalls, Life's A Pudding, Faber and Faber, London 1939

Geoffrey Page, Hear the Boat Sing, The History of Thames Rowing Club, Kingswood, London 1991

Colin Porter, Rowing to Win, Stanley Paul, London, 1959

Colin Porter, A Very Public Servant, Access Press, Bassendean WA, 2005

Andrew Ruddle, Rowing on the Thames Tideway and the expansion of London 1850-1900, Open University abstract, 2000

R P P Rowe and C M Pitman, Rowing, The Badminton Library, Longman Green, London 1898

Neil Wigglesworth, The Social History of English Rowing, Frank Cass, London, 1992

Neil Wigglesworth, Victorian and Edwardian Boating from Old Photographs, Batsford, London, 1988

W B Woodgate, Boating, The Badminton Library, Longman Green, London 1888

General

Asa Briggs, Victorian Things, Batsford 1988

Chris Cook and John Stevenson, Modern British History 1714-1995, Longman, London, 1996

Stephen Croad, Liquid History, The Thames Through Time, English Heritage and Batsford, London, 2003

Charles Dickens Jr, Dickens's Dictionary of the Thames from its source to the Nore 1885, Macmillan, London, 1885

Steve Fairbairn, Fairbairn of Jesus, Bodley Head, London, 1931

Judith Flanders, The Victorian House, Harper Perennial, London, 2003

Dorian Gerhold, Putney and Roehampton Past, Wandsworth Historical Society 1994, Historical Publications Ltd.

Bette Hill with Neil Ewart, The Other Side of the Hill, Stanley Paul, London 1976

Graham Hill, Life at the Limit, William Kimber, London 1969

David Kynaston, The City of London, A World of Its Own 1815-1890, Pimlico, London 1994

Peter Lovesay, The Official Centenary History of the Amateur Athletic Association, Guinness Superlatives, 1979

Oliver Philpot, Stolen Journey, Hodder and Stoughton, London 1950

R N Rose, The Field 1853 to 1953, Michael Joseph, London

A N Wilson, After the Victorians, Hutchinson, London, 2005

Footnotes

CHAPTER 1

1 *The Almanack*, 1862
2 Halladay, Rowing in England
3 Josias Nottidge, dinner speech 1857 dinner
4 F E Thorn, letter quoting his father,
a founding member,
The Times, 1926,
5 Edmund Belfour, vice-president LRC,
dinner speech 1858
6 Slug and Lettuce

CHAPTER 2

1 Letter from Mr P B Cooper of Bird Place,
Henley-on-Thames, to H H Playford dated
25 June 1854: 'I shall have much pleasure in
welcoming both you and your boats and have
given orders that the latter shall be taken
care of upon their arrival on my premises.'

CHAPTER 3

1 Macmillan's Magazine
2 Page, Hear the Boat Sing
3 W H Eyre in Lehmann's The Complete
Oarsman; Page, Hear the Boat Sing
4 E C Morley, Richmond Herald, 28
December 1907

CHAPTER 4

1 *The Field*, 10 August 1861
2 *Bell's Life*, 11 August 1861
3 F Playford, dinner speech 1857
4 Rowe and Pitman, Rowing and Punting
5 Woodgate, Boating
6 Woodgate, Boating

CHAPTER 5

1 Page, Hear the Boat Sing
2 See also Chapter 8
3 Page puts the first meeting in 1866
and the start of Hare and
Hounds in 1867; Lovesay's history of the
AAA gives the dates as 1867 and 1868
4 Bryon Butler, Oxford Dictionary of
National Biography
5 S LeBlanc-Smith in Rowing,
Rowe and Pitman
6 S LeBlanc-Smith in Rowing,
Rowe and Pitman
7 Lehmann, The Complete Oarsman
8 Mendenhall, The Harvard-Yale Boat Race
9 *The Field*, 1 March 1873
10 Rose, *The Field*, 1953
11 *The Field*, 12 April 1873
12 *The Lancet*, 2 October 1869
13 Mendenhall, The Harvard-Yale Boat Race
14 Halladay, Rowing in England
15 Dodd, The Story of World Rowing

16 S LeBlanc-Smith in Rowing,
Rowe and Pitman
17 See books by Dodd, Halladay,
Wigglesworth
18 Burnell, The Brilliants
19 R C Lehmann, Rowing

CHAPTER 6

1 Cash account 11 March 1859 to 8 March
1860 (£153 on premises, £55 on cutters,
£42 on repairs of boats)
2 See also Chapter 2
3 Newens Marine
4 LRC press release, 1989
5 See also Chapter 8
6 Woodgate, Boating
7 Woodgate, Boating
8 See also Chapter 3
9 The Cigar is at Marlow RC
10 Woodgate, Boating
11 VEB is Bootsbau Berlin;
The Dreissigackers founded Concept 2
12 LRC boat inventory 1 March 2004

CHAPTER 7

1 Fédération Internationale des Sociétés
d'Aviron (FISA)
2 See Chapter 8
3 Carter, Furnivall Sculling Club
4 Sir Bertram Cubitt, *Rowing* magazine

CHAPTER 8

1 Quoted in *The Badminton Magazine*,
May 1914
2 See also Chapter 3
3 Mendenhall, The Harvard-Yale Boat Race
4 *The Field*, 16 September 1876
5 A Nisbet, LRC 1856-1981
6 Nisbet to F H 'Dinty' Moore, 4 April 1984
7 G C Drinkwater, Report of LRC for 1930
8 D St J Gogarty, Report of LRC for 1934
9 Martin Bristow, *Regatta*, September 1988
10 See also Chapter 5
11 P H Jackson, Report of LRC for 1938
12 J D Sturrock, Report of LRC for 1938
13 P H Jackson, Report of LRC for 1935
14 B S Beazley, Report of LRC for 1936
15 M P Lee, Report of LRC for 1937
16 M P Lee, Report of LRC for 1938
17 C Dimont, *Rowing*, June 1966

CHAPTER 9

1 Page, Hear the Boat Sing
2 Page, Hear the Boat Sing
3 Fairbairn, Steve Fairbairn on Rowing
4 Squadron-Leader F E Hellyer,
The Syncopated Eight 1929
5 Captain's report, 1932
6 Martin Bristow, *Regatta*, August 1988

7 Dodd, The Story of World Rowing
8 Jackson, Report of LRC, 1936
9 Alan Burrough, Steve Fairbairn on Rowing

CHAPTER 10

1 See Chapter 5
2 *The Times*, 17 May 1938
3 C Dodd, The Story of World Rowing
4 See various writers on Rowing;
F Cunningham, A dialogue with
Steve and Stan, *Regatta*, November 1989
5 H B Playford (1949), revised M Pottle,
Stephen Fairbairn, Oxford Dictionary
of National Biography, 2004
6 *The Times*, 1 June 1931;
Fairbairn on Rowing
7 I Fairbairn, Ed, The Complete
Steve Fairbairn
8 D Kynaston, The City of London
9 G C Boase, revised J P Hopson, Oxford
Dictionary of National Biography, 2004
10 G O Nickalls in G Nickalls, Life's
a Pudding
11 Guy and Vivian won 11 Goblets between
them in the 1890s
12 J Slinn, Oxford Dictionary of National
Biography, 2004; D Kynaston,
The City of London
13 See Chapter 4
14 See Chapters 5 and 8
15 P Newbolt, Oxford Dictionary
of National Biography, 2004
16 K Prior, Oxford Dictionary
of National Biography, 2004
17 See Chapter 5
18 P Barker, Rowing's Olympic Founding
Fathers
19 G Dunnage, W Foster, F Potter,
W Dunnage, W Farrar, J Paine,
A A Casamajor, H H Playford
20 Göran Buckhorn, Rowing at the
Stockholm Olympics, Mystic Seaport
Museum
21 G Nickalls, Life's a Pudding

CHAPTER 11

1 Roy Meldrum was author of Rowing and
Sculling and coached Lady Margaret Boat
Club in a style described by Hylton Cleaver
of the *Evening Standard* as 'neither Fairbairn
nor orthodox... a wholly admirable blend of
all that is best in watermanship.'
2 *Evening Standard*, 5th November 1953
3 Dodd, The Story of World Rowing
4 Matthew Pinsent, Olympic champion
1992-2004
5 Emil Zátopek was a Czech Olympic
champion runner

6 *Regatta*, July 2003
7 Porter, A Very Public Servant
8 Edwards, The Way of a Man with a Blade
9 At St Neots London were rowing as Metropolitan and UL as Tyrian
10 J R L Anderson, *The Guardian*, 30 November 1965 and 3 December 1965

CHAPTER 12
1 S Crosse, LRC 1856 to 1981
2 P Coni, LRC 1856 to 1981

CHAPTER 13
1 Vernon Trophy for the fastest club on the tideway
2 Lightweight crew classified as average weight not greater than 70 kilos (11 stone); no individual weighing more than 72.5 kilos (11 stone 5 pounds) — FISA 1973
3 C Dodd, *The Guardian*, 25 August 1975
4 M Spracklen, The Lightweight Story, *British Rowing Almanack*, 1976
5 N Read, LRC 1856 to 1981
6 R Burnell, British Crews Abroad, *British Rowing Almanack*, 1978
7 N Read, LRC 1856 to 1981
8 GB: Ian Wilson (Thames Tradesmen), Stuart Wilson (Nottingham BC), Colin Barratt (Hereford), Nick Howe (Molesey). This crew rowed as LRC in the Wyfold
9 C Dodd, British crews abroad, *British Rowing Almanack*, 1978
10 M Sweeney, Olympic Regatta, *British Rowing Almanack*, 1981
11 Birkmyre is a former Olympic double sculling partner of George Justicz and rowed for Ariel (Bristol) and Stourport
12 Formerly the Royal Singapore Yacht Club
13 See glossary
14 *The Guardian*, 19 February 1981. Crew: Jim Clark (Thames Tradesmen), John Beattie, Martin Cross, Ian McNuff
15 South Africa's multi-racial rowing federation agreed not to compete in FISA events to retain its membership
16 Doug Melvin, Daniel Topolski, David Tanner, Terry O'Neill
17 LRC/UL: Ian McNuff, John Beattie, Adam Clift, Martin Cross, Richard Budgett, Tom Cadoux-Hudson, Richard Stanhope, John Bland, cox Alan Sherman
18 Haining became world lightweight single sculling champion for three consecutive years from 1993 to 1995
19 'Selected' crews at Henley are kept apart in the draw
20 Howe rowed for Lea in 1985 and Nautilus Lightweights in 1988-89

21 The twelve-oar's Henley crew was Mike Williams, Keith Mason, Paul Fitzwilliam, Mike Baldwin, Keith Ticehurst, Nigel Smith, Peter Harrison, George Plumtree, Richard Twallin, Peter Hilditch, Richard Philips, Simon Rippon and cox Simon Jefferies
22 The Ladies' Plate ranks second to the Grand at Henley, and was exclusively for academic institutions from 1854 to 1966
23 Henderson was a member of LRC in 1989

CHAPTER 14
1 *The Guardian*, 30 January 1993
2 Coni was awarded the FISA medal of honour; the press centre was voted best of 1986 by the International Sports Writers' Association
3 See Chapters 11 and 13
4 See Chapter 12
5 LRC Newsletter, September 1993
6 See Chapter 11
7 LRC Newsletter, August 1991
8 *The Guardian*, 30 January 1993
9 *The Guardian*, 15 July 1993. See also C Dodd, *Regatta*, August 1993
10 *The Guardian*, 12 February 1993
11 Peter Coni, Tubby Owen and Graham Beech
12 Interview, *Rowing* magazine, 1986
13 In 2005 including Chris Drury, Rob Mackenzie, Colin O'Malley, Richard Philips, Tam Richmond and Ian Watson
14 P Coni, LRC Newsletter, December 1986
15 LRC Newsletter, November 1972
16 *The Times*, 16 July 1971; LRC Newsletter, September 1971
17 See Chapter 9
18 P Coni, LRC Newsletter, April 1988
19 O Philpot, Stolen Journey
20 LRC Newsletter, Spring 1999
21 O Bryant, *Regatta*, November 1996
22 *Rowing*, April 1956
23 LRC Newsletter, September 1971
24 S Rippon, LRC Newsletter, May 2003
25 H R A Edwards, The Way of a Man with a Blade
26 R Burnell, Oxford Dictionary of National Biography, 2004
27 See Chapter 11
28 C Dimont, LRC Newsletter, January 1973
29 G Hill, Life at the Limit
30 See Chapter 11
31 H Cleaver, Rowing, June 1956; Obituary, *The Daily Telegraph*, 6 March 2004; LRC Newsletter, April 2004

CHAPTER 15
1 *Regatta*, August 1992
2 LRC: M A Chappell, A J Veal, M D Free, M Halstead, cox F E King
3 GB Olympic champions 1992: coxed pair — J Searle, G Searle, cox G Herbert; coxless pair — S Redgrave, M Pinsent
4 LRC B, Wyfold winners: Marcus Williams, Sean Sinclair, Robin Williams, Bill Baker; LRC A: Neil Thompson, John Warnock, Rob Dauncey, Angus Dodd
5 LRC won the eights, coached by Tam Richmond
6 *Regatta*, August 1994; HRR Records, 1994 Boulogne and Lyon: D Fauche, P Lot, M Andrieux, J-C Rolland Treviris and Böllberg: T Weishaupt, A Hajek, S Volkert, A Steiner Molesey: J Searle, R Obholtzer, G Searle, T Foster
7 Sean Bowden and John Wilson
8 Williams became chief coach for GB lightweights after the 2005 Boat Race
9 Chris Bates (NCRA), Ian Watson, Jonty Williamson, Bill Baker. Baker subbed for Andy Butt whose wife went into labour on regatta Friday. Bates, Watson and Williamson were also in the Ladies' eight
10 Martin Harris, Gordon Gillespie, Simon Woods, Angus Macpherson, Rupert Hare, Ben Hopkins, Tom Atkinson, Theodore Hudson, cox Lotte Miller
11 GB 1998 and 1999: James Brown, John Warnock with Notts County's Jim McNiven and Dave Lemon
12 Nick Wakefield, Diego and Javiere Aguirregomezcorta, Ian Watson
13 The Visitors', second in status to the Stewards', was previously open only to academic crews
14 HRR Records, 2003
15 *Regatta*, August 2003
16 Phil Vondra won this event in 1995, and Jonathan Curran was to do so in 2002
17 Phil Beard, Johnny Smith, Andy MacFarlane, John McGrail, Stephen 'Richo' Craig, Stuart Masterson, Pete Robertson, Dan Pring, cox Martin Haycock
18 Mark Watkin, Rob McKenzie, Mark Evans, Colin O'Malley
19 M Watkin, LRC archive
20 HRR Records, 2004
21 LRC Newsletter, August 2002
22 LRC Double Sculls winners: R Prentice and M Spencer 1976; N Kittoe and R Redpath (UL Tyrian) 1993

Index

Entries referring to illustrations appear in italics